ACTIVITY WOR

SIDE by SIDE

Plus

Steven J. Molinsky • Bill Bliss

with

Carolyn Graham

Contributing Authors

Jennifer Bixby • Elizabeth Handley
Dorothy Lynde

Illustrated by

Richard E. Hill

To The Teacher

Side by Side Plus Activity Workbook 4 provides supplemental activities to accompany *Side by Side Plus Student Book 4*. The all-skills activities include listening comprehension practice and GrammarRaps in the Audio Program available on the Pearson English Portal. New material in this edition includes activities to support the Student Book Gazette lessons and a new workbook section offering focused practice with life-skill competencies and employment topics. A complete Answer Key enables students to use the Workbook independently for self-study.

(*Side by Side Plus Test Prep Workbook 4*, available separately, offers test preparation practice through achievement tests for all units of the program. The tests are also available as reproducibles included with *Side by Side Plus Teacher's Guide 4*.)

Side by Side Plus Activity Workbook 4

Pearson Education, 221 River Street, Hoboken, NJ 07030

Staff credits: The people who make up the *Side by Side Plus* team, representing content creation, design, manufacturing, marketing, multimedia, project management, publishing, rights management, and testing are Pietro Alongi, Allen Ascher, Rhea Banker, Elizabeth Barker, Lisa Bayrasli, Elizabeth Carlson, Jennifer Castro, Tracey Munz Cataldo, Diane Cipollone, Aerin Csigay, Victoria Denkus, Dave Dickey, Daniel Dwyer, Wanda España, Oliva Fernandez, Warren Fischbach, Pam Kirshen Fishman, Nancy Flaggman, Patrice Fraccio, Irene Frankel, Aliza Greenblatt, Lester Holmes, Leslie Johnson, Janet Johnston, Caroline Kasterine, Barry Katzen, Ray Keating, Renee Langan, Jaime Lieber, Amy McCormick, José Antonio Méndez, Julie Molnar, Alison Pei, Pamela Pia, Stuart Radcliffe, Jennifer Raspiller, Kriston Reinmuth, Mary Perrotta Rich, Tania Saiz-Sousa, Katherine Sullivan, Paula Van Ells, Kenneth Volcjak, Paula Williams, and Wendy Wolf.

Text composition: TSI Graphics, Inc.
Illustrations: Richard E. Hill

The authors gratefully acknowledge the contributions of Pam Kirshen Fishman and Tina Carver in the development of the original *Side by Side* program.

ISBN-13: 978-0-13-834317-0

Printed in the United States of America
5 2025

Contents

A FOR MANY YEARS

STUDENT BOOK PAGES **1–14**

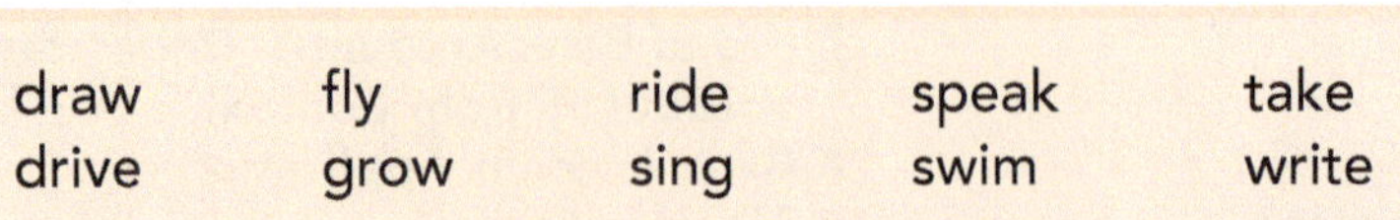

1. My son Timmy ___swims___ very well. ___He's swum___ for many years.

2. Rita __________ guitar lessons. __________ __________ lessons for many years.

3. Harry __________ a truck. __________ __________ a truck for many years.

4. I __________ Italian. __________ __________ Italian for many years.

5. My wife and I __________ in a choir. __________ in a choir for many years.

6. Glen __________ poetry. __________ __________ poetry for many years.

7. Abigail __________ her bicycle to work. __________ it to work for many years.

8. Dave __________ cartoons. __________ __________ cartoons for many years.

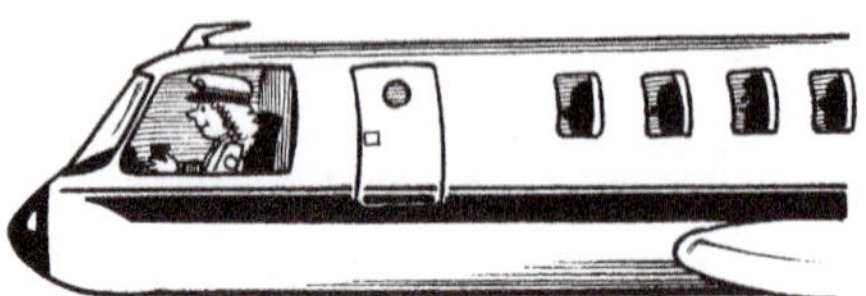

9. Fran __________ airplanes for Trans-Globe Airlines. __________ __________ airplanes for Trans-Globe Airlines for many years.

10. My grandfather __________ beautiful flowers in his garden. __________ __________ beautiful flowers in his garden for many years.

B A LITTLE WHILE AGO

do	eat	feed	give	go	see	take	write

1. A. ___Have___ the employees ___gone___ on strike yet?
   B. Yes, ___they have___. ___They went___ on strike a little while ago.
2. A. __________ Alice __________ a break yet?
   B. Yes, __________. __________ a break a little while ago.
3. A. __________ you __________ your homework yet?
   B. Yes, __________. __________ it a little while ago.
4. A. __________ you and Susie __________ breakfast yet?
   B. Yes, __________. __________ breakfast a little while ago.
5. A. __________ Frank __________ out the paychecks yet?
   B. Yes, __________. __________ them out a little while ago.
6. A. __________ Monica __________ her report yet?
   B. Yes, __________. __________ it a little while ago.
7. A. __________ you __________ the cats yet?
   B. Yes, __________. __________ them a little while ago.
8. A. __________ Thomas __________ his new son yet?
   B. Yes, __________. __________ him a little while ago.

C LISTENING 

Listen and decide what is being talked about.

1. (a.) songs
   b. clothes
2. a. a horse
   b. a letter
3. a. a language
   b. a book
4. a. a concert hall
   b. a lake
5. a. e-mail
   b. my new bicycle
6. a. cartoons
   b. newspaper articles
7. a. a movie
   b. inventory
8. a. a van
   b. a letter
9. a. friends
   b. flowers

D IN A LONG TIME

be	do	eat	get	give	go	ride	see	swim	take	write

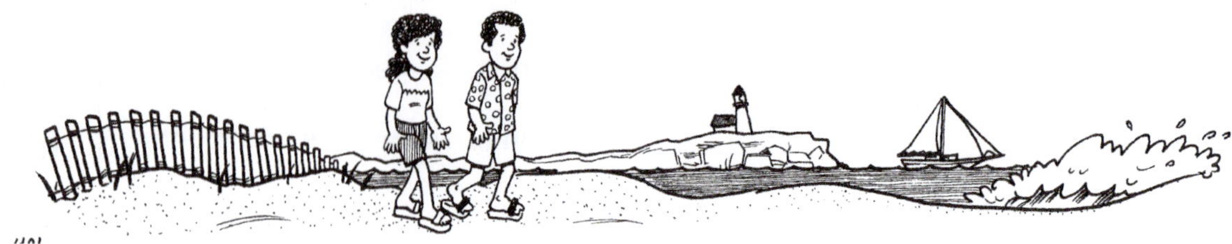

1. A. ___Have___ you and your husband ___taken___ a walk on the beach recently?
   B. No, ___we haven't___. ___We haven't taken___ a walk on the beach in a long time.
2. A. __________ Emily __________ a letter to her grandparents recently?
   B. No, __________. __________ to her grandparents in a long time.
3. A. __________ your husband __________ a raise recently?
   B. No, __________. __________ a raise in a long time.
4. A. __________ you __________ bowling recently?
   B. No, __________. __________ bowling in a long time.
5. A. __________ people __________ in the lake outside of town recently?
   B. No, __________. __________ there in a long time.
6. A. __________ your car __________ at the repair shop recently?
   B. No, __________. __________ at the repair shop in a long time.
7. A. __________ you and your wife __________ a movie recently?
   B. No, __________. __________ a movie in a long time.
8. A. __________ Diane __________ her motorcycle recently?
   B. No, __________. __________ it in a long time.
9. A. __________ you __________ at a nice restaurant recently?
   B. No, __________. __________ at a nice restaurant in a long time.
10. A. __________ George __________ anything interesting recently?
    B. No, __________. __________ anything interesting for a long time.
11. A. __________ I __________ you any difficult tests recently?
    B. No, __________. __________ us a difficult test in a long time.

E GrammarRap: *Have You Gone to the Zoo?*

Listen. Then clap and practice.

A. Have you gone to the zoo?
B. Yes, I have.
I went to the zoo last May.
And how about you? Have you gone there, too?
A. No, I haven't. I'm going today.

A. Have you seen the news?
B. Yes, I have.
I saw the news at seven.
And how about you? Have you seen it, too?
A. No, I haven't. I'll see it at eleven.

A. Have you done your laundry?
B. Yes, I have.
I did my laundry last Sunday.
And how about you? Have you done yours, too?
A. No, I haven't. I'll do it next Monday.

A. Have you taken your driving test?
B. Yes, I have.
I took it last November.
And how about you? Have you taken it, too?
A. No, I haven't. I'll take it in September.

F WHAT ARE THEY SAYING?

be	have	know	own	play	sing	want	work

since	for

1. A. How long ___has___ Jonathan ___known___ how to ski?
   B. ___He's known___ how to ski ___for___ the past ten years.
2. A. How long __________ your daughter __________ the measles?
   B. ______________ the measles __________ last Friday.
3. A. How long __________ you ________________ the violin?
   B. ______________ the violin __________ several years.
4. A. How long __________ Mr. and Mrs. Chang __________ their own house?
   B. ____________________ their own house __________ more than a year.
5. A. How long __________ your brother Tom __________ opera?
   B. ______________ opera __________ he moved to Italy last year.
6. A. How long __________ your daughter __________ to be a singer?
   B. ____________________ to be a singer __________ she was ten years old.
7. A. How long __________ you and Kathy __________ at the mall?
   B. ______________ at the mall __________ a few months.
8. A. This lecture is extremely long. How long __________ we __________ here?
   B. ______________ here __________ more than two hours.

G LISTENING

Listen and complete the sentences.

1. (a.) three years.
   b. last year.
2. a. a long time.
   b. they started high school.
3. a. 1999.
   b. fifteen years.
4. a. 1966.
   b. thirty-five years.
5. a. last weekend.
   b. four days.
6. a. I was a young boy.
   b. several years.
7. a. last spring.
   b. three months.
8. a. I moved here.
   b. the past ten years.
9. a. he moved to Boston.
   b. the past twenty years.

H WHAT'S THE QUESTION?

1. How long have you had a toothache?

I've had a toothache for the past two days.

2. ______ your daughter ______?

She's wanted to be a teacher since she was a child.

3. ______ your husband ______?

He's been in the hospital for more than a week.

4. ______ your children ______?

They've known how to swim since they were young.

5. ______ you and your wife ______?

We've owned our own home for twenty years.

I WRITE ABOUT YOURSELF

1. I know how to ....

   I've known how to .... (since/for) ....

2. I like to ....

   I've liked to .... (since/for) ....

3. I own ....

   I've owned .... (since/for) ....

4. I want to ....

   I've wanted to .... (since/for) ....

5. I have ....

   I've .... (since/for) ....

6. I'm ....

   I've been .... (since/for) ....

J HOW LONG?

1. A. How long has George been waiting for a taxi?

   B. He's been waiting for a taxi for ______ half an hour.

2. A. How long has Julie been practicing the piano?

   B. ______ early this afternoon.

3. A. How long have you been feeling sick?

   B. ______ the past few days.

4. A. How long have I been talking?

   B. ______ an hour and fifteen minutes.

5. A. How long have Stacy and Tom been going out?

   B. ______ last summer.

6. A. How long has your car been making strange noises?

   B. ______ a few weeks.

7. A. How long have you been doing sit-ups?

   B. ______ twenty minutes.

8. A. How long has Howard been snoring?

   B. ______ midnight.

K LISTENING 

Listen and choose the correct answer.

1. a. He bought his TV a few weeks ago.
   (b.) His TV hasn't been working well.

2. a. She's been going to college.
   b. She's been working at a bank.

3. a. They've been waiting in a restaurant.
   b. They've been shopping in a supermarket.

4. a. Peter and Jane have been going to high school.
   b. Peter and Jane have been dating.

5. a. Their ceiling has been leaking.
   b. Their landlord has been complaining.

6. a. They've been writing all day.
   b. They've been riding their bicycles.

L WHAT ARE THEY SAYING?

1. A. Something is the matter with my daughter Debbie.
   B. What seems to be the problem?
   A. She has a fever. And she's crying a lot.
   B. How long ______has she been crying______?
   A. ______She's been crying______ since yesterday afternoon.
   B. Can you bring her to see me at 2:00?
   A. Yes, I can. We'll be at your office at 2:00.

2. A. Mr. Burns? We're having some problems in our apartment.
   B. Oh? What's wrong?
   A. The ceiling is leaking. There's water all over the living room.
   B. How long ____________________?
   A. ____________________ since Monday morning.
   B. I'm glad you called me. I'll come over right away.

3. A. I'm afraid Michael is having some problems in school.
   B. Oh? What's the matter?
   A. He's been fighting with the other children.
   B. How long ____________________ with the other children?
   A. ____________________ with them for the past few weeks.
   B. That's very serious. I'll talk to him about it as soon as I get home.
   A. Thank you. I hope that helps.

(continued)

4. A. Hello, Charlie? This is Mrs. Graves. I'm afraid I've got some problems with my car.

   B. What's wrong with it?

   A. The engine is making a lot of noise.

   B. How long ______________________________ a lot of noise?

   A. ______________________________ a lot of noise since last week.

   B. Can you bring it in on Wednesday morning?

   A. Wednesday morning? That's fine. See you then.

5. A. We're having a terrible vacation!

   B. That's a shame! What's happening?

   A. It's raining. And it won't stop!

   B. How long ______________________________?

   A. ______________________________ since we arrived here three days ago.

   B. That's too bad. I hope it stops raining soon.

   A. So do I!

6. A. I'm having a problem with my neighbors.

   B. That's too bad. What's the problem?

   A. Their dogs bark all the time. They bark in the morning, they bark in the afternoon, and they bark all night.

   B. How long ______________________________?

   A. ______________________________ for several weeks.

   B. Have you talked to your neighbors?

   A. Yes. And they haven't done anything. I'm very frustrated.

M WHAT ARE THEY SAYING?

bake	build	do	give	make	see	sell	take	write

1. I'm very tired. ___I've been giving___ piano lessons all day. ___I've given___ more than fifteen lessons since this morning.

2. I'm exhausted. ________________ cakes since early this morning. ________ never ____________ so many cakes in one day before.

3. We've been busy. ________________ tee shirts at the mall all afternoon. ________ already ____________ more than 75.

4. My children must be tired. ________________ sandcastles on the beach all morning. Look! ________ already ____________ 9 or 10!

5. I need a break. ________________ inventory all day. ________ never ____________ inventory for so many hours before.

6. Dr. Wilson looks very tired. ________________ patients since 8 A.M. I think ____________ more than 20.

7. You must be tired. ________________ reports all day. ________ never ____________ so many reports in one day before.

8. I'm exhausted! ________________ smoothies all day. Believe it or not, I think ________ already ________ well over a hundred since we opened this morning.

9. Okay. You can stop. ________________ sit-ups for more than an hour. ________ probably ________ more than a hundred.

N THEY'VE BEEN WORKING VERY HARD

The Sanchez family is having a big family reunion this weekend. Mr. and Mrs. Sanchez and their children have been working very hard to get ready for the big event.

bake	hang up	look	make	plant	sing	throw out	vacuum	wash	write

1. Mr. Sanchez ___has been washing___ windows. ___He's___ already ___washed___ more than twenty windows.

2. __________ also ______________________ carpets. __________ already ________________ all the carpets on the first floor of their house.

3. Mrs. Sanchez ________________________ decorations. __________ already ______________ balloons in the living room and the dining room.

4. __________ also __________________ casseroles. __________ already __________________ five chicken casseroles and five tuna casseroles.

5. Their son, Daniel, ________________________ flowers and bushes. __________ already ______________ yellow roses in their yard and two beautiful bushes near the front door.

6. __________ also _______________________________ old newspapers. __________ already _________________ all the old newspapers that were in their basement.

7. Their daughter, Gloria, ________________________. __________ already ________________ ten apple pies and three dozen chocolate chip cookies.

8. __________ also __________________ poems about each member of the family. __________ already __________________ a poem about her brother and a poem about her grandparents.

9. And while they've been working, the whole Sanchez family ______________________ songs. __________ already __________________ more than fifty of their favorite songs.

10. Everybody in the Sanchez family is looking forward to the reunion. ____________________ forward to it for several months. In fact, they have never __________________ forward to anything as much as this weekend's family reunion.

O THEY HAD DONE THAT BEFORE

1. Last night I was looking forward to having the piece of chocolate cake I *(put)* ___had put___ in the refrigerator. But when I opened the refrigerator, it was gone! Somebody *(eat)* ________________ it!

2. Janet was very tired at work yesterday. She was exhausted because her husband *(snore)* ________________ all night the night before and she hadn't slept.

3. Fred couldn't eat any lunch yesterday. He *(be)* ____________ to the dentist that morning, and his mouth still hurt.

4. I didn't go out with Bill last Saturday night. I was upset because he *(go)* ____________ out with my friend Denise the night before.

5. Jerry couldn't read his e-mail yesterday. He *(leave)* ____________ his glasses at a concert the night before.

6. The man who delivered my computer couldn't assemble it because he *(assemble)* __________ never ____________ one before.

7. Jack didn't want to go to work yesterday. He was upset because he *(have)* ______________ a terrible day at work the day before.

8. I fell asleep in Professor Baker's class yesterday. As soon as he started to speak, I realized that he *(give)* ______________ the same lecture the week before.

9. We didn't watch *Jungle Adventure* on TV last night because we *(see)* ____________ it twice at the movie theater.

10. Albert didn't buy anything at the mall last weekend because he *(spend)* ________________ all his money at the mall the weekend before.

11. I didn't wear my pink-and-purple striped shirt to work yesterday. I wanted to, but then I remembered that I *(wear)* ______________ it to work a few days before.

12. Frederick wanted to take a day off last week, but he decided that wasn't a very good idea because he *(take)* ________________ two days off the week before.

13. My children didn't want spaghetti for dinner last night because I *(make)* ________________ it for dinner three times the week before.

P BY THE TIME

1. By the time I *(get)* ___got___ to the bank, it *(close)* ___had___ already ___closed___.

2. By the time I *(do)* ________ my monthly report, my supervisor *(go)* ________ already ____________ home.

3. By the time we *(arrive)* ____________ at the church, Jennifer and Jason *(get)* ________ already ____________ married.

4. By the time we *(drive)* ____________ to the ferry, it *(sail)* ________ already ____________ away.

5. By the time my friend *(bring)* ____________ over his hammer, I *(borrow)* ________ already _______________ one from my neighbor.

6. By the time the interviewer from the Blake Company *(call)* ____________ me back, I *(take)* ________ already ____________ a job with the Drake Company.

7. By the time the doctor *(see)* ____________ my mother, she *(be)* _______________ in the emergency room for three hours.

8. By the time we *(find)* ____________ our seats at the concert hall, the symphony *(begin)* ________ already ____________.

9. By the time my taxi *(drop)* ____________ me off at the train station, the train *(leave)* ________ already ____________.

10. By the time I *(stop)* ____________ speaking, I realized that at least half the audience *(fall)* ________ ____________ asleep.

Q WHAT HAD THEY BEEN DOING?

1. I came down with the flu last week, and I had to cancel my camping trip. I was so disappointed. I *(plan)* ___had been planning___ it for several months.

2. Tom and his girlfriend, Kathy, *(go out)* ______________ for more than five years. When they broke up last week, everybody was very shocked.

3. Brian injured himself and wasn't able to participate in last week's swimming competition. He was extremely disappointed. He *(train)* ______________ for it for months.

4. All our neighbors were surprised when the Carters sold their house last month and moved to a condominium in Arizona. They *(live)* ______________ in our city all their lives.

5. The students in Mr. Frank's eighth-grade English class were upset when he suddenly decided to cancel the school play. They *(rehearse)* ______________ for it all year.

6. I heard that Jonah got sick and couldn't take the SAT test. What's he going to do? He *(prepare)* ______________ for the test since the beginning of the year.

7. I was disappointed that the jewelry store downtown went out of business last month. Everybody says the store *(have)* ______________ a lot of financial problems.

8. We were all surprised when Brenda quit her job at the bank the other day. She *(work)* ______________ there for more than fifteen years.

9. Nobody was surprised when Barry was fired from his job at the Langley Company. He *(come)* ______________ to work late, and he *(fall)* ______________ asleep at his desk every afternoon.

10. It's a shame we arrived late for the space launch. We *(look)* ______________ forward to it all year.

11. My daughter Diane played the piano magnificently at her recital last night. I'm not surprised. She *(practice)* ______________ for the recital for several months.

R GRAMMARRAP: *I Had Been Planning to Call Fernando*

Listen. Then clap and practice.

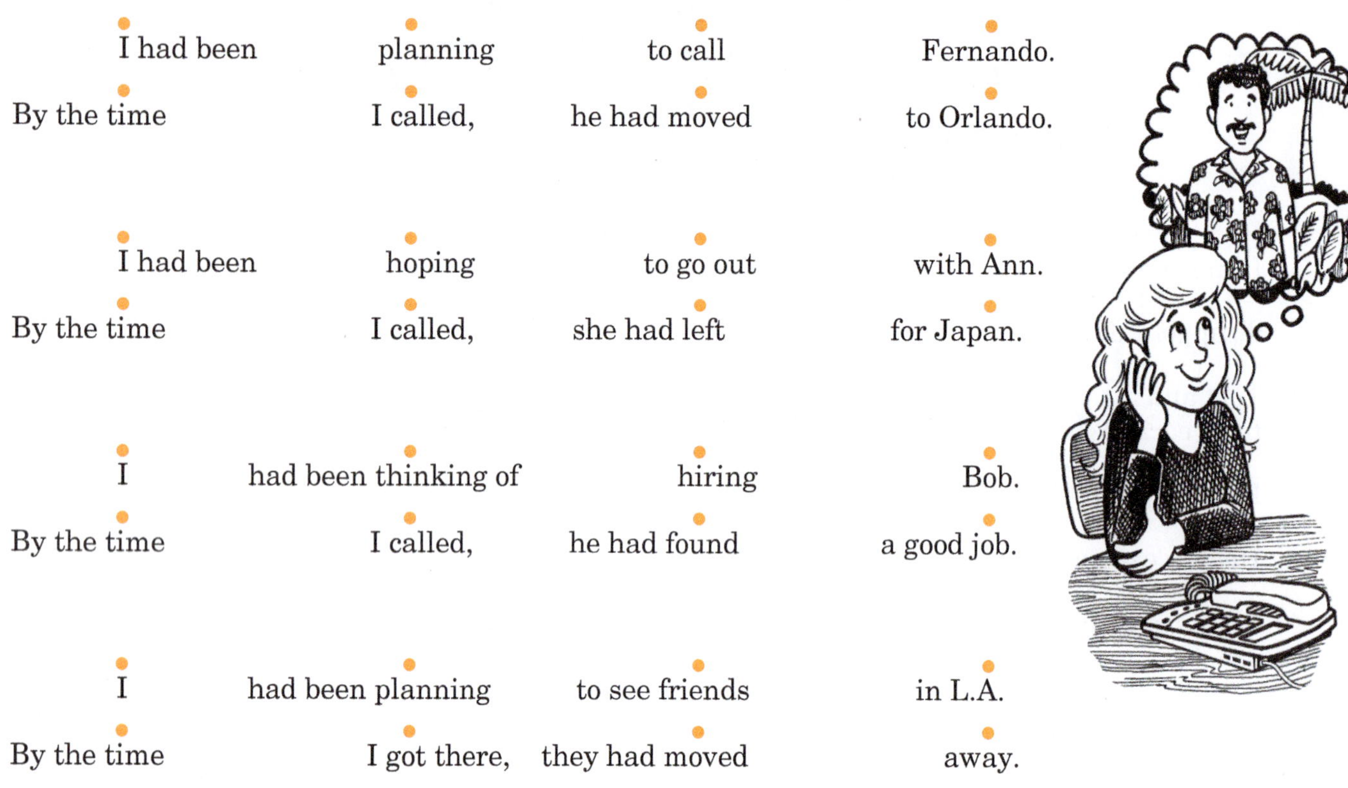

I had been planning to call Fernando.
By the time I called, he had moved to Orlando.

I had been hoping to go out with Ann.
By the time I called, she had left for Japan.

I had been thinking of hiring Bob.
By the time I called, he had found a good job.

I had been planning to see friends in L.A.
By the time I got there, they had moved away.

S LISTENING

Listen to each word and then say it.

bother	both	busy	boss
1. this	6. think	11. music	16. sink
2. father	7. birthday	12. doesn't	17. disappointed
3. they're	8. Theodore	13. days	18. guess
4. that	9. throat	14. because	19. serious
5. weather	10. Martha	15. loves	20. looks

T WHAT ARE _TH_EY _S_AYING?

Fill in the missing letters and then read the conversation aloud.

s th

A. My bro_t__h_er _T__h_eodore doe__n't ____ink he can go to ____e ____eater wi____ u__ tomorrow becau__e he ha__ a __ore ____roat.

B. Ano____er __ore ____roat? ____at's terrible! Didn't he ju__t get over one la__t ____ursday?

A. ____at's right. Believe it or not, ____is is ____e ____ird __ore ____roat he'__ had ____is mon____. My poor bro____er alway__ get__ __ick when ____e wea____er i__ very cold.

B. I hope it i__n't __eriou__ ____is time.

A. I don't ____ink __o. ____eodore __ays hi__ __ore ____roat isn't bo____ering him too much, but bo____ my mo____er and fa____er __ay he'll have to re__t in bed for at lea__t a few day__. ____ey're worried becau__e he i__n't eating any____ing, and ____ey don't ____ink he look__ very heal____y.

B. ____en I gue____ he won't be going to ____e __unday concert ei____er.

A. Probably not. And he'__ very di__appointed. He really love__ cla____ical mu__ic.

B. Well, I'm __orry our plan__ fell ____rough. Plea__e tell ____eodore I hope he feel__ better __oon. Oh, I almo__t forgot. My little si__ter Mar____a is having a __mall bir____day celebration today at ____ree ____irty. Would you like to come?

A. Ye__, of cour__e. ____ank you very much.

A WHAT SHOULD THEY HAVE DONE?

STUDENT BOOK PAGES 15–30

buy	get	go	have	keep	see	sit	speak	study	take

1. Angela was late this morning. She *should have gotten* to the train station earlier.

2. I'm really upset. I burned my cookies. I ______________________ them out of the oven sooner.

3. All the students failed Mrs. Baker's math exam. They ______________________ harder.

4. I got sick because the chili was too spicy. I ______________________ the chicken.

5. Sally went to the beach yesterday, and it started to rain. She ______________________ to the museum.

6. We hated the science fiction movie in Cinema One. We ______________________ the drama in Cinema Two.

7. Nobody could hear you at the meeting. You ______________________ louder.

8. I couldn't hear anything she said. I definitely ______________________ closer.

9. I'm sorry I threw away my ex-girlfriend's letters. I ______________________ them.

10. We're sorry we bought the small TV. We ______________________ the large one.

B GOOD ADVICE

1. I'm sorry. I can't read this.
   a. You shouldn't have written so legibly.
   (b.) You should have written more legibly.

2. I was stuck in traffic for two hours this morning.
   a. You should have driven to work.
   b. You shouldn't have driven to work.

3. Janet had a terrible stomachache last night.
   a. She shouldn't have eaten all the ice cream in her refrigerator.
   b. She should have eaten all the ice cream in her refrigerator.

4. Mr. Hopkins was uncomfortable at the beach.
   a. He shouldn't have worn a jacket and tie.
   b. He should have worn a jacket and tie.

5. We didn't like the movie on TV last night.
   a. You shouldn't have watched something else.
   b. You should have changed the channel.

6. Brian is confused in his Advanced Spanish class.
   a. He shouldn't have taken Beginning Spanish.
   b. He should have taken Beginning Spanish.

C YOU DECIDE: *Uncle Charlie's Advice*

should have	shouldn't have

All my life, my Uncle Charlie has always given me advice. He started giving me advice when I was a young boy.

1. Mom was angry because she tripped and fell when she came into my room this morning.

   Well, you should have ....
   ....,
   and you shouldn't have ....
   ....

2. My parents were upset because I got a terrible grade on my last English test.

   ....
   ....
   ....

3. I wanted to go to the school dance with Amy, but by the time I asked her, she already had another date.

   ....
   ....
   ....

(continued)

Uncle Charlie was still giving me advice as I got older, got married, and had children.

Even now that I'm retired, Uncle Charlie STILL gives me advice.

7. I looked everywhere, but I couldn't find my glasses this morning!

8. I took my granddaughter to the opera last week, and she didn't like it!

9. I have a terrible backache. I played basketball with some of the kids in the neighborhood.

D WHAT MIGHT HAVE HAPPENED?

might have | may have

1. A. I wonder why Louise was late for work this morning.
   B. She *(might / miss)* might have missed the bus.
2. A. What happened to all the ice cream in the refrigerator?
   B. I'm not sure. The children *(may / eat)* may have eaten it.
3. A. I wonder why Donald isn't wearing his new watch.
   B. He *(may / break)* ______________________ it.
4. A. I called Aunt Gertrude all morning, and she wasn't home.
   B. She *(might / go)* ______________________ shopping.
5. A. Lucy didn't come to English class all last week.
   B. She *(may / be)* ______________________ sick.
6. A. I wonder why Nancy and Larry didn't come to my birthday party.
   B. They *(might / forget)* ______________________ about it.
7. A. It's 10 o'clock, and the Baxters haven't arrived at the party yet.
   B. Hmm. They *(might / lost)* ______________________ the directions.

E WHAT'S THE ANSWER?

1. My daughter is sick. She has a bad cold.
   (a.) She may have played with Timmy. He has a cold.
   b. She should have played with Timmy. He has a cold.
2. I wonder why Bertha didn't want to see the Eiffel Tower when she was in Paris.
   a. She should have seen it already.
   b. She might have seen it already.
3. James arrived late for the meeting.
   a. He should have called to tell us.
   b. He may have been late.
4. Rita decided to study Italian in college.
   a. She might have wanted to learn the language her grandparents speak.
   b. She shouldn't have wanted to learn the language her grandparents speak.
5. I wonder why we haven't seen our next-door neighbors recently.
   a. They should have gone on vacation.
   b. They might have gone on vacation.
6. We didn't like the food at that restaurant.
   a. We shouldn't have gone there.
   b. We may have gone there.

F I DON'T UNDERSTAND IT!

1. Grandma __could have watched__ anything on TV last night. Why did she watch an old western she had already seen several times?
2. Tom went to his prom last night. He ______________ any tuxedo he wanted to. Why did he wear a purple one?
3. I don't understand it. My daughter ______________ anybody she wanted to. Why did she marry Herbert?
4. Your friends ______________ their bicycles anywhere. Why did they ride them downtown during rush hour? It's very dangerous!
5. I don't understand it. My son ______________ anything he wanted to. Why did he become a magician?
6. Those children ______________ at the new skating rink in the center of town. Why did they skate on the town pond?
7. Barbara ______________ any course she wanted to. I wonder why she's taking first-year French for the fourth time!
8. Richard Rockford ______________ in any movie he wanted to. I wonder why he's in this awful movie!
9. You ______________ anything you wanted to. Why did you make carrot soup with onions?
10. The Wilsons ______________ their new son anything they wanted to. I wonder why they named him Mortimer!
11. Norman ______________ his living room any color. I wonder why he painted it black!
12. Those tourists ______________ at any restaurant in town. Why did they eat at MacDoodle's?
13. Frank and his wife ______________ to a lot of interesting places for their vacation. Why did they go to Greenville?
14. I don't understand it. Sally ______________ her composition about anything she wanted to. Why did she write about termites?

G GrammarRap: *He Should Have Studied Harder* 

Listen. Then clap and practice.

He should have studied harder.
He could have done his best.
He should have gotten a good night's sleep.
Then he might have passed the test.

She shouldn't have packed so much clothing.
She didn't need all that stuff.
She shouldn't have taken four bathing suits.
One may have been enough.

I should have taken a shorter break.
I shouldn't have come back at three.
I missed a meeting at half past two.
Now my boss is mad at me.

They shouldn't have moved to the suburbs.
They shouldn't have bought a car.
They should have stayed in the city,
Where everything's close, not far.

We should have studied Spanish
Before we went to Spain.
We could have spoken with the people there
The minute we left the plane.

H WHAT HAPPENED?

1. A. Albert has been in a terrible mood all day.

   B. I know. He *(get up)* __must have gotten up__ on the wrong side of the bed this morning.

2. A. Susie has a terrible stomachache.

   B. She *(eat)* ______________________ too many cookies for dessert.

3. A. I think I know you.

   B. I think I know you, too. We *(meet)* ______________________ before.

4. A. It's raining, and I can't find my umbrella.

   B. You *(leave)* ______________________ it at the office.

5. A. I didn't hear a word you said at the meeting.

   B. You didn't? I *(speak)* ____________________________ too softly.

6. A. The boss gave everyone in our office a raise yesterday!

   B. He did? He *(be)* ______________________ in an excellent mood.

7. A. Ellen and her boyfriend, Bob, have stopped talking to each other.

   B. Really? They *(break up)* ______________________________.

8. A. Beverly isn't driving an old car anymore.

   B. I know. She *(buy)* ________________________ a new one.

9. A. Johnny woke up crying in the middle of the night.

   B. I know. I heard him. He *(have)* ______________________ a bad dream.

10. A. The Gleasons' new living room sofa is beautiful.

    B. I know. It *(cost)* ______________________ a lot of money!

11. A. When I saw Donna this morning, she looked upset.

    B. Oh, no! She *(do)* ______________________ badly on her science test.

I YOU DECIDE: *What Must Have Happened at the Millers' House?*

When Barbara and Edward Miller got home last Saturday afternoon, they found their front door was open and everything in the house was out of place. Someone must have broken into their house while they were out!

The first thing they saw was their attractive living room sofa. It was dirty and wet. Someone must have .... 1. Then they found their expensive new lamps on the floor. Someone must have .... 2. Their beautiful glass bowl from Italy wasn't in its usual place on the piano. Someone must have .... 3. Their computer was on, and there was a message on the screen. It said, " .... 4." Someone must have .... 5. They looked for their fax machine, but they couldn't find it. Someone must have .... 6.

Then they looked in the kitchen and found that the kitchen cabinets were all open. Someone must have .... 7. There was also an empty bottle of soda in the kitchen. Someone must have .... 8. And then they found that Barbara's car keys were missing! Someone must have .... 9. The door to the back porch was open, and the dog wasn't in the yard. Someone must have .... 10.

The Millers were very upset. They couldn't believe what had happened while they were out.

J YOU DECIDE: *Might Have / Must Have*

1\.

What did the Baxters name their new baby boy?

I'm not sure. They might have .... , or they might have ....

Didn't they want to name him after the president?

You're right. Then they must have ....

2\.

Where did Elizabeth go on her vacation this year?

I'm not sure. She might have .... , or she might have ....

She sent me a picture of herself on a safari.

Oh. Then she must have ....

3\.

What did Howard have for dinner at the restaurant last night?

I'm not sure. He might have .... , or he might have ....

Didn't you see tomato sauce all over his tie?

No, I didn't. Then he must have ....

4. What vegetables did Martha plant in her garden this year?

I'm not sure. She might have ....
.............................., or she might have ....
....

The last three times I went to her house, we had carrot juice, carrot cake, carrot cookies, and carrot pie!

Oh. Then she must have ....
....

5. What did Mr. and Mrs. Williams do for their wedding anniversary?

I'm not sure. They might have ....
.............................., or they might have ....
....

My brother saw them at the most expensive restaurant in town.

Oh. Then they must have ....
....

6. Poor Angela! Her car wouldn't start this morning. How did she get to work?

I'm not sure. She might have ....
.............................., or she might have ....
....

I think she asked her brother if his bicycle was working.

Oh. Then she must have ....
....

(continued)

7.

K GrammarRap: *What Must Have Happened?* 

Listen. Then clap and practice.

Jonathan looks happy.
He must have gotten hired.
Mortimer looks very sad.
He must have gotten fired.

Timothy is quite upset.
He must have failed the test.
Jennifer is smiling.
She must have done her best.

Melanie looks nervous.
She must have lost her keys.
Her dog looks very anxious, too.
He must have gotten fleas.

Marvin came home late last night.
He must have missed the train.
His coat and hat and shoes were wet.
He must have walked in the rain.

L WHAT'S THE WORD?

could have	might have	should have
couldn't have	must have	shouldn't have

1. It's a very cold day. I ___should have___ worn a sweater. I'm sorry I didn't.
2. Mrs. Johnson never forgets her appointment with the dentist. But yesterday she forgot. I'm sure she ______________ been very busy.
3. I ______________ called you yesterday. I was in an important meeting all day.
4. Our English teacher was late for class today. He ______________ overslept, or the bus______________ been late. I'm not sure.
5. Abigail is very absent-minded. Last week she got on the wrong train. She's very lucky. She ______________ wound up in Canada!
6. I called your apartment all afternoon, and nobody answered. You ______________ gone out.
7. I ______________ gone skiing with you last Saturday. I had to take care of my niece.
8. My washing machine is broken. The repairperson said I never ______________ tried to wash four pairs of sneakers and five pairs of jeans at the same time.
9. I wonder why my cousin Greg didn't want to come to the movie with us last night. He ______________ seen it already. I'm not sure.
10. We ______________ gone sailing on a windy day. We ______________ gotten seasick!
11. You ______________ swept your front porch. It looks so clean!

M LISTENING

Listen and choose the correct answer.

1. (a.) He must have gone to bed very late.
   b. He should have been very tired.
2. a. She must have called them later.
   b. She shouldn't have called them so late.
3. a. He should have missed the bus.
   b. He may have missed the bus.
4. a. You could have caught a cold.
   b. You should have done that.
5. a. He might have gotten a promotion.
   b. He must have been disappointed.
6. a. They should have rehearsed more.
   b. They must have remembered their lines.
7. a. She must have been home.
   b. She might have gone away.
8. a. He could have hurt himself!
   b. He shouldn't have hurt himself!

N WHAT DOES IT MEAN?

Choose the correct answer.

1. Monica overslept.
   a. She came to work late.
   b. She stayed at a friend's house.
   c. She got up too early.

2. My doctor doesn't write legibly enough.
   a. He doesn't write enough.
   b. He doesn't write very often.
   c. I can't read anything he writes.

3. Vincent wound up in jail.
   a. He was dizzy.
   b. He asked a police officer to help him.
   c. He got arrested.

4. Eleanor was almost electrocuted.
   a. Now she's a senator.
   b. Now she's in the hospital.
   c. Now she's an electrician.

5. I owe you an apology.
   a. I'll pay you back.
   b. How much did it cost?
   c. I'm sorry I shouted at you.

6. They ate the entire pizza.
   a. They ate half the pizza.
   b. They ate all the pizza.
   c. They ate just a little pizza.

7. Martha is very understanding.
   a. She understands everything.
   b. She's very sympathetic.
   c. I understand everything she says.

8. He got up on the wrong side of the bed.
   a. Is he in a better mood now?
   b. Did he hurt himself?
   c. He didn't make his bed.

9. Their children refused to go.
   a. They didn't want to go.
   b. They wanted to go.
   c. They went there and returned.

10. We handed over the money.
    a. We held the money.
    b. They returned the money.
    c. We gave them the money.

11. They were having financial problems.
    a. They were having health problems.
    b. They were having family problems.
    c. They were having money problems.

12. Did your landlord evict you?
    a. Yes. We had to move.
    b. Yes. We envied them.
    c. Yes. We enjoyed the apartment.

13. Tony skipped work yesterday.
    a. He came to work early.
    b. He didn't come to work.
    c. He came to work late.

14. We ran up a very large bill.
    a. We spent a lot of money.
    b. We were very tired.
    c. We had never jogged so far.

15. Mrs. Grumble yelled at everybody today.
    a. She was ecstatic.
    b. She must have been in a good mood.
    c. She was very irritable.

16. He didn't act confidently at his interview.
    a. He didn't arrive on time.
    b. He didn't talk enough about his skills.
    c. I can't read anything he writes.

O LISTENING

Listen to each word and then say it.

1. fill—feel
2. filling—feeling
3. fit—feed
4. his—he's
5. it—eat
6. knit—need
7. live—leave
8. living—leaving
9. rich—reach
10. still—steal
11. this—these
12. wig—week
13. will—we'll
14. Tim—team
15. hit—heat

P HAVE YOU HEARD? 

Listen and complete the sentences.

fill	feel

1. (a.) . . . today?
   b. . . . out this income tax form?

still	steal

2. a. . . . cars?
   b. . . . ride your bicycle to work?

this	these

3. a. . . . sneakers?
   b. . . . school?

knitted	needed

4. a. . . . a new sweater.
   b. . . . a new briefcase.

live	leave

5. a. . . . in a small house.
   b. . . . early every day.

living	leaving

6. a. . . . on the third floor.
   b. . . . on the next plane.

his	he's

7. a. . . . very tired.
   b. . . . alarm clock is broken.

It	Eat

8. a. . . . some potatoes instead.
   b. . . . wasn't very fresh.

this	these

9. a. . . . math problems.
   b. . . . homework assignment.

wig	week

10. a. . . . we're going to be busy.
    b. . . . needs a shampoo.

rich	reach

11. a. . . . New York?
    b. . . . and famous?

fill	feel

12. a. . . . it out right away.
    b. . . . a lot better soon.

fit	feed

13. a. . . . the animals very often.
    b. . . . me. They're too small.

It	Eat

14. a. . . . is my favorite recipe.
    b. . . . a little more.

still	steal

15. a. . . . go to high school.
    b. . . . cars anymore.

his	he's

16. a. . . . test was canceled.
    b. . . . getting married soon.

A WHO DID IT?

3

STUDENT BOOK PAGES 31–46

1. A. Did Picasso paint the *Mona Lisa*?

   B. No. The *Mona Lisa* was painted by Leonardo da Vinci.

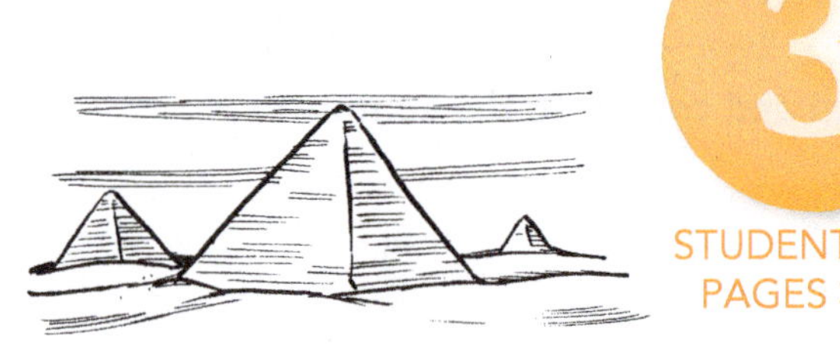

2. A. Did the Romans build the pyramids?

   B. No. The pyramids ______________ by the Egyptians.

3. A. Did the chef serve you dinner at the Ritz?

   B. No. Dinner ______________ by four waiters.

4. A. Did Bruce Springsteen compose "Yesterday"?

   B. No. "Yesterday" ______________ by John Lennon and Paul McCartney.

5. A. Did Ponce de León discover America?

   B. No. America ______________ by Christopher Columbus.

6. A. Did Charles Dickens write *Hamlet*?

   B. No. *Hamlet* ______________ by William Shakespeare.

7. A. Did Queen Elizabeth wear this beautiful gown?

   B. No. This gown ______________ by Jacqueline Kennedy.

8. A. This movie is incredible! Did Fellini direct it?

   B. No. It ______________ by Steven Spielberg.

9. A. Did your parents take this prom picture of you and your girlfriend?

   B. No. This picture ______________ by a photographer.

10. A. Did your mother bake this delicious cake?

    B. No. This cake ______________ by my father.

B YOU DECIDE: *At the Museum*

1. This car *(own)* was owned by the president of .... It *(make)* ________ by the .... Company in .... *(year)*.

2. This airplane *(fly)* ________ by .... in .... *(year)*. It *(design)* ________ ________ by ....

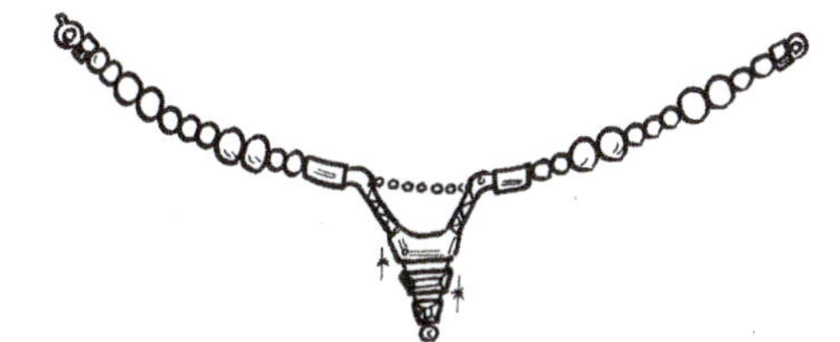

3. This beautiful necklace *(wear)* ________ ________ by the famous actress .... It *(give)* ________ to her by .... It *(leave)* ________ to the museum by her children.

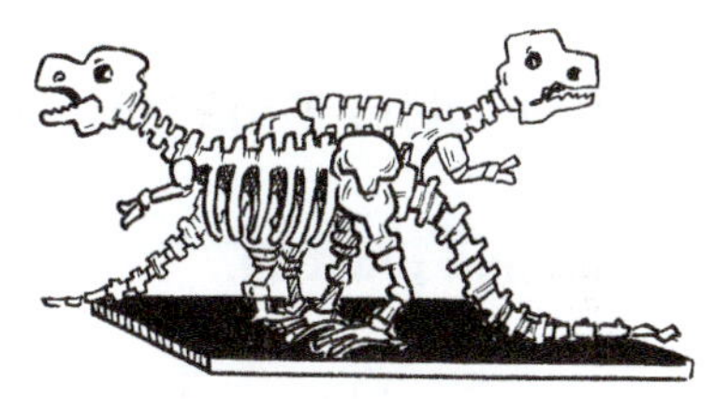

4. These dinosaur skeletons *(find)* ________ ________ by .... in Africa in .... *(year)*. Unfortunately, they *(forget)* ________ by the museum for many years.

5. This letter *(write)* ________ by .... to .... , but it *(send)* ________ never ________ . It *(discover)* ________ recently between the pages of an old book.

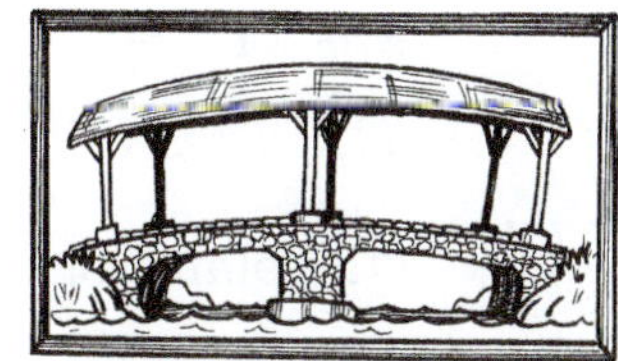

6. This impressive bridge *(build)* ________ ________ in .... *(city)* more than 300 years ago. It *(begin)* ________ ________ in 1520, and it *(finish)* ________ until 1600.

(continued)

7. This is one of ....'s earliest operas. It *(compose)* ________ ________ in .... *(year)*, and it *(sung)* ________ for the first time in .... *(year)*.

8. This portrait ....
....
....
....
....

C GRAMMARRAP: *Who Took This Wonderful Photo of Jill?*

Listen. Then clap and practice.

A. Who took this wonderful photo of Jill?
B. I think it was taken by her brother Bill.

A. Who built that beautiful house on the hill?
B. I think it was built by my cousin Phil.

A. Who wrote this interesting book about dance?
B. I think it was written by someone in France.

A. Who drew the plans for this elegant palace?
B. I think they were drawn by a woman from Dallas.

A. Who sang that wonderful Mexican tune?
B. I think it was sung by a man from Cancún.

A. Who did this beautiful picture of snow?
B. I think it was done by Vincent Van Gogh.

D IT'S TOO LATE

Aunt Louise is a kind and generous person, but she's a little lazy. She wants to help her friends and family, but she never thinks about helping them until it's too late.

1. A. I'll be glad to help you do the dishes.

   B. Thank you, Aunt Louise, but ___they've___ already ___been done___.

2. A. Can I set the table for you?

   B. That's very nice of you, but __________ already __________.

3. A. Do you want me to iron the clothes today?

   B. Thanks, Aunt Louise, but __________ already __________.

4. A. I'll be glad to make Grandpa's doctor's appointment.

   B. That's very kind of you, but __________ already __________.

5. A. I think I'll take down the party decorations.

   B. Don't bother. __________ already __________.

6. A. Here. I'll sweep the floor.

   B. I appreciate it, but __________ already __________.

7. A. I'll be glad to buy flowers for the table.

   B. Thank you, Aunt Louise, but __________ already __________.

8. A. Do you want me to hang up the new portrait?

   B. I guess you haven't looked in the hall. __________ already __________.

E LISTENING

Listen and decide what is being talked about.

1. (a.) the cookies
   b. the bed
2. a. the train
   b. the movie
3. a. the packages
   b. the letter
4. a. the scarf
   b. the fireplace
5. a. the presents
   b. the children
6. a. the bicycles
   b. the letters
7. a. the song
   b. the portrait
8. a. the books
   b. the cats
9. a. the meeting room
   b. the alarm

F NOTHING IS READY!

- [ ] make the beds
- [ ] sweep the porch
- [ ] prepare the salad
- [ ] feed the cat
- [ ] put the children to bed

A. What are we going to do? All our friends will be arriving soon, and nothing is ready. The beds *haven't been made* ¹. The porch __________ ². The salad __________ ³. The cat __________ ⁴. And the children __________ ⁵ to bed. I'm really upset.

B. Don't worry. Everything will be okay. We still have some time.

G AT THE HOSPITAL

- [x] take Mrs. Johnson's blood pressure
- [x] give Ms. Blake her injection
- [x] do Mr. Tanaka's cardiogram
- [x] tell Mrs. Wong about her operation
- [x] send Mr. Bacon home

A. How have all the patients been this morning? Have there been any problems?

B. Everything is fine, Doctor.

A. How is Mrs. Johnson this morning? *Has* ¹ her blood pressure *been taken* ² yet?

B. Yes, it has. And it wasn't as high as it was yesterday.

A. That's good. And __________ ³ Ms. Blake __________ ⁴ her injection?

B. Yes, she has. And we'll give her another at two o'clock.

A. What about Mr. Tanaka? __________ ⁵ his cardiogram __________ ⁶?

B. Yes. It __________ ⁷ an hour ago.

A. Mrs. Wong looks upset. __________ ⁸ she __________ ⁹ about her operation?

B. Yes. I explained everything to her, and I think she understands.

A. And finally, is Mr. Bacon ready to leave the hospital?

B. He's MORE than ready! __________ ¹⁰ already __________ ¹¹ home!

H CAN WE LEAVE SOON?

- [x] stop the mail
- [x] turn off the lights
- [ ] set the alarm
- [ ] take out the garbage

A. Can we leave soon?

B. I think so. The mail has been stopped [1], and the lights ______________ [2].

A. Great!

B. Wait a minute! ______________ [3] the house alarm ______________ [4]?

A. No, it hasn't. But don't worry about it. I'll do it right away.

B. And now that I think of it, ______________ [5] the garbage ______________ [6]?

A. I'm not sure. Why don't I go and see?

I CROSSWORD

Across

2. The paychecks were ______ this morning.
4. Has the kitchen floor been ______ yet?
7. The Christmas presents were ______ in the attic last year.

Down

1. This picture was ______ by my daughter.
2. I hope your homework has already been ______.
3. This dress was ______ by Oleg Cassini.
5. The beds have already been ______.
6. That terrible speech was ______ by the president of our company.

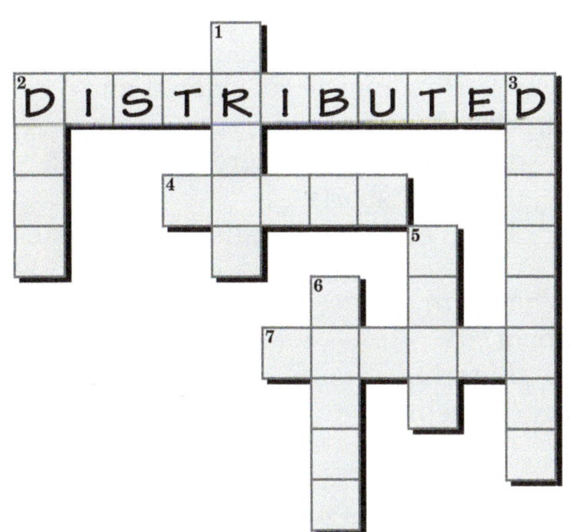

J ERNEST HEMINGWAY

Read and then answer the questions below.

Ernest Hemingway is considered one of the most important modern American writers. He wrote six novels and more than fifty short stories. He also wrote many poems and newspaper articles.

Hemingway's books are lively and exciting. They are full of fighting, traveling, sports, love, and war. Hemingway's life was also lively and exciting.

When he was a young high school student, Hemingway played football, boxed, and wrote for the school newspaper. He ran away from home when he was fifteen years old, but he returned and finished high school in 1917. He never went to college.

Hemingway wanted to fight in World War I, but he was rejected by the army. Instead, he went to war as an ambulance driver and was badly injured.

In 1921, Hemingway went to Paris and started writing seriously. He stayed there for six years. His first novel, *The Sun Also Rises*, was written when he was still in Paris. It made him very famous.

In 1937, Hemingway went to Spain as a journalist to write about the Spanish Civil War. In 1944 he returned to Europe and wrote newspaper articles about World War II. Although he wasn't in the army, it is believed he did more fighting than writing during the war.

What's the Answer?

1. Why is Hemingway considered an important writer?
   a. He wrote many interesting works.
   b. He liked sports.
   c. He lived in many different countries.

2. What *didn't* Ernest Hemingway write about?
   a. Fighting.
   b. Traveling.
   c. Cooking.

3. What did Hemingway do when he was fifteen years old?
   a. He ran a long way.
   b. He left home.
   c. He went to high school.

4. Which of these statements about Hemingway is true?
   a. He finished high school.
   b. He went to college.
   c. He didn't play any sports in high school.

5. Why didn't Hemingway serve in the army?
   a. He wanted to fight.
   b. The army didn't want him.
   c. He didn't want to fight.

6. Which of these statements about Hemingway *isn't* true?
   a. He was a journalist for a while.
   b. He wrote about the Spanish Civil War.
   c. *The Sun Also Rises* was written in Spain.

K A ROBBERY

Mr. and Mrs. Wilson *(rob)* ___were___1 ___robbed___2 last month. Their TV, their computer, and all of their beautiful living room furniture *(steal)* ______3 ______4. In fact, nothing *(leave)* ______5 ______6 in the living room except the rug. Fortunately, Mrs. Wilson's gold necklace *(take)* ______7 ______8. She was glad because it had been *(give)* ______9 to her by her husband many years ago.

The thief *(see)* ______10 ______11 driving away from the house in a small black van. The neighbors called the police, and the man *(arrest)* ______12 ______13. He *(send)* ______14 ______15 to jail for seven years.

A day after the robbery, the living room furniture, the computer, and the TV *(return)* ______16 ______17. The sofa had *(rip)* ______18 ______19, but fortunately everything else was okay.

L LISTENING

Listen and choose the correct answer.

1. (a.) Yes. It's already been fixed.
   b. No. It hasn't been swept yet.
2. a. Yes. It's already been set.
   b. Yes. It's already been set up.
3. a. It was written by my uncle.
   b. It was taken by my wife.
4. a. I'm sorry. They've already been sung.
   b. I'm sorry. They've already been hung.
5. a. He was hurt in an accident.
   b. He was offered a better job.
6. a. She's already been lent.
   b. She's already been sent.
7. a. Yes. It's been rejected.
   b. Yes. It's been approved.
8. a. She was hired by the Blaine Company.
   b. She was fired by the Blaine Company.
9. a. They've already been hung.
   b. They've already been sung.
10. a. Yes. It's already been baked.
    b. Yes. It's already been set.
11. a. It's already been read.
    b. It's already been played.
12. a. She's been taken to the hospital.
    b. She's been invited to a wedding.

M YOU DECIDE: *A Famous Composer*

...........................1 is an extremely talented composer. She has written many beautiful sonatas. Her compositions *(perform)* have 2 been 3 performed 4 in Asia, in the United States, and in ....5. Her symphonies are often *(hear)* ________ 6 on the radio.

Ms. ....7 started to compose music when she was ....8 years old. She *(give)* ________ 9 ________ 10 a composition book for her birthday, and she knew right away that she wanted to be a composer.

In 1985, she sent some of her sonatas and a symphony to the ....11 Symphony Orchestra, but all these early compositions *(reject)* ________ 12 ________ 13. Ms. ....14 was disappointed, but she continued to compose. Finally, in 1994, several of her sonatas *(recorded)* ________ 15 ________ 16 by the ....17 Symphony Orchestra.

It took many years before Ms. ....18's music *(appreciate)* ________ 19 ________ 20. At first, her music *(consider)* ________ 21 ________ 22 strange because it was new and different, and it *(understand)* ________ 23 not easily ________ 24. Most people couldn't hear the beautiful melodies. Today, of course, Ms. ....25 is highly *(respect)* ________ 26 by composers all over the world.

In 1996, she wrote her most famous symphony called "...........................27." A year later, it *(used)* ________ 28 ________ 29 as the music in a very successful movie. Since then, she has written three other symphonies that *(play)* ________ 30 ________ 31 ________ 32 all over the world.

In 2001, Ms. ....33 *(hurt)* ________ 34 ________ 35 badly in a car accident. She composed a sonata about this terrible accident. In 2002, Ms. ....36 *(choose)* ________ 37 ________ 38 best composer of the year. She *(invite)* ________ 39 ________ 40 to play her music at the White House in Washington, D.C.

N WHAT ARE THEY SAYING?

bake	promote	rewrite	take in
clip	repair	set up	wash

1. A. The president is concerned. Is his speech ready?
   B. It'll be ready soon. ___It's___ ___being rewritten___.
2. A. Why are you taking the bus to work?
   B. My car was in an accident. ________ still ______________________.
3. A. Is this Bob's Bakery? I'm calling about the cake I ordered.
   B. I'm sorry. It isn't ready yet. ________ still ______________________.
4. A. Should I pick up my pants at the tailor's?
   B. Not yet. ____________ still ______________________.
5. A. Is Carla going to quit her job at the Internet company?
   B. No. She's decided to stay because ______________________ next week.
6. A. Is the meeting room ready?
   B. Not yet. ________ still ______________________.
7. A. What happened to the shirt I wore to the baseball game yesterday?
   B. ______________________. It was very dirty.
8. A. Hello. This is Mrs. Vickers. When is my poodle going to be ready?
   B. Very soon. His hair ______________________ right now.

O GRAMMARRAP: *Spring Cleaning* 

Listen. Then clap and practice.

The family's getting organized.
The beds are being made.
The kitchen's being swept and cleaned.
The bills are being paid.
The sheets and towels are being washed
And dried and put away.
The rugs are being vacuumed.
Spring cleaning starts today.

P A FACTORY TOUR

Good morning, and welcome to your tour of Bob and Betty's Ice Cream Factory. We make the best ice cream in the world, and you're going to see how we do it! You'll learn a lot about how ice cream *(made)* ___is___ 1 ___made___ 2 at Bob and Betty's! Let's begin.

In this room, cream *(take)* ______ 3 ______ 4 out of our large refrigerators. Then the cream *(put)* ______ 5 ______ 6 into this machine. The cream *(mix)* ______ 7 ______ 8 for about forty minutes in this machine. While the cream is mixing, sugar *(pour)* ______ 9 ______ 10 slowly into the cream by our ice cream makers.

In the next room, the flavors *(prepare)* ______ 11 ______ 12. Today we are making banana nut ice cream. Right now, different kinds of nuts *(chop)* ______ 13 ______ 14 ______ 15 in a large chopper. It's a very expensive machine, but it chops the nuts very quickly. Also, bananas *(slice)* ______ 16 ______ 17 ______ 18 in our new computer-controlled slicing machine.

When the nuts and bananas are ready, they *(add)* ______ 19 ______ 20 to the sugar and cream in a special machine that *(invent)* ______ 21 ______ 22 by Betty a few years ago.

The ice cream *(keep)* ______ 23 ______ 24 in a large cold room until it *(sent)* ______ 25 ______ 26 by trucks all over the country.

That is the end of our tour. Thank you for visiting our factory, and we invite you to go to our tasting room, where our delicious ice cream can *(enjoy)* ______ 27 ______ 28 by all our visitors.

Q WHAT DOES IT MEAN?

Choose the correct answer.

1. I've got to take in my suit.
   (a.) It's too big.
   b. It's too small.
   c. It's too hot.

2. You're required to go to the meeting.
   a. You might go to the meeting.
   b. You don't have to go to the meeting.
   c. You have to go to the meeting.

3. Lois ran up a big phone bill.
   a. She talked on the telephone a lot.
   b. She didn't use her cell phone.
   c. The phone company gave her a phone.

4. Ms. Johnson was promoted.
   a. She was hired.
   b. She was given a more important job.
   c. She was fired.

5. Parking is permitted here.
   a. You can't park here.
   b. You can park here.
   c. You have to park here.

6. Tom is distributing the mail right now.
   a. He's giving it to everyone.
   b. He's sending it to everyone.
   c. He's opening the mail for everyone.

7. I was rejected by Harvard University.
   a. I'll work there next year.
   b. I'll be a student there next year.
   c. I'll attend another college next year.

8. You'll be allowed to vote when you're older.
   a. You'll be required to vote.
   b. You'll be permitted to vote.
   c. You'll want to vote.

9. She was offered the position.
   a. She was given the job.
   b. She was told about the position.
   c. She was taken off the position.

10. Where are the decorations?
    a. They've already been offered.
    b. They've already been set.
    c. They've already been hung up.

11. This is a beautiful portrait.
    a. Who directed it?
    b. Who invented it?
    c. Who painted it?

12. I'm going overseas to work.
    a. My boss is going to watch me.
    b. I'm going to work in another country.
    c. I'm going to work near the water.

13. I'm confident about the future.
    a. I'm concerned about the future.
    b. I'm confused about the future.
    c. I'm positive about the future.

14. My son was chosen "Student of the Month."
    a. He must be afraid.
    b. He must be thrilled.
    c. He must be hung up.

R LISTENING 

Listen and choose the correct answer.

1. (a.) When will it be finished?
   b. When was it finished?

2. a. When will it be ready?
   b. How long ago did you finish?

3. a. They've been made.
   b. They're being made.

4. a. I didn't receive mine.
   b. Someone is distributing them.

5. a. It's being set up.
   b. It's been set up.

6. a. I see. When will it be ready?
   b. Good. I'll come over right away.

7. a. When will they be ready?
   b. How long have they been ready?

8. a. I don't want to disturb them.
   b. How long ago did you feed them?

✓ CHECK-UP TEST: Chapters 1–3

A. Complete the sentences.

Ex. My son can swim very well. ___He's___ ___swum___ for many years.

1. Can you speak Chinese? I can speak it very well. __________ ____________ it for many years.
2. Can you ride horses? My daughter __________ ____________ horses for a long time.
3. When did you take your break? I __________ ____________ my break yet.
4. When are you going to eat lunch? I'm hungry. I __________ ____________ lunch yet.
5. When are you going to write your composition? I __________ ____________ mine yet.

   Bob ____________ his composition a little while ago.
6. How long __________ you and your husband ____________ married?
7. My daughter __________ ____________ studying English for the past few hours.
8. Paul didn't see a movie last weekend. He __________ ____________ a movie the weekend before.
9. By the time I got to the plane, it __________ already ____________ off.
10. I'm sorry to hear that Debbie and her boyfriend broke up. They __________ __________

    ____________ out for several years.

B. Complete the sentences.

could have	might have	must have	should have	shouldn't have

(give) *Ex.* You ___shouldn't___ ___have___ ___given___ Howard eggs for breakfast. He's allergic to them.

(practice) 1. Boris has won every chess game he's played today. He ___________ ___________

_________________ a lot.

(do) 2. I don't have anything to wear today. I _________ ________ ________ my laundry.

(leave) 3. Timmy can't find his homework. He __________ ________ ________ it at home,

or he __________ ________ ________ it on the bus. He can't remember.

(build) 4. The Ace Corporation __________ __________ ____________ their office building anywhere. It was a mistake to build it here.

(study) **5.** You did very well on your test. You __________ __________ __________ a lot.

(wear) **6.** It's hot in here. I __________ __________ __________ a heavy sweater to work today.

(feed) **7.** You __________ __________ __________ Rex. He's been hungry all morning.

(fall) **8.** Terry shouldn't have stood on that broken chair. She __________ __________ __________.

(spend) **9.** I __________ __________ __________ ten dollars, or I __________ __________ __________ twelve dollars. I can't remember.

C. Complete the sentences.

(write) *Ex.* This poem ___was___ ___written___ in 2001.

(draw) **1.** This picture __________ __________ by a famous artist.

(repair) **2.** I can't drive my car to work. __________ still __________ __________.

(give) **3.** My wife __________ __________ __________ a raise twice this year.

(teach) **4.** Every student should __________ __________ a foreign language.

(do) **5.** Nobody has to do the dishes. __________ already __________ __________.

(take in) **6.** Your pants aren't ready yet. __________ still __________ __________.

(choose) **7.** Margaret __________ __________ "Employee of the Year."

(make) **8.** This is a very interesting novel. I think it should __________ __________ into a movie.

(send) **9.** Grandma is still in the hospital. She __________ __________ __________ home yet.

D. Listening

Listen and choose the correct answer.

Ex. (a.) When was it completed?
b. When will it be completed?

1. a. When will you finish taking them?
b. When did you finish taking them?

2. a. How much longer will it take?
b. How long ago did you hang them up?

3. a. They're being made.
b. They've been made.

4. a. When was it completed?
b. When will it be done?

5. a. Good. I'll pick it up soon.
b. When will it be ready?

A INVENTIONS THAT CHANGED THE WORLD

Read the article on student book page 47 and answer the questions.

SIDE by SIDE Gazette

STUDENT BOOK PAGES **47–50**

1. Alexander Fleming discovered ______.
   a. bacteria
   b. X-rays
   c. an antibiotic
   d. mold

2. The first screws were ______.
   a. mass-produced
   b. made of wood
   c. used to hold things together
   d. small

3. The first Nobel Prize in Physics was for ______.
   a. the screw
   b. the telephone
   c. the television
   d. the X-ray machine

4. Alexander Graham Bell was NOT ______.
   a. deaf
   b. a teacher
   c. a doctor
   d. an inventor

5. The first telephone call was made ______.
   a. in 1895
   b. to Thomas Watson
   c. to Alexander Graham Bell
   d. by Thomas Watson

6. Computers were very large before the invention of ______.
   a. the telephone
   b. the X-ray machine
   c. the television
   d. the microchip

7. The first ______ was built for the army.
   a. computer
   b. telephone
   c. television
   d. X-ray machine

8. The first television was made of ______.
   a. paper and glass
   b. needles and a bicycle
   c. common household objects
   d. wires and tubes

B FACT FILE

Look at the Fact File on student book page 47 and answer the questions.

1. The Fact File presents information in the form of ______.
   a. a graph
   b. a major invention
   c. a time line
   d. an article

2. The Fact File helps the reader understand the article about inventions because ______.
   a. it gives the information in a visual form
   b. it summarizes the article
   c. it gives opinions about inventions
   d. it tells about the lives of inventors

3. The microscope was invented ______ years after the printing press.
   a. 50
   b. 100
   c. 140
   d. 150

4. ______ in the twentieth century.
   a. CDs were NOT invented
   b. X-rays were NOT discovered
   c. Penicillin was NOT discovered
   d. Gas-powered cars were NOT invented

C AROUND THE WORLD

Read the information on student book page 48 and answer the questions.

1. This information is presented in the form of ______.
   a. an article
   b. photographs with captions
   c. a chart
   d. a timeline

2. ______ was built in the 12th century.
   a. The Taj Mahal
   b. The Great Wall of China
   c. The Temple of Angkor Wat
   d. Machu Picchu

3. ______ was a city.
   a. Stonehenge
   b. The Taj Mahal
   c. The Colosseum
   d. Tenochtitlan

4. ______ is older than the Colosseum.
   a. Machu Picchu
   b. Stonehenge
   c. The Taj Mahal
   d. The Temple of Angkor Wat

5. ______ is a modern wonder of the world.
   a. Machu Picchu
   b. The Great Wall of China
   c. The Temple of Angkor Wat
   d. The Panama Canal

6. The Taj Mahal and the Pyramids were both built ______.
   a. in Egypt
   b. more than 1000 years ago
   c. for the dead
   d. with machines

7. 200,000 to 300,000 people ______.
   a. built Tenochtitlan
   b. lived in Tenochtitlan
   c. live in Mexico City
   d. built the Taj Mahal

8. No one knows ______.
   a. why Shah Jahan built the Taj Mahal
   b. why the Egyptians built the Pyramids
   c. who built Stonehenge
   d. why the Temple of Angkor Wat was built

9. ______ was definitely NOT a place of worship.
   a. The Colosseum
   b. Stonehenge
   c. The Temple of Angkor Wat
   d. Machu Picchu

10. People say that the Great Wall is visible from the moon because it is ______.
    a. in the mountains
    b. very tall
    c. very bright
    d. very long

11. Machu Picchu was *abandoned* in the 1500s means ______.
    a. everybody left
    b. construction was finished
    c. it was destroyed
    d. it was dedicated

12. Which sentence best *summarizes* this information?
    a. These places were constructed for religious purposes.
    b. The world is full of modern and ancient wonders.
    c. The United Nations helps preserve these wonders.
    d. These are the most popular places to visit in the world.

D AROUND THE WORLD: Writing

What is another wonder of the world that you know about? Write a paragraph about it. Use some of these words in your paragraph: *begun, built, completed, constructed, dedicated, designed, established, inhabited, preserved, rebuilt, repaired, used.*

E INTERVIEW

Read the interview on student book page 49 and answer the questions.

1. Sam Turner has been a photojournalist ______.
   a. since he was ten
   b. since he won a competition
   c. for ten years
   d. for twenty years

2. He grew up in Australia because ______.
   a. his parents were American
   b. his parents were Australian
   c. his parents worked there
   d. he loved the Outback

3. Many people encouraged him to study photography because ______.
   a. he took many family trips
   b. they were impressed by his photos
   c. he was given a camera
   d. he went to photography school

4. His photography is inspired by ______.
   a. his parents
   b. his camera
   c. the national photo competition
   d. nature

5. His most important life event was ______.
   a. winning a photo contest
   b. hiking to the top of Mt. Everest
   c. climbing to the base of Mt. Everest
   d. returning to Mt. Everest

6. You can infer that he would NOT be inspired to take photographs of ______.
   a. the Statue of Liberty
   b. the Grand Canyon
   c. the Mississippi River
   d. Yellowstone National Park

F YOU'RE THE INTERVIEWER!

Interview a classmate, a neighbor, or a friend. Use the chart below to record the person's answers. Then share what you learned with the class.

What is something you are very interested in? How did you become interested in that?	
What has been the most memorable event in your life so far?	
What do you dream about doing someday?	

G FUN WITH IDIOMS

Choose the best response.

1. I was blown away by the cost of the dinner.
   a. I know. It was very windy.
   b. I was surprised, too.
   c. I didn't enjoy it either.
   d. I also thought it was delicious.

2. My bus was held up by the parade.
   a. My bus was stuck in traffic, too.
   b. Yes. I saw your bus in the parade.
   c. I'm glad you arrived early.
   d. I agree. It was a colorful parade.

3. Since you didn't call me, I was left in the dark about our plans.
   a. Yes. It was dark when I called.
   b. I'm sorry the lights went out.
   c. I'm sorry you didn't know.
   d. I'm sorry it was dark.

4. Tom was given the ax last week.
   a. That's wonderful news!
   b. I'm sure he's very happy.
   c. That's a very unusual gift.
   d. What a shame!

H WE'VE GOT MAIL!

Choose the words that best complete each sentence.

1. The wheel ______ in 3500 B.C.
   a. is invented c. was invented
   b. invented d. has invented

2. The Taj Mahal ______ in the 17th century.
   a. was built c. built
   b. has built d. was building

3. All students ______ to take the final exam.
   a. be required c. requiring
   b. are required d. have required

4. The instructions ______ on the board.
   a. were writing c. wrote
   b. written d. were written

5. The stop sign ______ by a truck last night.
   a. is hit c. was hit
   b. hit d. was being hit

6. Children should not ______ to see that movie.
   a. allow c. are allowed
   b. allowed d. be allowed

Choose the sentence that is correct and complete.

7. a. The oil in my car was changing.
   b. The oil in my car be changed.
   c. The oil in my car being changed.
   d. The oil in my car was changed.

8. a. He be taken to the hospital.
   b. He took to the hospital.
   c. He was taken to the hospital.
   d. He was took to the hospital.

9. a. The new curtains were hung.
   b. The new curtains be hung.
   c. The new curtains been hung.
   d. The new curtains being hung.

10. a. The house built in 1953.
    b. The house was built in 1953.
    c. The house has built in 1953.
    d. The house being built in 1953.

11. a. She been told about the meeting.
    b. She not be told about the meeting.
    c. She being told about the meeting.
    d. She wasn't told about the meeting.

12. a. The winner be chosen soon.
    b. The winner chose soon.
    c. The winner will be chosen soon.
    d. The winner was chose soon.

I "CAN-DO" REVIEW

Match the "can do" statement and the correct sentence.

____ 1. I can tell about my work experience.
____ 2. I can ask about the duration of an activity.
____ 3. I can tell about the duration of an activity.
____ 4. I can evaluate my own activities.
____ 5. I can make a deduction.
____ 6. I can apologize.
____ 7. I can express agreement.
____ 8. I can express uncertainty.
____ 9. I can offer to do something.
____ 10. I can react to good news.

a. I've been waiting for the plumber all morning.
b. Tony must have missed the bus.
c. Do you want me to do the dishes?
d. I'm sorry.
e. I've flown airplanes for many years.
f. I'm not sure.
g. That's wonderful!
h. How long have you been studying for the test?
i. I think so, too.
j. I shouldn't have eaten that entire dessert.

A THEY DIDN'T SAY

STUDENT BOOK PAGES 51–64

A. Were you just talking to George and Janet on the phone?

B. Yes. They called from California.

A. How are they?

B. They're fine.

A. The last time I heard from them, they were building a new house. Where are they living now?

B. I don't know _____where they're living now_____ 1. They didn't say.

A. Where is Janet working?

B. I have no idea ________________ 2. She didn't say.

A. How are their children?

B. I'm not sure ________________ 3. They didn't say.

A. Tell me about George. When will he be starting his new job?

B. I don't know ________________ 4. He didn't say.

A. I really miss George and Janet. When are they going to come to New York?

B. I'm not sure ________________ 5. They didn't say.

A. When will their new house be finished?

B. I don't know ________________ 6. They didn't say.

A. What have they been doing since we saw them last summer?

B. I have no idea ________________ 7. They didn't say.

A. Why haven't they e-mailed us?

B. I'm not sure ________________ 8. They didn't say.

A. This is ridiculous! I'm going to call them tonight. What's their telephone number?

B. I'm sorry. I don't know ________________ 9. They didn't say.

B I'M NOT THE PERSON TO ASK

1. A. What does this painting mean?
   B. I have no idea ___what this painting means___.
2. A. Why does Robert always get to school so early?
   B. I don't know ______.
3. A. When did the ice cream truck come by?
   B. I have no idea ______.
4. A. Where does Margaret work?
   B. I don't remember ______.
5. A. How did Sam break his arm?
   B. I don't know ______.
6. A. Why did Alice rewrite her novel?
   B. I have no idea ______.
7. A. What time does the concert begin?
   B. I'm not sure ______.
8. A. When does the bank open tomorrow?
   B. I have no idea ______.
9. A. What did we do in French class yesterday?
   B. I can't remember ______.
10. A. Where did Mom and Dad go?
    B. I have no idea ______.
11. A. How much does a quart of milk cost?
    B. I don't know ______.

C TOO MANY QUESTIONS!

A. Daddy, when did you learn to drive?

B. I can't remember ___when I learned to drive___ [1].
It was a long time ago.

A. Why doesn't Grandma drive?

B. I don't know ______ [2].
You'll have to ask her.

A. Daddy, I've been thinking . . . Why is the sky blue?

B. I don't know ______ [3].

A. How do birds learn to fly?

B. I'm not sure ______ [4].

A. Why are clouds white?

B. I don't know ______ [5].

A. What time does the zoo open tomorrow?

B. I'm sorry. I don't know ______ [6].

A. Daddy, do you remember the mouse that was in our attic last winter?

B. Yes, I do.

A. Where is that mouse now?

B. I don't know ______ [7].

A. Daddy, why ...... [8]?

B. I have no idea ...... [9].

A. Daddy, when ...... [10]?

B. I don't remember ...... [11].

A. When will we be home?

B. I hope we'll be home soon.

D WHAT ARE THEY SAYING?

1. Do you know _______?
   a. what time it is
   b. what time is it
2. Could you possibly tell me _______?
   a. when will the train arrive
   b. when the train will arrive
3. Can you tell me _______?
   a. where do they live
   b. where they live
4. I'm not sure _______.
   a. how long they're going to stay
   b. how long are they going to stay
5. I'm sorry. I have no idea _______.
   a. when will she be back
   b. when she'll be back
6. Could you possibly tell me _______?
   a. how I can get there from here
   b. how can I get there from here
7. I can't remember _______.
   a. why does she want to talk to me
   b. why she wants to talk to me
8. Do you have any idea _______?
   a. whose glasses are these
   b. whose glasses these are
9. Could you please tell me _______?
   a. how much this costs
   b. how much does this cost
10. I don't remember _______.
    a. what are our plans for the weekend
    b. what our plans are for the weekend

E LISTENING 

Listen and decide what is being talked about.

1. a. a bus
   b. a movie
2. a. a word
   b. a person
3. a. a cake
   b. a photograph
4. a. a bicycle
   b. a car
5. a. a movie
   b. a train
6. a. a plane ticket
   b. a TV
7. a. the packages
   b. the restrooms
8. a. the books
   b. the animals

F GRAMMARRAP: *Do You Know How Long This Flight Will Take?* 

Listen. Then clap and practice.

A. Do you know how long this flight will take?
Do you know what kind of food they'll make?
Do you know what movie they'll show on the plane?
Do you know what time we'll get to Spain?

B. I don't know how long this flight will take.
I'm not sure what kind of food they'll make.
I don't know what movie they'll show on the plane.
I have no idea when we'll get to Spain.

G YOU DECIDE: *What Are They Saying?*

Answer the questions with any vocabulary you wish.

1\. How much does this bicycle cost?

A. Can you tell me how much this bicycle costs?

B. ....

....

2\.

A. Could you possibly tell me ______________________?

B. ....

....

3\.

A. Do you have any idea ______________________?

B. ....

....

4\.

A. Could you tell me ______________________?

B. ....

....

5\.

A. Can you tell me ______________________?

B. ....

....

6. How long have we been driving?

A. Do you have any idea ________________

________________________________?

B. ....

....

7. Why is Johnny sitting in a puddle?

A. Can you tell me ________________

________________________________?

B. ....

....

8. When does the post office open?

A. Do you by any chance know __________

________________________________?

B. ....

....

9. What's in the "Chicken Surprise Casserole"?

A. Could you please tell me __________

________________________________?

B. ....

....

10. When will you be getting out of here?

A. Do you know ________________

________________________________?

B. ....

....

H GrammarRap: *Mystery People*

Listen. Then clap and practice.

A. What did he do?
B. I don't know what he did.
A. Why did he hide?
B. I don't know why he hid.
A. Where did he go?
B. I don't know where he went.
A. What did he spend?
B. I don't know what he spent.

A. What did she say?
B. I don't know what she said.
A. What did she read?
B. I don't know what she read.
A. Where was her purse?
B. I don't know where it was.
A. What does she do?
B. I don't know what she does.

A. What did they buy?
B. I don't know what they bought.
A. What did they bring?
B. I don't know what they brought.
A. What did they sell?
B. I don't know what they sold.
A. Who did they tell?
B. I'm not sure who they told.

I WHAT ARE THEY SAYING?

1. Do you know _______?
   (a.) whether parking is permitted here
   b. if is parking permitted here

2. Can you tell me _______?
   a. if will the library be open tomorrow
   b. if the library will be open tomorrow

3. Do you by any chance know _______?
   a. whether it's going to rain this weekend
   b. if is it going to rain this weekend

4. Could you please tell me _______?
   a. whether does this bus stop at the mall
   b. if this bus stops at the mall

5. Do you have any idea _______?
   a. if they were upset
   b. whether were they upset

6. Can you possibly tell me _______?
   a. if the bus will be arriving soon
   b. if will the bus be arriving soon

7. Do you know _______?
   a. whether they're coming to our party
   b. if are they coming to our party

8. Can you tell me _______?
   a. whether did I pass the test
   b. if I passed the test

9. Does our superintendent know _______?
   a. if the plumber is coming soon
   b. whether is the plumber coming soon

10. Do you by any chance know _______?
    a. whether I'm going to be fired
    b. if am I going to be fired

J LISTENING

Listen and decide where these people are.

1. (a.) a beach
   b. a parking lot

2. a. a department store
   b. a laundromat

3. a. a playground
   b. a theater

4. a. a parking garage
   b. a parking lot

5. a. a train station
   b. a gas station

6. a. a classroom
   b. a restaurant

7. a. a bakery
   b. a lake

8. a. a post office
   b. a supermarket

9. a. a zoo
   b. a bank

K GRAMMARRAP: *Gossip* 

Listen. Then clap and practice.

A. Do you know whether David is dating Diane?
Do you know if Irene is married to Stan?
Can you tell me if Bob is in love with Elaine?
Do you know if they really met on a plane?

B. I don't know whether David is dating Diane.
I'm not sure if Irene is married to Stan.
I can't tell you if Bob is in love with Elaine.
And I really don't know if they met on a plane.

L RENTING AN APARTMENT

Questions to Ask the Rental Agent

1. Has it been rented yet?
2. Is there an elevator in the building?
3. Does the kitchen have a microwave?
4. Are pets allowed?
5. Is there a bus stop nearby?
6. Does the landlord live in the building?
7. Does the apartment have an Internet connection?
8. ....
9. Can I see the apartment today?

A. Hello. This is Mildred Williams. I'm calling about the apartment at 119 Appleton Street. Can you tell me ______ if it's been rented yet ______ 1 ?

B. Not yet. But several people have called. Would you like to see it?

A. Yes, but first I have a few questions. According to the newspaper, the apartment is on the fifth floor. Can you tell me ______________________ 2 ?

B. Yes. As a matter of fact, there are two elevators.

A. I see. And do you know ______________________ 3 ?

B. It has a dishwasher, but it doesn't have a microwave.

A. Also, do you by any chance know ______________________ 4 ?

B. I don't know. I'll check with the landlord.

A. Can you tell me ______________________ 5 ?

B. Yes. The downtown bus stops in the front of the building.

A. That's very convenient. Can you also tell me ______________________ 6 ?

B. Yes, he does. And all the tenants say he takes very good care of the apartments.

A. Do you know ______________________ 7 ?

B. Yes, it does. It's a very modern building.

A. And could you please tell me .... 8 ?

B. I'm not sure. I'll have to find out and let you know.

A. You've been very helpful. Do you know ______________________ 9 ?

B. Certainly. Stop by our office at noon, and I'll take you to see it.

M YOU DECIDE: *The College Visit*

Ask the Admissions Office

1. How many students go to your school?
2. Do I have to take any special examinations?
3. How do I get an application form?
4. Are the classes difficult?
5. Are the dormitories noisy?
6. What kind of food do you serve in the cafeteria?
7. What do students do on weekends?
8. How much does your school cost?
9. ....
10. ....

Hello. My name is Robert Johnson, and I'm interested in studying at your college. I'd like to ask you a few questions.

Certainly. My name is Ms. Lopez. I'll be happy to answer your questions.

1. Can you tell me ___how many___ ___students go to___ ___your school___?

....

2. Do you know ______ ______ ______?

....

3. Can you tell me ______ ______ ______?

....

(continued)

4. Also, could you tell me ______________

____

______________________________________?

5. I've heard the dormitories are large.

Do you know __________________________

______________________________________?

6. Do you by any chance know __________

____

______________________________________?

7. Can you tell me ____________________

____

______________________________________?

8. I'm a little worried about expenses.

Can you tell me ____________________

______________________________________?

9. Can you also tell me ....

....

....?

10. And do you know ....

....

....?

A IF

STUDENT BOOK PAGES 65–78

1. My doctor says that if I exercise every day, _______ healthier.
   a. I'm
   (b.) I'll be

2. If Alan _______ stuck in traffic today, he'll be late for work.
   a. gets
   b. will get

3. If _______ the lottery tomorrow, I'll have a lot of money.
   a. I'll win
   b. I win

4. If we get to the theater early, _______ to get good seats.
   a. we're able
   b. we'll be able

5. If you decide to apply for a promotion, _______ probably get it.
   a. you'll
   b. you

6. If they _______ to pay the rent next week, their landlord will call them.
   a. forget
   b. will forget

7. If Amanda oversleeps this morning, _______ the bus.
   a. she misses
   b. she'll miss

8. If you _______ for Jack Strickland, you'll have an honest president.
   a. will vote
   b. vote

9. If the weather is warm, _______ to the beach tomorrow.
   a. I'll go
   b. I go

10. If _______ Melanie, I'm sure I'll be happy for the rest of my life.
    a. I'll marry
    b. I marry

B SCRAMBLED SENTENCES

1. late she'll lot tonight. to at If do, has work Barbara the a office

   If Barbara has a lot to do, she'll work late at the office tonight.

2. attic energetic, he'll his If this clean Tom weekend. feels

   _______________________, _______________________

3. cake about decide have to If diet, I'll I dessert. forget for my

   _______________________, _______________________

4. income weather tomorrow, the home nice If I'll forms. stay isn't my tax fill out and

   _______________________, _______________________

5. clinic see I If I'll cold Dr. Lopez. still a go tomorrow, have the to and

   _______________________, _______________________

C YOU DECIDE: *If*

1. If I'm in a good mood, ...
2. .... if I'm in a bad mood.
3. If .... ,
   he'll speak more confidently.
4. .... , you'll be disappointed.
5. If I can afford it, ...
6. .... , we'll be very surprised.
7. If I'm invited to the White House, ...
8. You'll get lost if ....
9. You'll regret it if ....
10. .... , you won't regret it.

D LISTENING

Listen and complete the sentences.

1. a. . . . I go to a movie.
   (b.) . . . I'll go to a concert.
2. a. . . . I'm on a diet.
   b. . . . I'll stay on a diet.
3. a. . . . we miss the train.
   b. . . . we'll miss the train.
4. a. . . . they rent a DVD.
   b. . . . they'll go dancing.
5. a. . . . we're late for school.
   b. . . . we'll have to walk to work.
6. a. . . . you miss the test.
   b. . . . you'll miss the exam.
7. a. . . . the teacher is boring.
   b. . . . the teacher will be bored.
8. a. . . . it isn't too expensive.
   b. . . . it won't cost as much.
9. a. . . . he complains to his boss.
   b. . . . he'll quit his job.
10. a. . . . you'll decide to visit me.
    b. . . . you want to go jogging.
11. a. . . . she has time.
    b. . . . she won't be too busy.
12. a. . . . I take them to the doctor.
    b. . . . I'll call the nurse.
13. a. . . . we have too much work.
    b. . . . we'll be too busy.
14. a. . . . she doesn't study.
    b. . . . she won't work harder.

E GRAMMARRAP: *If It Rains, I'll Take a Taxi* 

Listen. Then clap and practice.

If it rains, I'll take a taxi.
If it snows, I'll take the train.
If it's sunny, I'll ride my brand new bike,
The one that was made in Spain.

If it's hot, they'll wear their sandals.
If it's cold, they'll wear their boots.
If the weather is nice, they'll go to the beach.
And swim in their bathing suits.

If the party starts at seven o'clock,
We'll plan to arrive at eight.
If we're tired, we'll come home early.
If we aren't, we'll get home late.

If I'm hungry, I'll have a midnight snack.
If I'm sleepy, I'll go to bed.
If I'm wide awake, I'll stay up late
With a book I haven't read.

F THEY MIGHT

1. Remember, if you plan to have your wedding outside, it _______.
   (a.) might rain
   b. rains

2. If we take the children to visit their grandparents, they _______ sore throats.
   a. might give
   b. might give them

3. If Marvin breaks up with Susan, he _______ trouble finding another girlfriend.
   a. might have
   b. might be

4. If you go to bed too late, _______ have trouble getting up on time for work.
   a. you might
   b. you'll might

5. If you don't take that job, you _______ it for the rest of your life.
   a. regret
   b. might regret

6. If you have trouble seeing well, _______ rejected by the army.
   a. I might be
   b. you might be

7. If our teacher tries to break up that fight, _______.
   a. he might get hurt
   b. he might hurt

8. If we take the children to see the skeletons at the museum, they _______.
   a. might scare
   b. might be scared

G YOU DECIDE: *What Might Happen?*

1. A. I still have a cold, and I feel terrible.

   B. That's too bad. Why don't you drink tea with honey?

   If ___you drink___ tea with honey, ...you might...

   ...feel better soon....

2. A. Should I put more pepper in the casserole?

   B. I'm not sure. If _______ more pepper in

   the casserole, ...

   ....

3. A. It's the boss's birthday tomorrow. Why don't we send her flowers?

B. I'm not sure. If ______________________

her flowers, ...

....

4. A. I'm thinking of skipping English class today,

B. I don't think you should. If ______________________

English class, ...

....

5. A. Mrs. Wong, I really enjoy taking violin lessons with you. I'm going to practice every day.

B. I'm happy to hear that. If ______________________

every day, ...

....

6. A. Good-bye!

B. Please don't stay away too long! If ______________

away for a long time, ...

....

7. A. Danny, I don't think you should go hiking in the woods by yourself.

B. Why not?

A. If ______________________ by yourself, ...

....

8. A. You've known each other for only a few weeks. I don't think you should get married so soon.

B. Why not?

A. If ______________________ so soon, ...

....

H YOU DECIDE: *What Might Happen?*

if ______________ might ______________

1. A. I don't think I'll ever learn to speak English well.

   B. Why don't you ....?

   If ____,

   ______you might learn______ to speak English better.

2. A. I feel exhausted.

   B. Why don't you ....?

   If ____,

   ________________________________ more energetic.

3. A. I can't fall asleep.

   B. Maybe you should ....

   If ____,

   ________________________________ more easily.

4. A. I've been feeling depressed lately.

   B. I think you should ....

   If ____,

   ________________________________ a lot better.

5. A. My girlfriend and I had a terrible argument. She won't go out with me anymore.

   B. Why don't you ....?

   If ____,

   ________________________________ with you again.

I WHAT'S THE POLITE ANSWER?

J LISTENING

Listen and choose the polite response.

1. (a.) I hope so. b. I hope not.
2. a. I hope so. b. I hope not.
3. a. I hope so. b. I hope not.
4. a. I hope so. b. I hope not.
5. a. I hope so. b. I hope not.
6. a. I hope so. b. I hope not.
7. a. I hope so. b. I hope not.
8. a. I hope so. b. I hope not.
9. a. I hope so. b. I hope not.
10. a. I hope so. b. I hope not.
11. a. I hope so. b. I hope not.
12. a. I hope so. b. I hope not.

K HOPES

1. A. Do you think it will rain tomorrow?

   B. I hope not. If ___it rains___ tomorrow, we'll have to cancel our picnic.

   And if ___we have to cancel___ the picnic, everybody will be disappointed.

   A. You're right. I hope ___it doesn't rain___ tomorrow.

2. A. Do you think it'll be cold tonight?

   B. I hope not. If ______________ tonight, our car won't start in the morning.

   And if our car ______________ in the morning, we'll have to walk to work.

   A. You're right. I hope ______________ tonight.

3. A. Do you think it'll be a hot summer?

   B. I hope not. If ________ a hot summer, the office will be very warm.

   And if the office ________ very warm, it'll be impossible to work.

   A. You're right. I hope ____________ a hot summer.

4. A. Do you think our TV will be at the repair shop for a long time?

   B. I hope not. If our TV ________ at the repair shop for a long time, we won't have anything to do in the evening.

   And if ______________ anything to do in the evening, we'll go crazy.

   A. You're right. I hope ____________ at the repair shop for a long time.

L THE EXAM

1. A. I've gotten up early every day this semester, and I haven't missed anything important.

   B. That's great! I hope 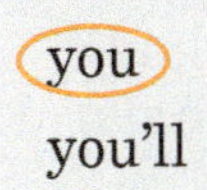 (you / you'll) get up early again tomorrow.

   It's the last class and the last exam.

   A. I know. (I / I'll) definitely get up early tomorrow.

2. A. Do you think tomorrow's exam will be difficult?

   B. I hope not. If (it will be / it's) difficult, I'll probably do poorly.

   And if (I do / I'll do) poorly, my parents (are / will be) disappointed.

3. A. What happened? You overslept and missed the exam!

   B. I have a terrible cold. I'm going to call my professor now.

   I hope she (isn't / doesn't be) angry. If she (will be / is) angry, (she / she'll) give me a bad grade.

4. A. What did your professor say?

   B. She said she hopes (I / I'll) feel better soon. If (I / I'll) feel better tomorrow, (I / I'll) take the exam at 2 o'clock.

   If (I'll be / I'm) still sick tomorrow, (I / I'll) take the exam on Wednesday morning.

M WHAT IF?

1. If my apartment _______ bigger, I would be more comfortable.
   a. was
   (b.) were

2. If you _______ more, you'd be stronger.
   a. exercised
   b. exercise

3. If it were a nice day today, _______ to the park.
   a. we'll go
   b. we'd go

4. If I _______ more, I'd be happy working here.
   a. got paid
   b. get paid

5. If I were going to be here this weekend, _______ a movie with you.
   a. I'll see
   b. I'd see

6. If _______ more friends in our apartment building, we'd be much happier living there.
   a. we had
   b. we have

7. If you _______ up your engine more often, you'd get better gas mileage.
   a. tune
   b. tuned

8. If _______ more, you'd feel more energetic.
   a. you sleep
   b. you slept

9. If she were more careful, _______ a better driver.
   a. she'd be
   b. she'll

10. If you _______ older, we'd let you stay up later.
    a. were
    b. are

11. If Rick and Rita had more in common, I'm sure _______ get along better with each other.
    a. they'd
    b. they

12. If the president _______ more concerned about the environment, he'd do something about it.
    a. is
    b. were

N LISTENING 

Listen and choose the correct answer based on what you hear.

1. a. George probably feels energetic.
   (b.) George probably feels tired.

2. a. The musicians aren't very talented.
   b. The musicians are talented.

3. a. He's very aggressive.
   b. He isn't aggressive enough.

4. a. Bob's car needs to be tuned up.
   b. Bob's car doesn't need to be tuned up.

5. a. They have a lot in common.
   b. They don't have a lot in common.

6. a. She cares a lot about her students.
   b. She isn't a very good teacher.

7. a. Their school needs more computers.
   b. Their school has enough computers.

8. a. The cookies aren't sweet enough.
   b. The cookies are sweet enough.

O YOU DECIDE WHY

1\. A. Mr. Montero, why doesn't my daughter Lisa get better grades in English?

B. She doesn't ......do her homework carefully......,

she doesn't ....,

she doesn't ....,

and she doesn't ....

If she ___did her homework carefully___,

if she ______________________________,

if she ______________________________,

and if she ______________________________,

______________________________ much better grades. She's a very intelligent girl.

2\. A. What's wrong with me, Dr. Green? Why don't I feel energetic anymore? I'm only thirty years old, and I feel exhausted all the time.

B. You don't ....,

you don't ....,

you don't ....,

and you ....

If you ______________________________,

if you ______________________________,

if you ______________________________,

and if you ______________________________ less,

______________________________ much more energetic.

(continued)

3. A. How do you like your new car?

B. It's better than my old one, but I really don't like it very much.

A. That's too bad. Why not?

B. It doesn't ____________________,

it doesn't ____________________,

I'm not ____________________,

and my husband ____________________.

If ____________________,

if ____________________,

if ____________________,

and if ____________________,

____________________ my car a lot more. I guess all cars have their problems.

P YOU DECIDE: *What Would You Do If . . . ?*

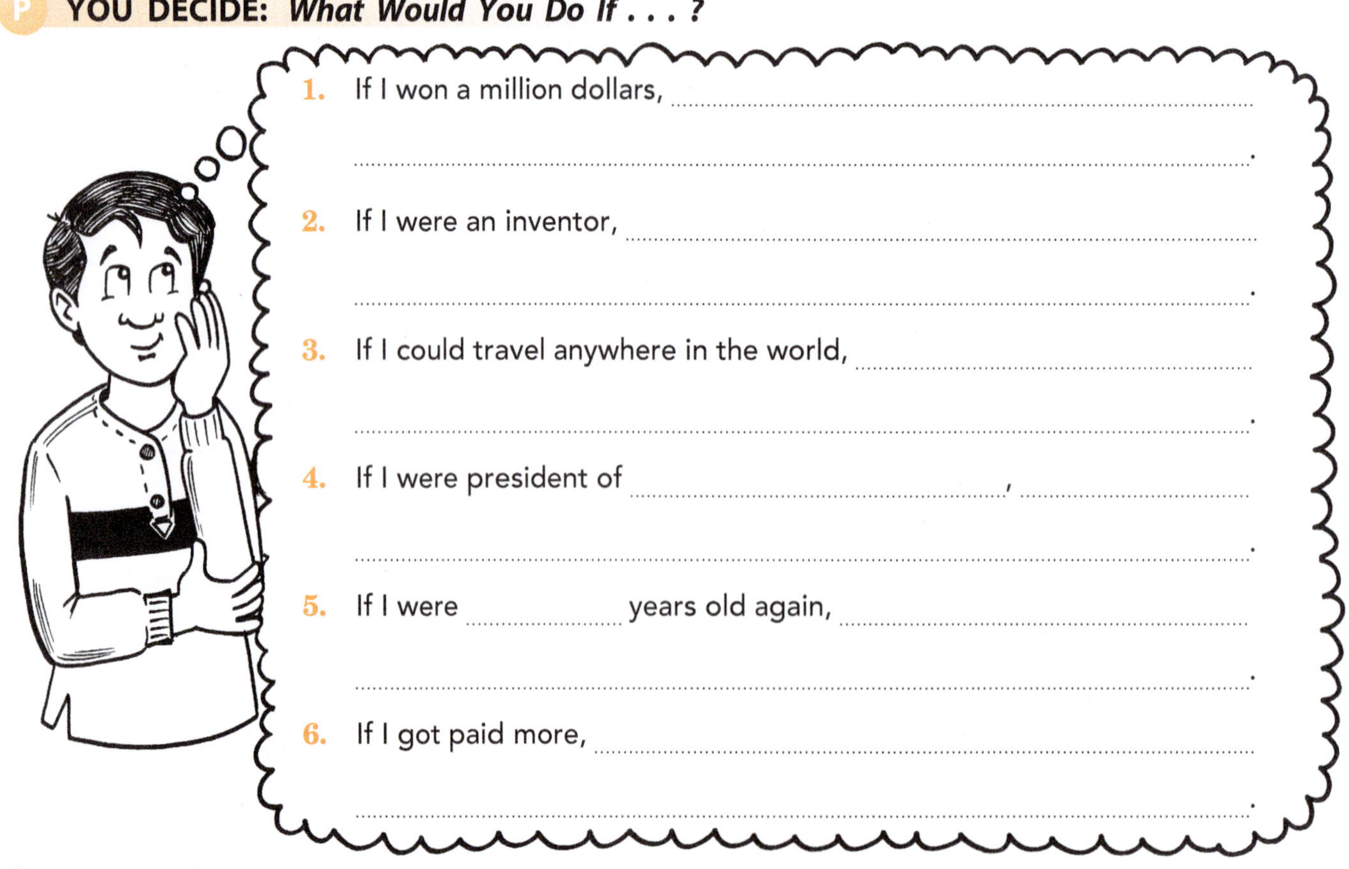

1. If I won a million dollars, ____________________
____________________.

2. If I were an inventor, ____________________
____________________.

3. If I could travel anywhere in the world, ____________________
____________________.

4. If I were president of ____________________, ____________________
____________________.

5. If I were ________ years old again, ____________________
____________________.

6. If I got paid more, ____________________
____________________.

Q MATCHING

d	1.	If this party weren't so boring,	a.	I wouldn't have so many accidents.
____	2.	If I didn't hate working here,	b.	I wouldn't be sneezing so much.
____	3.	If I didn't have a big exam tomorrow,	c.	you wouldn't have so many problems with it.
____	4.	If I weren't such a careless driver,	d.	we wouldn't want to leave so early.
____	5.	If I weren't a vegetarian,	e.	people wouldn't have to wait for me.
____	6.	If I weren't always late,	f.	I wouldn't go hiking every weekend.
____	7.	If I weren't allergic to cats,	g.	I wouldn't be so nervous.
____	8.	If they weren't in love,	h.	I wouldn't always order vegetables.
____	9.	If I didn't like the outdoors so much,	i.	the neighbors wouldn't be complaining.
____	10.	If your car weren't so old,	j.	I wouldn't be looking for another job.
____	11.	If we didn't make so much noise,	k.	they wouldn't hold hands all the time.

R YOU DECIDE: *What Are They Saying?*

(continued)

4. Ted went out with Jean on Monday, with Jane on Tuesday, with Joan on Wednesday, and with Jen on Thursday.

He must ______________________________.

5. My neighbors spend every weekend at the beach. Last weekend they went water-skiing, and this weekend they're going sailing.

They must really ______________________________.

6. My daughter got the highest grade in her class.

She must ______________________________, and you must ______________________________.

7. I'm going to miss something important in school tomorrow.

Really? You must ______________________________.

8. Last weekend I made three pies and four cakes. This weekend I'm going to make cookies.

No kidding! You must ______________________________.

9. My son is going to be the star of his school play this weekend.

He must ______________________________, and you must ______________________________.

10. My husband has been watching a football game on TV all day, and there's a big game he's going to watch tonight.

He must really ______________________________, and you must ______________________________.

11. You've been complaining about this movie since it started. You must ______________________________.

S IF

1. Rita works overtime every night. She must want to get a raise.

   If _____she didn't want to get_____ a raise,

   she _____wouldn't work overtime_____ every night.

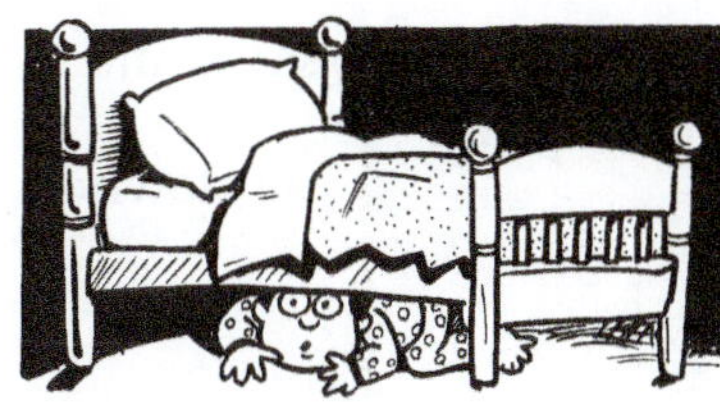

2. Jimmy is hiding under the bed. He must be afraid of the dark.

   If ______________________________ of the dark,

   he ______________________________ under the bed.

3. Stephanie runs ten miles every day. She must want to win the marathon this weekend.

   If ______________________________ the marathon,

   she ______________________________ ten miles every day.

4. My friend Gary wears a green shirt every day. He must love the color green.

   If ______________________________ the color green,

   he ______________________________ a green shirt every day.

5. My sister Karen makes a lot of mistakes on her homework. She's very careless.

   If ______________________________,

   she ______________________________ a lot of mistakes on her homework.

6. Gregory goes to the health club every day. He must want to lose weight.

   If ______________________________ weight,

   he ______________________________ to the health club every day.

(continued)

7. Andy is all dressed up. He must have a big date tonight.

If ______________________ a big date tonight,

he ______________________ all dressed up.

8. I'm driving very slowly because there's a police car behind me.

If ______________________ a police car behind me.

I ______________________ so slowly.

T YOU DECIDE: *Why Don't Mr. and Mrs. Miller Like Their Neighborhood?*

Mr. and Mrs. Miller don't like their neighborhood because ....,

..............................,

..............................,

..............................,

and ....

If ______________________,

if ______________________,

if ______________________,

and if ______________________,

______________________ their neighborhood a lot more.

U GRAMMARRAP: *If I Lived Near the Sea* 

Listen. Then clap and practice.

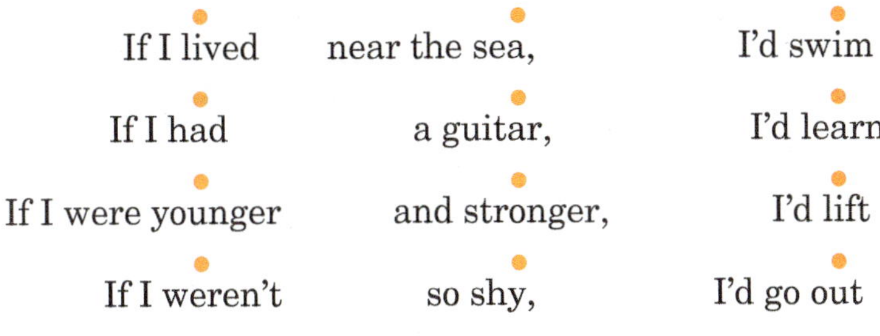

If I lived near the sea, I'd swim every day.
If I had a guitar, I'd learn how to play.
If I were younger and stronger, I'd lift heavy weights.
If I weren't so shy, I'd go out on more dates.

If Tom could speak Spanish, he'd travel to Spain.
If Ann had a raincoat, she'd walk in the rain.
If Jack were an actor, he'd star in a play.
If we weren't so busy, we'd go sailing today.

V GRAMMARRAP: *If I Didn't Like Desserts* 

Listen. Then clap and practice.

If I didn't like desserts, I wouldn't eat cake.
If I didn't like meat, I wouldn't eat steak.
If I weren't so happy, I wouldn't be smiling.
If I weren't working late, I wouldn't be filing.

If she didn't like pets, she wouldn't have a cat.
If he didn't play baseball, he wouldn't have a bat.
If they weren't so clumsy, they wouldn't always fall.
If you weren't my friend, I wouldn't always call.

W LISTENING

Listen to each word and then say it.

1. might
2. maybe
3. mushroom
4. summer
5. improve
6. remember
7. poems
8. warm
9. famous
10. night
11. never
12. noon
13. sunny
14. Sunday
15. increase
16. explain
17. telephone
18. fantastic

X NORMAN'S BROKEN KEYBOARD

Norman's keyboard is broken. The m's and the n's don't always work. Fill in the missing m's and n's and then read Norman's letters aloud.

1.

Dear A_m_y,

I really e_n_joyed visiti__g you i__ your __ew apart__e__t. It's o__e of the __icest apart__e__ts I've ever see__. I liked everythi__g about it: the __oder__ kitche__ a__d bathroo__, the elega__t livi__g roo__ and di__i__g roo__, a__d the su____y bedroo__s. I ca__'t believe there's eve__ a garde__ with le__o__ and ora__ge trees i__ fro__t of the buildi__g. I thi__k you'll be very happy i__ your __ew __eighborhood. It's certai__ly very co__ve__ie__t to be so __ear a super__arket, a __ovie theater, a__d a trai__ statio__.

I'__ looki__g forward to seei__g you agai__ a__d __eeti__g your __ew __eighbors.

Si__cerely,

__or__an

2.

To Who__ It __ay Co__cer__:

I a__ writi__g to reco____e__d __ax __iller for the job of co__puter progra____er at the ABC Co__puter Co__pa__y. Duri__g the __i__e years I've k__ow__ hi__, he's bee__ a__ excelle__t e__ployee a__d a ki__d a__d ho__est frie__d. He's __ever __issed a day's work at our co__pa__y, a__d he's always bee__ o__ ti__e. But __ost i__porta__t, __ax __iller really u__dersta__ds what __akes a good co__puter progra____er.

Si__cerely,
__or__a__ Brow__
__a__ager
XYZ Co__puter Co__pa__y

3.

Dear Bria__,

I just fi__ished readi__g your __ost rece__t poe__s, a__d i__ __y opi__io__, they're a__azi__g. The poe__ about the e__viro____e__t is very origi__al, but __y favorite o__es are "__issi__g __y __other" a__d "U__der __y U__brella."

Accordi__g to __y wife a__d frie__ds, you're beco__i__g fa__ous i__ __a__y foreig__ cou__tries, a__d your poe__s are bei__g tra__slated i__to Russia__, Chi__ese, Ger__a__, Spa__ish, a__d Japa__ese. I thi__k that's fa__tastic!

Have you begu__ writi__g your __ew __ovel yet? I wo__der whe__ we'll be heari__g more about it.

__or__a__

4.

Dear __ichael,

Re__e__ber whe__ you explai__ed to __e how to __ake your __other's fa__ous chicke__ a__d __ushroo__ casserole? Well, I __ade so__e for di____er last __ight, a__d I'__ afraid so__ethi__g __ust have go__e wro__g. I__ight have bur__t the chicke__, or __aybe I did__'t put i__ e__ough o__io__s a__d __ushroo__s. I do__'t k__ow what happe__ed, but I k__ow I __ust have __ade so__e __istakes because __obody e__joyed it very __uch. To__ and __a__cy did__'t co__plai__, but they said yours was __uch __ore delicious.

Do you thi__k you could se__d your __other's recipe to __e by e-__ail so I ca__ try it again? Whe__ you explai__ed it to __e, I should have writte__ it dow__.

__or__a__

✓ CHECK-UP TEST: Chapters 4–5

A. Fill in the blanks.

Ex. *(What time does the plane arrive?)*

Could you please tell me ____what time the plane arrives____?

1. *(When will the next train be leaving?)*

   Can you tell me ____?

2. *(Was Michael at work yesterday?)*

   Do you know ____?

3. *(How much does this suit cost?)*

   Can you please tell me ____?

4. *(Is there a laundromat nearby?)*

   Could you tell me ____?

5. *(Why did David get up so early?)*

   Do you know ____?

6. *(Did Martha take her medicine this morning?)*

   Do you know ____?

7. *(How long have we been waiting?)*

   Do you have any idea ____?

B. Complete the sentences.

Ex. If we can afford it, ____we'll take____ a vacation next summer.

1. I'll send you an e-mail if I ______________ the time.
2. If Uncle Fred were more careful, ______________ a better driver.
3. If Mrs. Bell didn't enjoy classical music, ____________________ to concerts every weekend.
4. If I ______________ a raise soon, I'll complain to my supervisor.
5. If you stay up too late tonight, ______________ get a good night's sleep.
6. We're having a picnic this Sunday. I hope ______________ rain.
7. Tomorrow is the most important game of the year. I hope our team ______________.

8. My parents ______________ extremely disappointed if I fail tomorrow's French test.

9. If you ______________ your dog more often, he wouldn't be so hungry.

C. Complete the sentences.

Ex. Albert doesn't have many friends because he isn't outgoing enough.

If he ___were___ more outgoing, ___he'd have___ a lot of friends.

1. Caroline feels tired all the time because she works too hard.

   If she ______________ so hard, ______________ so tired all the time.

2. David doesn't get good grades in school because he doesn't study enough.

   If he ______________ more, ______________ better grades.

3. Allison and Paul don't get along with each other because they don't have enough in common.

   If they ______________ more in common, ______________ better with each other.

4. Nellie is very careless. She makes a lot of mistakes when she types.

   If she ______________ so careless, ______________ a lot of mistakes.

D. Listening

Listen and complete the sentences.

Ex. (a.) . . . I'll play tennis.
b. . . . I'd play tennis.

1. a. . . . I'd be late for work.
   b. . . . I'll be late for work.

2. a. . . . I wouldn't make so many mistakes.
   b. . . . I won't make so many mistakes.

3. a. . . . you didn't study for the test.
   b. . . . you don't study for the test.

4. a. . . . I'd see a movie.
   b. . . . I'll see a movie.

5. a. . . . she'll go out with you.
   b. . . . she'd go out with you.

A THE MUSIC OF WISHES AND HOPES

SIDE by SIDE Gazette

STUDENT BOOK PAGES 79–82

Read the article on student book page 79 and answer the questions.

1. Which song was made popular by a singing group?
   a. "If I Were a Rich Man"
   b. "If I Were a Bell"
   c. "If I Had a Hammer"
   d. "If I Could Change the World"

2. ______ of the songs described in the article were first performed in musicals.
   a. Two
   b. Three
   c. Four
   d. None

3. In ______ of the songs, the wish is for wealth.
   a. one
   b. two
   c. three
   d. four

4. Lee Ann Womack is a ______.
   a. folk singer
   b. rock singer
   c. Broadway singer
   d. country music singer

5. You can infer that a Grammy Award is given for ______.
   a. songs
   b. books
   c. acting
   d. writing a poem

6. In "If I Had a Million Dollars," the word *exotic* means ______.
   a. expensive
   b. beautiful
   c. unusual
   d. very large

7. In all of these songs, the common wish of the singers is to have ______.
   a. love
   b. peace
   c. time
   d. happiness

8. From this article, you can infer that the music of wishes and hopes is ______.
   a. always about relationships
   b. found in many different types of music
   c. the most popular music theme
   d. loved by everyone

B MUSIC LYRICS AND METAPHORS

A *metaphor* is a figure of speech. It describes two different things or people as being the same in some way. Answer these questions about metaphors in the article.

1. In the song from the musical *Guys and Dolls*, a happy Sarah describes herself as ______.
   a. a gambler at a gate
   b. the man she loves
   c. a swinging bell
   d. a ringing bell

2. In the song from the movie *Phenomenon*, the singer's metaphor is that he and the girl he loves ______.
   a. would go to the center of the universe
   b. would get married
   c. would be a king and queen
   d. would change the world

3. In another song in the article, saving money in a bank is compared to ______.
   a. saving money to buy a house
   b. winning a Grammy Award
   c. saving time in a bottle
   d. being rich

4. Another famous song in the article describes using a hammer as a metaphor for ______.
   a. building a house for a family
   b. working for peace
   c. ringing a bell
   d. singing a song

C FACT FILE

Look at the Fact File on student book page 79 and answer the questions.

1. The word ______ is the most popular of the three words in song titles.
   a. "hope"
   b. "wish"
   c. "if"

2. The word ______ is not in any of the song titles in the article.
   a. "hope"
   b. "wish"
   c. "if"

D AROUND THE WORLD

Read the article on student book page 80 and answer the questions.

1. You make a wish if you catch something in ______.
   a. Jamaica
   b. Japan
   c. Korea
   d. Ireland

2. If you hear coins splash into water three times in ______, your wishes will come true.
   a. the United States
   b. Asia
   c. South America
   d. Europe

3. Make a wish when you blow out candles on a cake ______
   a. in the evening
   b. at midnight
   c. on your birthday
   d. when you look at the moon

4. Coins are used for making wishes in ______ of the traditions described in the article.
   a. two
   b. three
   c. four
   d. five

5. ______ of the traditions described in the article involve looking at the sky.
   a. One
   b. Two
   c. Three
   d. Four

6. People in the United States are likely to make a wish with a wishbone on ______.
   a. Valentine's Day
   b. July 4th
   c. Thanksgiving
   d. New Year's Day

7. "Star light, star bright, first star I see tonight" is a ______.
   a. wish
   b. tradition
   c. custom
   d. poem

8. In the New Year's Eve tradition with grapes, the *chimes* of the clock refer to ______.
   a. the sounds of the clock
   b. the hands of the clock
   c. grapes
   d. midnight

9. If you throw a *pebble* into a well to make a wish, you throw ______.
   a. a leaf
   b. a nut
   c. a small stone
   d. a candle

10. The tradition for making wishes with ______ requires two people.
   a. a wishbone or a coin
   b. a nut or a leaf
   c. candles or grapes
   d. a wishbone or a nut

E INTERVIEW

Read the interviews on student book page 81 and answer the questions.

1. The man on the left wouldn't want to quit his job because _______.
   a. he has too much free time
   b. he loves his job
   c. he works very hard
   d. he wouldn't know how to use his time

2. _______ of the people would stop working.
   a. One
   b. Two
   c. Three
   d. Four

3. _______ of the people would help family members.
   a. One
   b. Two
   c. Three
   d. Four

4. _______ of the people would save the money.
   a. One
   b. Two
   c. Three
   d. Four

5. You can infer that *debts* are _______.
   a. money you owe
   b. banks
   c. people
   d. jobs

6. One man would give money to charities. You can infer that _______.
   a. he's retired
   b. he already has a lot of money
   c. he's generous
   d. he works

F YOU'RE THE INTERVIEWER!

Interview a classmate, a neighbor, or a friend. Use the chart below to record the person's answers. Then share what you learned with the class.

What would you do if you won a million dollars?	
Would you keep working or going to school? Why or why not?	
Would you give money to people? Who would you give it to?	
Would you give any money to charities? Which ones?	

G FUN WITH IDIOMS

Match the question and the correct answer.

_____ 1. What would you say to someone who always makes you feel happy?

_____ 2. What would you say if someone hurt your feelings very badly?

_____ 3. What would you say to someone you would do anything for?

_____ 4. What would you say to a friend who often ignores you?

a. You're breaking my heart.

b. You light up my life.

c. You're a heel!

d. You've got me wrapped around your little finger.

H WE'VE GOT MAIL!

Choose the words that best complete each sentence.

1. We hope they _______ on time for dinner.
   a. will
   b. are
   c. will be
   d. be

2. He hopes he _______ a raise.
   a. is going to get
   b. will get
   c. is getting
   d. gets

3. They hope it _______ tomorrow.
   a. is raining
   b. will rain
   c. doesn't rain
   d. won't rain

4. She hopes the bus _______ late.
   a. isn't
   b. won't be
   c. is going to be
   d. will be

5. I hope I _______ for the team.
   a. will be chosen
   b. am chosen
   c. will choose
   d. am choosing

6. We hope we _______ the train.
   a. won't miss
   b. are missing
   c. don't miss
   d. aren't going to miss

Choose the sentence that is correct.

7. a. If I was tired, I wouldn't go with you.
   b. If I weren't tired, I would go with you.
   c. If I weren't tired, I will go with you.
   d. If I wasn't tired, I would go with you.

8. a. If she wasn't busy, she would help us.
   b. If she isn't busy, she would help us.
   c. If she weren't busy, she would help us.
   d. If she was busy, she would help us.

9. a. If he is sick, I would call the doctor.
   b. If he were sick, I will call the doctor.
   c. If he was sick, I would call the doctor.
   d. If he were sick, I would call the doctor.

10. a. If it weren't funny, I wouldn't laugh.
    b. If it weren't funny, I won't laugh.
    c. If it wasn't funny, I wouldn't laugh.
    d. If it wasn't funny, I won't laugh.

11. a. If I was you, I would leave now.
    b. If I was you, I will leave now.
    c. If I were you, I would leave now.
    d. If I will be you, I would leave now.

12. a. She was upset if he is late.
    b. She will be upset if he was late.
    c. She were upset if he would be late.
    d. She would be upset if he were late.

I "CAN-DO" REVIEW

Match the "can do" statement and the correct sentence.

_____ 1. I can ask for information.
_____ 2. I can say that I don't know something.
_____ 3. I can apologize.
_____ 4. I can express uncertainty.
_____ 5. I can make a suggestion.
_____ 6. I can ask about future plans.
_____ 7. I can ask for advice.
_____ 8. I can express hopes.
_____ 9. I can express agreement.
_____ 10. I can make a deduction.

a. I'm not really sure.
b. The boss must be in a bad mood.
c. Could you tell me what time our plane leaves?
d. What are you going to do this weekend?
e. Do you think I should go to work with this cold?
f. You're right.
g. I'm sorry.
h. Why don't you check with the librarian?
i. I don't know when my car will be fixed.
j. I hope the economy improves next year.

A WHAT'S THE WORD?

6

STUDENT BOOK PAGES 83–94

1. I think the children ______ scared if the lights went out.
   a. will be
   (b.) would be

2. I think your parents would be angry if you ______ school tomorrow.
   a. skipped
   b. skip

3. I think Jim would be disappointed if I ______ his party.
   a. was missing
   b. missed

4. Do you think I would be happier if I ______ rich?
   a. was
   b. were

5. I think the children would be excited if it ______.
   a. snowed
   b. snows

6. I think the neighbors ______ annoyed if I practiced the drums now.
   a. would be
   b. are going to be

7. I think this pizza would be better if it ______ more cheese on it.
   a. have
   b. had

8. I think we would be unhappy if our teacher ______ a test today.
   a. gave
   b. gives

9. Do you think Bob ______ jealous if I got into law school?
   a. would be
   b. is going to be

10. I think my sister would be upset if I ______ her new computer.
    a. use
    b. used

B IF

1. I know I would be scared if a robber *(be)* ___were___ in my house.
2. Do you think Amy would be jealous if I *(go out)* ________________ with her boyfriend?
3. I'm sure I would be concerned if I *(get lost)* ________________ in New York City.
4. I'm positive Johnny would be upset if he *(have)* ________________ the flu on his birthday.
5. I know that my doctor would be pleased if I *(eat)* ________________ healthier foods.
6. I'd be very upset if I *(lose)* ________________ the keys to my car.
7. My wife would be upset if I *(quit)* ________________ my job.
8. All the neighbors would be unhappy if the landlord *(sell)* __________ our apartment building.

C YOU DECIDE: *If*

1. A. Do you think Mom would be happy if I .... ?

   B. Of course ___she would___. ___She'd be___ very happy. That's a wonderful idea.

2. A. Do you think Dad would be angry if I .... ?

   B. I'm sure ______________. ______________ very angry. That's a terrible idea.

3. A. Do you think the boss would be pleased if I .... ?

   B. I'm positive ______________. ______________ very pleased.

4. A. Do you think our grandchildren would be disappointed if we .... ?

   B. Of course ______________. ______________ very disappointed.

5. A. Do you think our teacher would be annoyed if we .... ?

   B. I'm afraid ______________. ______________ very annoyed.

6. A. Do you think my wife would be upset if I .... ?

   B. Of course ______________. ______________ very upset.

D WHAT'S THE WORD?

1. If I ______ you, I wouldn't miss Grandma's birthday party.
   a. was
   (b.) were

2. If you ______ a gallon of ice cream, you'd probably feel sick.
   a. ate
   b. eat

3. If you always practiced the guitar at two in the morning, I'm sure ______ evicted from your building.
   a. you'll be
   b. you'd be

4. If I were you, ______ your children to play a musical instrument.
   a. I encourage
   b. I'd encourage

5. If you ______ at the meeting late, you'd probably be embarrassed.
   a. arrived
   b. arrive

6. If I ______ the money, I would definitely buy a better car.
   a. have
   b. had

7. If today were Saturday, ______ until noon.
   a. I'd sleep
   b. I'll sleep

8. If the mayor raised taxes, people ______ vote for him in the next election.
   a. won't
   b. wouldn't

9. If he ______ me more often, I'd be very pleased.
   a. visits
   b. visited

10. To tell the truth, I ______ the phone if I were you.
    a. wouldn't answer
    b. won't answer

11. If you said you could come home tomorrow, ______ very happy.
    a. we're
    b. we'd be

12. If our teacher ______ easier, I'm sure I'd get better grades.
    a. was
    b. were

E LISTENING

Listen and complete the sentences.

1. a. . . . you'll look very old.
   (b.) . . . you'd look very old.

2. a. . . . I'll call you.
   b. . . . I'd call you.

3. a. . . . you'll probably get carsick.
   b. . . . you'd probably get carsick.

4. a. . . . I'll clean my yard.
   b. . . . I'd clean my yard.

5. a. . . . he'll be upset.
   b. . . . he'd probably be upset.

6. a. . . . you'll be very cold.
   b. . . . you'd be very cold.

7. a. . . . I won't be very happy.
   b. . . . I'm not very happy.

8. a. . . . you'll probably regret it.
   b. . . . you'd probably regret it.

9. a. . . . you'll miss something important.
   b. . . . you miss something important.

10. a. . . . you'll probably lose your shirt.
    b. . . . you'd probably lose your shirt.

11. a. . . . I'd call the landlord.
    b. . . . I'll call the landlord.

12. a. . . . you'd be very sorry.
    b. . . . you'll be very sorry.

F PERSONAL OPINIONS

1. A. I'm thinking of going skating this afternoon.

   B. I wouldn't go skating this afternoon if I were you. It's very warm. If you ___went___ skating today, ___you'd___ probably ___fall___ into the pond.

2. A. I'm thinking of tuning up my car myself.

   B. I wouldn't do that. If I were you, ________ call Charlie, the mechanic. ________ definitely ________________ ________ correctly.

3. A. I'm thinking of going to the prom with Larry.

   B. You are?! I wouldn't do that if I were you. If you ________ to the prom with Larry, ________ probably ____________ a terrible time.

4. A. I'm thinking of painting my house red.

   B. Really? I wouldn't paint it red if I were you. If ________________ your house red, ________________ look awful!

5. A. I'm thinking of driving downtown this morning.

   B. I ____________________ downtown if I were you. If ______________ downtown, ________ probably get stuck in a lot of traffic.

6. A. I'm thinking of having a party this weekend while my parents are away.

   B. I __________________ a party if I were you. If ________ ____________ a party, I'm sure your parents ______________ very upset.

(continued)

7. A. I'm thinking of seeing the new Julie Richards movie this weekend.

B. To tell the truth, I ____________________ it if I were you.

It's terrible! If ____________ it, ____________ probably be very bored.

8. A. I'm thinking of buying a parrot.

B. I wouldn't buy a parrot if I ____________ you. If ____________ ____________ a parrot, ________________ make a lot of noise!

9. A. I'm thinking of ....

B. I wouldn't ....

If ....,

....

G GrammarRap: *If I Were You*

Listen. Then clap and practice.

A. What color do you think I should paint my house?
B. If I were you, I'd paint it blue.

A. What time do you think I should leave for the plane?
B. If I were you, I'd leave at two.

A. What food do you think I should serve my guests?
B. If I were you, I'd serve them stew.

A. Where do you think I should go with my kids?
B. If I were you, I'd go to the zoo.

H WHAT DO THEY WISH?

1. The Johnson family has a small car. They wish they ______ a larger one.
   a. have
   (b.) had

2. I work the night shift at the factory. I wish I ______ the day shift.
   a. worked
   b. work

3. I'm disappointed with my new haircut. I ______ it weren't so short.
   a. wish
   b. wished

4. Barbara has two children. She wishes she ______ three.
   a. has
   b. had

5. I always forget to check the messages on my answering machine. I wish I ______ to check them.
   a. remembered
   b. remember

6. My boyfriend is a cook. He ______ he were a mechanic.
   a. wishes
   b. wished

7. I'm sick and tired of working. I wish I ______ on vacation.
   a. was
   b. were

8. I live in Minnesota, but I wish I ______ in Florida.
   a. live
   b. lived

9. I send e-mails to my girlfriend every day. I wish she ______ back to me.
   a. wrote
   b. writes

10. I enjoy making big holiday meals for my family. I wish I ______ washing the dishes, too.
    a. enjoy
    b. enjoyed

I LISTENING 

Listen and complete the conversations.

1. a. . . . it is.
   (b.) . . . it were.

2. a. . . . you talk more.
   b. . . . you talked less.

3. a. . . . it were easier.
   b. . . . I were easier.

4. a. . . . he daydreams more.
   b. . . . he daydreamed less.

5. a. . . . they're scarier.
   b. . . . they were scarier.

6. a. . . . you sang more softly.
   b. . . . you sing softly.

7. a. . . . it has e-mail.
   b. . . . it had e-mail.

8. a. . . . I worked near my house.
   b. . . . I work near my house.

9. a. . . . I was married.
   b. . . . I were married.

10. a. . . . it were larger.
    b. . . . it was smaller.

11. a. . . . he is working.
    b. . . . he were working.

12. a. . . . you called more often.
    b. . . . you call more often.

J I WISH

1. ___I wish I felt___ better today. I really don't feel well at all.

2. ________ it ________. When it's 5:00, I can leave work.

3. ________________ as well as my sister does. She has a magnificent voice.

4. ________________ history. Teaching history is much more interesting than teaching driver's ed.

5. ________ our teacher ________ us less homework. She gives us a lot of homework every day.

6. ________________. I think dogs are the best pets in the world.

K YOU DECIDE: *What Does Teddy Wish?*

My friend Teddy isn't very happy. He's never satisfied with anything.

1. Teddy lives in the suburbs. He wishes ....
2. Teddy's father is a dentist. He wishes ....
3. His mother teaches English at his school. He wishes ....
4. Teddy has two older sisters. He wishes ....
5. Teddy's father drives a used car. He wishes ....
6. Teddy plays the trombone. ....
7. A lot of Teddy's friends ...., but Teddy doesn't. He wishes ....
   ....
8. Also, ... He wishes ....
   ....

L LOOKING FOR A JOB

A. I wonder if you could help me. I'm looking for a job as a repairperson.

B. Most of the repair shops in town want to hire people who can repair many different kinds of things. For example, can you repair TVs?

A. I wish ___I could___ 1, but TVs are very complicated.

B. That's too bad. If ________ 2 repair TVs, ________ 3 able to find a job more easily. Hmm. *Freddy's Fix-It Shop* is looking for someone who can repair DVD players.

A. The truth is, I'm very good at repairing CD players, but I can't repair DVD players.

B. That's too bad! If ________________ 4, *Freddy's Fix-It Shop* ________ 5 VERY interested in you.

A. *Freddy's Fix-It Shop* is one of the best repair shops in town. I wish ________ 6 repair DVD players.

B. Well, *We Fix It!* is also a repair shop, and they're looking for someone who can repair CD players and .... 7. They also want someone who can .... 8.

A. I'm afraid I can't ________________ 9.

B. What a shame! If ________________ 10, *We Fix It!* ________ 11 interested in you. Maybe you should think about finding another kind of job. What else can you do?

A. Let's see. I used to be a waiter, but I hurt my back, so I can't do that anymore.

B. I wish you ________ 12 be a waiter. If ________ 13 a waiter, ________ 14 any trouble finding a job. There must be other things you can do. For example, can you .... 15 ?

A. Not really.

B. That's too bad, because if ________________ 16, ________ 17 send you for an interview with the .... 18 Company. I'm sorry, but those are all the jobs I have today. I wish ________ 19 help you. Come back next week. Maybe I'll have something then.

M CHOOSE

1. If the children were asleep, ______ have some peace and quiet in the house.
   (a.) we'd be able to
   b. we couldn't
   c. we'll

2. If I saw you more often, ______ get to know each other better.
   a. we couldn't
   b. we could
   c. we can

3. If you were more talented, ______ be in the movies.
   a. you'll
   b. you can
   c. you'd be able to

4. If the TV weren't so loud, ______ concentrate on my homework.
   a. I will
   b. I could
   c. I can't

5. If Ms. Evans weren't so busy, ______ speak with her now.
   a. you could
   b. you couldn't
   c. you wouldn't be able to

6. If he didn't live in the suburbs, ______ get to work faster.
   a. he'll
   b. he won't be able to
   c. he could

7. If you had more spare time, ______ learn to knit.
   a. you could
   b. you can
   c. you'll

8. If Ms. Jackson made more money, ______ buy a new computer.
   a. she couldn't
   b. she'd be able to
   c. she can

9. If I were more athletic, ______ play on the school basketball team.
   a. I could
   b. I can
   c. I couldn't

10. If he weren't so clumsy, ______ dance better.
    a. he will
    b. he can't
    c. he'd be able to

N LISTENING 

Listen and decide what the person is talking about.

1. (a.) speaking a language
   b. writing a language

2. a. flowers
   b. vegetables

3. a. my driver's license
   b. a raise

4. a. the bus
   b. school

5. a. food
   b. money

6. a. preparing taxes
   b. watching TV

O YOU DECIDE WHY

A. I'm really annoyed with our neighbors upstairs.

They always ....,

they always ....,

and they're ....

B. I know.

I wish ______________________________________,

I wish ______________________________________,

and I wish ______________________________________.

We should probably speak to the landlord.

P GRAMMARRAP: *I Wish* 

Listen. Then clap and practice.

I wish I had a more interesting job.
I wish I made more money.
I wish I were sitting and reading a book.
On a beach where it's warm and sunny.

I wish we lived on a quiet street.
I wish our neighbors were nice.
I wish our roof weren't leaking.
I wish we didn't have mice.

I wish I could be on a sports team.
I wish I were six feet tall.
I wish I knew how to play tennis.
I wish I could throw a ball.

Q WHAT DOES IT MEAN?

1. I had trouble answering the questions.
   (a.) The questions were confusing.
   b. The questions were amusing.
   c. I answered all the questions three times.

2. I'm positive we're having a test tomorrow.
   a. I'm afraid we might have a test.
   b. I'm sure we're having a test.
   c. I think we'll probably have a test.

3. We can't convince him to take the job.
   a. He wants to take the job.
   b. He can't take the job.
   c. He won't take the job.

4. Carl is happy he moved to the suburbs.
   a. He prefers the city.
   b. He likes taking care of his yard.
   c. He likes the noise in the city.

5. Mrs. Randall wants to teach something else.
   a. She wants to teach the same thing again.
   b. She wants to teach at a different time.
   c. She wants to teach a different subject.

6. The Super Bowl is next Sunday. I'm going to invite a friend over to watch it on TV.
   a. I'm thinking about my Super Bowl plans.
   b. I'm having a big Super Bowl party.
   c. I'm going to the Super Bowl.

7. Amy and Dan don't have enough in common.
   a. They don't get paid enough.
   b. They don't have enough clothes.
   c. They aren't interested in the same things.

8. We live in a high-rise building.
   a. Our house is in the mountains.
   b. Our building has many floors.
   c. Our building isn't very large, but the rents are high.

9. Ronald is sick and tired of his job.
   a. He's in the hospital.
   b. He's unhappy.
   c. He's taking medicine.

10. My sister Nancy is never annoyed.
    a. She's never upset.
    b. She's never in a good mood.
    c. She never enjoys anything.

11. My cousin Norman dropped out of school.
    a. He skipped a few classes.
    b. He quit school.
    c. He ran away from school very quickly.

12. Our apartment has a view of the park.
    a. We can see the park from our window.
    b. We can't see the park from our apartment.
    c. We can hear the park very well.

13. I'd like some peace and quiet around the house.
    a. Our house is very quiet.
    b. Our house is very large.
    c. Our house is very noisy.

14. Ever since I heard we were going to have an important exam next week, I've been concentrating on my work.
    a. I've been complaining more about it.
    b. I've been paying more attention to it.
    c. I've been worrying more.

15. I'm afraid your brakes are getting worse.
    a. They need to be replaced.
    b. They need to be rehearsed.
    c. They need to be tuned up.

16. My brother-in-law started a new business, and he lost his shirt.
    a. He's looked everywhere for it.
    b. It was successful.
    c. His business wasn't very successful.

R SOUND IT OUT!

Listen to each word and then say it.

bread			break		
1. fell	3. eggs	5. pleasure	1. paid	3. ate	5. plays
2. special	4. athletic	6. many	2. space	4. operation	6. main

Listen and put a circle around the word that has the same sound.

1. sweater:	grade	gets	parade
2. main:	take	let	terrible
3. ready:	away	great	Ted
4. operation:	upset	paid	pepper
5. paint:	rest	vacation	said
6. complain:	then	said	Spain
7. spend:	sprain	Jane	when
8. tell:	friend	weigh	receive

Now make a sentence using all the words you circled, and read the sentence aloud.

9. .... my ...., he'll .... a .... in ....

10. toothpaste:	best	play	past
11. hate:	hat	eight	head
12. special:	tennis	came	cat
13. lesson:	late	great	let's
14. upset:	skate	made	next
15. pleasure:	mail	Wednesday	plane
16. friend:	Fred	wait	same

Now make a sentence using all the words you circled, and read the sentence aloud.

17. .... with .... at .... o'clock.

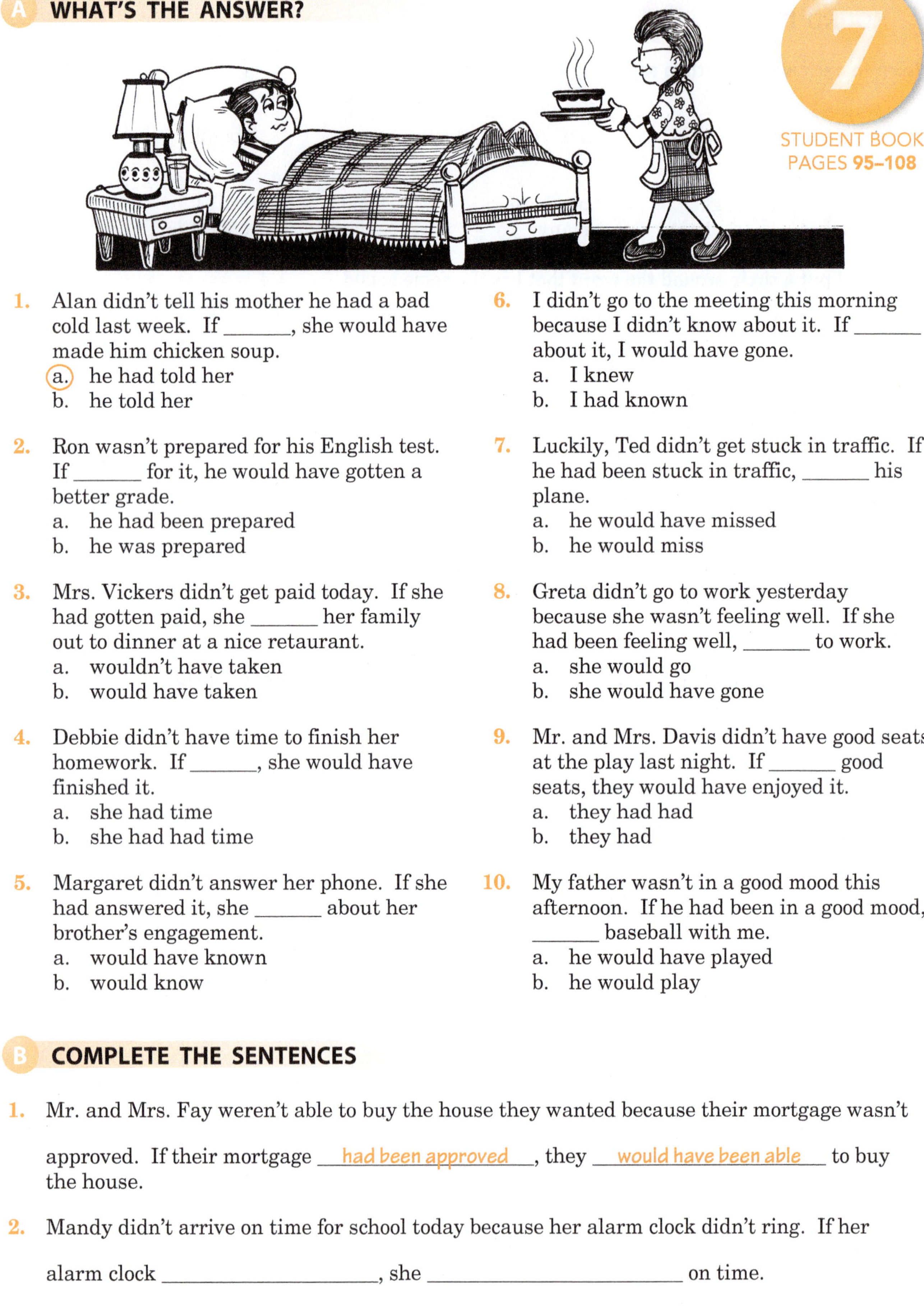

A WHAT'S THE ANSWER?

7

STUDENT BOOK PAGES 95–108

1. Alan didn't tell his mother he had a bad cold last week. If ______, she would have made him chicken soup.
   (a.) he had told her
   b. he told her

2. Ron wasn't prepared for his English test. If ______ for it, he would have gotten a better grade.
   a. he had been prepared
   b. he was prepared

3. Mrs. Vickers didn't get paid today. If she had gotten paid, she ______ her family out to dinner at a nice retaurant.
   a. wouldn't have taken
   b. would have taken

4. Debbie didn't have time to finish her homework. If ______, she would have finished it.
   a. she had time
   b. she had had time

5. Margaret didn't answer her phone. If she had answered it, she ______ about her brother's engagement.
   a. would have known
   b. would know

6. I didn't go to the meeting this morning because I didn't know about it. If ______ about it, I would have gone.
   a. I knew
   b. I had known

7. Luckily, Ted didn't get stuck in traffic. If he had been stuck in traffic, ______ his plane.
   a. he would have missed
   b. he would miss

8. Greta didn't go to work yesterday because she wasn't feeling well. If she had been feeling well, ______ to work.
   a. she would go
   b. she would have gone

9. Mr. and Mrs. Davis didn't have good seats at the play last night. If ______ good seats, they would have enjoyed it.
   a. they had had
   b. they had

10. My father wasn't in a good mood this afternoon. If he had been in a good mood, ______ baseball with me.
   a. he would have played
   b. he would play

B COMPLETE THE SENTENCES

1. Mr. and Mrs. Fay weren't able to buy the house they wanted because their mortgage wasn't approved. If their mortgage ___had been approved___, they ___would have been able___ to buy the house.

2. Mandy didn't arrive on time for school today because her alarm clock didn't ring. If her alarm clock ____________________, she ____________________ on time.

3. Sam wasn't happy because he didn't win the tennis game.

If he ______________ the tennis game, he ______________ happy.

4. My friends didn't get dressed up because they didn't know about the party. If they ______________ about the party, they ______________ dressed up.

5. My daughter didn't learn to play the piano well because she didn't practice every day.

If she ______________ every day, she ______________ to play the piano well.

6. We weren't on time for the wedding because we didn't take our map with us.

If we ______________ our map with us, we ______________ on time.

7. Cindy didn't stop at the traffic light because she didn't notice it.

If she ______________ it, she definitely ______________.

8. We didn't have good seats for the concert because we didn't buy our tickets early enough.

If we ______________ our tickets early enough, we ______________ good seats.

C YOU DECIDE: *What Would Happen If . . . ?*

1. I had a terrible time on my vacation!

The weather wasn't ......warm enough......,
I didn't take ....,
I wasn't able to ....,
the hotel didn't have ....,
.... weren't ....,
and .... didn't write to me while I was away.
If the weather ______had been warmer______,
if I ______________________________,
if I ______________________________,
if the hotel ______________________________,
if ______________________________,
and if ______________________________ while I was away,
I'm sure I ______would have enjoyed______ my vacation.

(continued)

2. I had a terrible job interview yesterday at the Trans-Tel Company. I didn't get the job, and I know why.

I didn't remember to ______________________________,

I didn't arrive ______________________________,

I didn't ______________________________,

I wasn't ______________________________,

and I wasn't ______________________________.

If I ______________________________,

if I ______________________________,

if I ______________________________,

if I ______________________________,

and if I ______________________________,

I'm sure I ______________________ a better job interview.

And if I ______________________ a better job interview,

maybe I ______________________ the job.

3. I didn't enjoy myself at my cousin's birthday party last night.

The music wasn't ______________________________,

the food wasn't ______________________________,

the people there weren't ______________________________,

______________________ wasn't ______________________,

and ______________________ didn't ______________________.

If the music ______________________________,

if the food ______________________________,

if the people there ______________________________,

if ______________________________,

and if ______________________________,

I'm sure I ______________________ myself at the party.

D WHAT'S THE ANSWER?

1. If I hadn't expected Maria to say "yes," I _______ her to marry me.
   (a.) wouldn't have asked
   b. wouldn't ask

2. If you hadn't set off the metal detector, you _______ searched.
   a. wouldn't get
   b. wouldn't have gotten

3. If Janet's mortgage _______ approved, she wouldn't have been able to buy a house.
   a. hadn't been
   b. wasn't

4. If I _______ problems with my printer last night, I wouldn't have turned in my paper late.
   a. didn't have
   b. hadn't had

5. If Timmy's report card _______ bad, his parents wouldn't have been upset.
   a. hadn't been
   b. wasn't

6. If we hadn't felt under the weather, we _______ home.
   a. didn't stay
   b. wouldn't have stayed

7. If Debbie _______ her leg, she wouldn't have missed the class trip.
   a. didn't sprain
   b. hadn't sprained

8. If the boss hadn't been upset, he _______ at everybody this morning.
   a. wouldn't have yelled
   b. wouldn't yell

9. If it _______ cold last week, there wouldn't have been ice on the pond.
   a. wasn't
   b. hadn't been

10. If I hadn't had a bad headache, I _______ to bed so early.
    a. wouldn't go
    b. wouldn't have gone

E LISTENING

Listen and choose the statement that is true based on what you hear.

1. a. She got the job.
   (b.) She didn't speak confidently.

2. a. He got fired.
   b. He arrived on time for work every day.

3. a. It rained.
   b. They didn't have to cancel the picnic.

4. a. He wasn't in a hurry.
   b. He made mistakes on his homework.

5. a. She didn't call them.
   b. She remembered their phone number.

6. a. The play wasn't boring.
   b. The audience fell asleep.

7. a. They weren't in the mood to go swimming.
   b. They went to the beach.

8. a. He didn't get a ticket.
   b. He was speeding.

9. a. She didn't write legibly.
   b. She wrote legibly.

10. a. He remembered the meeting.
    b. He didn't go to the meeting.

F HOW I BECAME A BASKETBALL PLAYER

A. Why did you decide to become a basketball player?

B. When I was very young, my uncle took me to basketball games every weekend, my grandparents bought me a basketball, and my parents sent me to basketball camp. When I was older, I played basketball in high school and college, and I went to basketball games whenever I could.

If my uncle ____hadn't taken me____ [1] to basketball games every weekend,

if my grandparents ________________________ [2] a basketball,

if my parents ________________________ [3] to basketball camp,

if I ________________________ [4] basketball in high school and college,

and if I ________________________ [5] to basketball games whenever I could,

I ____wouldn't have become____ [6] a basketball player.

G I'M REALLY GLAD

I'm really glad I went to Five-Star Business School.

If ____I hadn't gone____ [1] to Five-Star,

I ____wouldn't have____ [2] learned information technology.

And if I ________________________ [3] information technology,

I ________________________ [4] a job at the Trans-Tel Company.

And if I ________________________ [5] a job at Trans-Tel,

I ________________________ [6] sent to Vancouver on business.

And if I ________________________ [7] sent to Vancouver on business,

I ________________________ [8] met your father.

And if I ________________________ [9] your father,

you ________________________ [10] born!

H WHY DIDN'T YOU TELL ME?

Why didn't you tell me today's English class was canceled? If you had told [1] me it was canceled, I ______ [2] to school this morning. And if I ______ [3] to school, I ______ [4] here when the repairperson came to pick up the computer. And if ______ [5] here when the repairperson came to pick it up, she ______ [6] able to take it to her repair shop. And if she ______ [7] able to take it to her shop, I'm sure she ______ [8] fixed it. And if she ______ [9] it, we would be on the Internet right now!

Why didn't you tell me you had invited your friends for dinner last night? If you ______ [10] me you had invited them, I definitely would have ______ [11] more food. If I ______ [12] more food, there would have been enough for everyone to eat. And if ______ [13] enough food for everybody to eat, we ______ [14] to Ziggy's Restaurant for dinner. And if we ______ [15] to Ziggy's for dinner, we ______ [16] sick. And if we ______ [17] sick, we ______ [18] had to go to the hospital. And if we ______ [19] to go to the hospital, we ______ [20] home, and you could ______ [21] your homework. And if you ______ [22] your homework, your teacher ______ [23] upset.

I YOU DECIDE: *Why Was Larry Late for Work?*

I'm sorry I was late for work this morning. I tried to get here on time, but everything went wrong.

First, ...

Then, ...

After that, ...

And also, ...

If ____,

if ____,

if ____,

and if ____,

I ______________________________ so late.

J GRAMMARRAP: *If They Hadn't* 

Listen. Then clap and practice.

If he hadn't been asked to dance in the show,
He wouldn't have slipped and broken his toe.

If she hadn't decided to learn to ski,
She wouldn't have fallen and hurt her knee.

If you hadn't lost the keys to your car,
You wouldn't have had to walk so far.

If we hadn't left our tickets at home,
We wouldn't have missed the flight to Rome.

K WHAT'S THE ANSWER?

1. Henry didn't enjoy the lecture. He wishes _______ home.
   a. he stayed
   (b.) he had stayed

2. I don't do my homework all the time. My teacher wishes _______.
   a. I did
   b. I had done

3. When I was young, I used to feel bad because I wasn't as athletic as the other students in my class. I wish _______ athletic.
   a. I was
   b. I had been

4. When we moved into this neighborhood, we were invited to a big neighborhood party. We wish _______.
   a. we had gone
   b. we went

5. We don't know if it's a girl or a boy. We wish _______.
   a. we knew
   b. we had known

6. I didn't read the instructions very carefully. I wish _______ them more carefully.
   a. I read
   b. I had read

7. My parents always worry about the future when they hear bad news on TV. I wish _______ so much.
   a. they hadn't worried
   b. they didn't worry

8. Mrs. Watson is concerned that her husband doesn't eat better food. She wishes _______ healthier things.
   a. he ate
   b. he had eaten

L COMPLETE THE SENTENCES

1. I'm a terrible dancer. I wish ____I had taken____ dance lessons when I was younger.
2. Amy didn't study for her math test, and she got a bad grade. She wishes ____________________ for it.
3. Fred doesn't enjoy working in the Accounting Department. He wishes ____________ in the Personnel Department.
4. I love dogs. I wish ____________ a dog when I was young. My mother didn't like dogs. She liked cats. We had five of them!
5. When my friends go skiing, I never go with them because I can't ski. I wish ____________ how to ski.
6. I'm really sorry I didn't see the new James Bond movie when it was playing downtown last month. I wish ____________ it.
7. My wife and I are both being transferred to our company's office on the east coast, and now we have to sell our house. We wish ____________ sell it.

M PATTY'S PARTY

These people didn't have a very good time at Patty's party last night.

1. I didn't have a very good time at Patty's party last night. I wish I *hadn't* *gone*. There were a lot of other things I could have done. I wish I ______ ______ something else.

2. Patty's party was outside, and it was very cold. If it ______ ______ so cold, I ______ ______ ______ more comfortable.

3. I'm very sorry that Claudia Crandall was at the party. She didn't stop singing and playing the guitar. I CERTAINLY wish she ______ ______ and ______ the guitar. She has the worst voice I've ever heard, and she plays the guitar VERY badly. If Claudia ______ ______ and ______ the guitar at the party, I ______ ______ ______ a headache all night!

4. I wish I ______ forget people's names all the time. Can you believe it? I couldn't remember Patty's sister's name. I wish I ______ ______ it. After all, if she ______ forgotten MY name, I ______ ______ liked it.

5. I wish I ______ ______ more people at the party. I didn't know anybody at all. If I ______ ______ more people, I ______ ______ ______ so lonely, and I ______ ______ ______ so out of place.

N GrammarRap: *They Wish They Hadn't*

Listen. Then clap and practice.

I wish I hadn't skied down the mountain.
I wish I had watched TV.
If I hadn't skied down the mountain,
I wouldn't have hurt my knee.

I wish I hadn't walked to the office.
I wish I had taken the train.
If I hadn't walked to the office,
I wouldn't have gotten caught in the rain.

I wish I hadn't typed so carelessly.
I wish I had done much better.
If I hadn't typed so carelessly,
I wouldn't have had to redo this letter.

I wish I hadn't swum in the ocean.
I wish I had gone to the park.
If I hadn't swum in the ocean,
I wouldn't have gotten scared by a shark.

I wish I hadn't used so much toothpaste.
I wish I had used much less.
If I hadn't used so much toothpaste,
I wouldn't have made such a mess.

O HOPES AND WISHES

1. A. I heard that I might get a promotion. Can you tell me if it's true?

   B. I wish I ___could tell___ you now, but I'm not supposed to say anything. I hope I ___can tell___ you soon.

2. A. Do you like your job?

   B. My job is very boring. I wish I ______________ someplace else. I'm looking for a job at an Internet company. I hope I ______________ one soon.

3. A. I wish Ricardo Palermo ______________ "Loving You" last night. He's the most fantastic singer I've ever heard.

   B. I certainly hope he ______________ it when I go to his concert on Saturday night.

4. A. I'm having trouble learning to speak English. I'm afraid I'm too old. I wish I ______________ English when I was younger.

   B. Don't be ridiculous! You do a lot better than many of the younger students in our class. They all wish they ______________ English as well as you.

5. A. I wish you ___________ have to leave on a business trip. I'm really going to miss you. I hope you ______________ a good time while you're away, but don't enjoy yourself TOO much!

   B. You know I'm going to miss you, too. I wish you ______________ going with me.

6. A. I had my yearly check-up today, and my doctor is a little concerned about my weight.

   B. What did the doctor say?

   A. He wishes I ______________ so heavy. He gave me a new diet that I'm going to try. I hope I ______________ a lot of weight.

P YOU DECIDE: *If*

1. I hope it doesn't rain this weekend. If it rains this weekend, ...

2. I wish I had more free time. If I had more free time, ...

3. I wish I didn't have to .... If I didn't have to ...., ...

4. I hope you can lend me .... If you can lend me ...., ...

5. I wish I had .... many years ago. If I had ...., ...

6. I hope .... is elected president. If .... is elected president, ...

7. I wish I knew more about .... If I knew more about ...., ...

8. I hope .... in the future. If ...., ...

Q WISH OR HOPE?

1. They (wish hope) they had taken their umbrellas today.
2. Timothy can't drive yet. He (wishes hopes) he were older.
3. I (wish hope) I find the right ingredients for the soup.
4. Mrs. Jones (wishes hopes) her son hadn't quit the baseball team.
5. John (wishes hopes) his shirt doesn't shrink in the washing machine.
6. I (wish hope) I didn't have to wait so long to see if I got accepted to college.
7. Tomorrow is Saturday. I (wish hope) I still don't feel "under the weather."
8. Mr. McDonald doesn't like his new house. He (wishes hopes) he had bought a condominium.
9. The minister is embarrassed. He (wishes hopes) he hadn't arrived late for the wedding.

R LISTENING 

Listen and complete the sentences.

1. a. . . . I wouldn't be so nervous.
   b. . . . I won't be so irritable.
2. a. . . . I'll be home right away.
   b. . . . I wouldn't be late.
3. a. . . . he'll have a lot more friends.
   b. . . . he'd be a lot happier.
4. a. . . . she wouldn't have gotten wet.
   b. . . . she'll be dry.
5. a. . . . we'd dance together.
   b. . . . we'll talk to each other all evening.
6. a. . . . I won't have to walk to work.
   b. . . . I wouldn't have to drive everywhere.

S LISTENING: *Hopes and Wishes* 

Listen and complete the sentences.

1. a. . . . he isn't sick.
   b. . . . he felt better.
2. a. . . . tomorrow's lesson is easier.
   b. . . . I understood English better.
3. a. . . . she visits me more often.
   b. . . . she still lived across the street.
4. a. . . . she can't work someplace else.
   b. . . . she can find another job.
5. a. . . . I had a dog or a cat.
   b. . . . I can get a pet.
6. a. . . . I'm a more graceful dancer.
   b. . . . I weren't so clumsy.
7. a. . . . you can come.
   b. . . . you could be there.
8. a. . . . she were more careful.
   b. . . . she finds it soon.
9. a. . . . they tasted good.
   b. . . . everybody likes chocolate.
10. a. . . . it were healthier.
    b. . . . it needs more sun.
11. a. . . . you knew more about fax machines.
    b. . . . you know how to fix it.
12. a. . . . she owned a more reliable car.
    b. . . . it starts on cold days.
13. a. . . . I had some.
    b. . . . we can borrow some.
14. a. . . . I had a better memory.
    b. . . . I can remember them.

T LISTENING 

Listen to each word and then say it.

1. beg—bay
2. check—shake
3. Fred—afraid
4. men—Main
5. met—made
6. never—neighbor
7. pepper—paper
8. set—say
9. pet—paid
10. wedding—waiting

U HAVE YOU HEARD? 

Listen and complete the sentences.

met made

1. a. . . . all the beds.
   (b.) . . . an old friend.

fell fail

2. a. . . . while they were skiing.
   b. . . . whenever they take a test.

teller tailor

3. a. . . . works in a bank.
   b. . . . takes in your clothes.

pepper paper

4. a. . . . in my notebook.
   b. . . . in the stew.

Fred afraid

5. a. . . . you might drown?
   b. . . . Smith?

met made

6. a. . . . any summer plans yet?
   b. . . . their new neighbors?

men Main

7. a. . . . Street bus is leaving.
   b. . . . are leaving the barber shop.

check shake

8. a. . . . hands.
   b. . . . with the mechanic.

wedding waiting

9. a. . . . at the bus stop.
   b. . . . was the happiest day of my life.

never neighbor

10. a. . . . just moved in yesterday.
    b. . . . flown in a helicopter before.

pet paid

11. a. . . . her income tax.
    b. . . . bird knows how to talk.

check shake

12. a. . . . hands with the ticket agent.
    b. . . . with the ticket agent.

fell fail

13. a. . . . most of my English exams.
    b. . . . asleep very late last night.

wedding waiting

14. a. . . . for us.
    b. . . . is at 11:00.

never neighbor

15. a. . . . is very noisy.
    b. . . . been to Hawaii.

Fred afraid

16. a. . . . I'll get hurt.
    b. . . . Jones. What's your name?

A WHAT DID THEY SAY?

8

STUDENT BOOK PAGES 109–124

1. Nick called. He told me __he was having__ problems with his car.
2. Carol and Don said ______________________ to our party this Saturday.
3. Aunt Alice promised ______________________ us sometime soon.
4. The waiter told us ______________________ to order our food.
5. Our boss told us ______________________ to retire next year.
6. Ronald told his supervisor that ______________________ his report yet.
7. Ruth called. She said ____________ home in bed because ____________ a bad cold.
8. Pierre called. He said our dog ____________ ready, and we ____________ pick her up now.
9. Bob said he ______________ me at the mall, but I ____________________ him.
10. Jane said ____________________ working overtime, so ________________ be able to go bowling with me.
11. Nancy told us __________________________ very hard, so she ____________ to take a vacation.

B MESSAGES

1.

Dear Mother,

I got an "A" on my biology test.

Love,
Amy

A. I just got an e-mail from my daughter in college.

B. Really? What did she say?

A. She said she had gotten an "A" on her biology test.

2. A. I received a note from Uncle Ralph today.

B. Oh, that's nice. What did he say?

A. He said ______________________________.

Dear Gloria,

I'm home from the hospital and I'm feeling much better.

Uncle Ralph

3.

Dear Sue and Mike,

We saw the Colosseum, but we haven't gone to the Vatican yet.

The Wilsons

A. The Wilsons sent us a postcard from Rome.

B. Oh, really? What did they say?

A. They said ______________________________.

4. A. I got an e-mail from my friend Richard today.

B. He hasn't written in a while. What did he say?

A. He said ______________________________.

Kathy,

I hope you can visit me when you come to Japan this summer.

Richard

5.

Dear Mr. Watson,

I'm sorry, but you aren't the right person for the job.

Sincerely,
Roberta Bennett

A. I received an e-mail from Ms. Bennett at the Apex Company.

B. Oh. You've been expecting her to write. What did she say?

A. She said ______________________________.

(continued)

6. A. Charlie, the plumber, left us a note.

B. Oh. What did he say?

A. He said ______________________________

______________________________.

Dear Mr. and Mrs. Blake,

I'm very busy, and I can't repair your dishwasher this week.

Charlie

7. Hi everyone!

We love Hawaii, and we're thinking of buying a condominium.

Love,

Grandma & Grandpa

A. We received a postcard from Grandma and Grandpa in Hawaii.

B. That's nice. Are they enjoying their vacation there?

A. Yes. They said ______________________________

______________________________.

8. A. I received an e-mail from my father last night.

B. What did he say?

A. He said ______________________________

____

______________________________.

Dear Brian,

I was hoping to send you more money for college, but I won't be able to because I'm having financial problems.

Dad

9. Dear Ann and Tom,

I'll be arriving ....

and I plan to ....

....

A. We received a note from Cousin George.

B. Oh. What did he say?

A. He said ______________________________

______________________________.

10. A. We got a letter from Aunt Clara today.

B. That's nice. What did she say?

A. She said ______________________________

____

______________________________.

Dear ....,

I have some good news.

I'm finally going to ....

....

....

11.

Dear ....,

You won't believe it, but ....

....

....

A. I received an e-mail from my friend Larry.

B. He hasn't written in a long time. What did he say?

A. He said ______________________________

____

______________________________.

C GRAMMARRAP: *What Did They Say?*

Listen. Then clap and practice.

I'm mad.

I'm sad.

A. What did he say?
B. He said he was mad.
A. What did she say?
B. She said she was sad.

I'm busy.

I'm dizzy.

A. What did she say?
B. She said she was busy.
A. What did he say?
B. He said he was dizzy.

I've been hired.

I've been fired.

A. What did she say?
B. She said she'd been hired.
A. What did he say?
B. He said he'd been fired.

We'll be late.

We'll wait.

A. What did they say?
B. They said they'd be late.
A. What did you say?
B. We said we would wait.

D WHAT'S THE ANSWER?

1. A. We can't fish here.
   B. Really? I was sure ______ fish here.
   a. we can
   (b.) we could

2. A. My husband wants to sell our house.
   B. Oh. I didn't know ______ to sell it.
   a. he wanted
   b. he had wanted

3. A. Has the meeting been canceled?
   B. I thought everybody knew it ______.
   a. was canceled
   b. had been canceled

4. A. Susan got a big promotion.
   B. That's nice. I didn't know ______ a promotion.
   a. she had gotten
   b. she got

5. A. My parents have moved to Miami.
   B. Yes. I knew ______ there.
   a. they moved
   b. they had moved

6. A. Our big sale starts tomorrow.
   B. Really? I didn't know ______ tomorrow.
   a. it starts
   b. it started

7. A. Do we have to work overtime today?
   B. I thought everybody knew ______.
   a. we had to work overtime
   b. we have to work overtime

8. A. The school picnic is going to be canceled.
   B. You're kidding! I didn't know the school picnic ______ to be canceled.
   a. was going
   b. is going

E LISTENING 

What did they say? Listen and choose the correct answer.

1. a. He said he had fixed their car last week.
   (b.) He said he could fix their car next week.
2. a. She said her daughter was going to have a baby in July.
   b. She said her daughter had had a baby in July.
3. a. He said that the meeting had been canceled.
   b. He said the meeting was important.
4. a. He said his wife was going to be promoted.
   b. He said his wife had been promoted.
5. a. She said she didn't believe the bus drivers were going on strike.
   b. She said she didn't know the bus drivers.
6. a. He said they had loved each other.
   b. He said they loved each other.
7. a. She said the monkeys had escaped from the zoo.
   b. She said she hadn't believed the monkeys would escape from the zoo.
8. a. He said he was nervous about his interview.
   b. He said he had been nervous about his interview.
9. a. She said her parents had sold their condominium and moved into a house.
   b. She said that her parents had sold their house.
10. a. She said she was going to quit her job.
    b. She said she had moved to Hollywood.

F YOU DECIDE: *What Happened While Paula Wilson Was Away?*

Paula Wilson just returned home after working in Australia for two years. She's talking to her old friend Steve.

A. Welcome home, Paula! I'm glad you're back. How have you been?

B. Fine. Tell me, what's happened since I've been away?

A. Well, your cousin Frank got married last month.

B. He did? I didn't know ___he had gotten married___ 1 last month. I wonder why he didn't write me.

A. He probably thought you knew. Have you heard about Aunt Martha? She's in the hospital.

B. Really? I had no idea ________________ 2. What happened? Did she have an accident?

A. No. Actually, she had a third heart attack last week.

B. That's terrible! I knew ________________ 3 having problems with her heart for the past several years, but I didn't know she ________________ 4 another heart attack. I hope she's okay. Tell me, how's your sister Eileen?

A. You probably haven't heard. She's going to become the president of her company next month.

B. That's wonderful! I knew she ________________ 5 promoted many times, but I didn't know she ________________ 6 the president of her company! That's very exciting news. And how are your children?

A. They've been doing very well. My son .... 7, and my daughter .... 8.

B. That's fantastic! I didn't know that your son ________________ 9 and your daughter ________________ 10.

A. By the way, have you heard about Nancy and Tom? They .... 11.

B. Really? I had no idea ________________ 12. A lot sure has happened recently!

G YOU WON'T BELIEVE IT!

1. My daughter asked me _______!
   a. do I like being old
   b. if I liked being old

2. My students asked me _______.
   a. why the test had been difficult
   b. why was the test so difficult

3. My dentist asked me _______.
   a. whether I ever brushed my teeth
   b. if do I ever brush my teeth

4. My boss asked me what time _______.
   a. did I go to bed last night
   b. I had gone to bed last night

5. My neighbor asked me _______.
   a. if I would sell him my car
   b. if will I sell him my car

6. The job interviewer asked me _______.
   a. where I had learned to spell
   b. where did I learn to spell

7. The salesperson in the store asked me _______!
   a. how old are you
   b. how old I was

8. My girlfriend asked me _______.
   a. if we could get married next month
   b. whether could we get married next month

9. My employees asked me _______.
   a. when was I going to give them raises
   b. when I was going to give them raises

10. My daughter's boyfriend asked me _______.
    a. if I dyed my hair
    b. do I dye my hair

H LISTENING

Listen and choose the correct answer.

1. Patty's father asked her _______.
   a. did she break up with Gary
   b. if she had broken up with Gary
   c. whether she had broken up with Larry

2. She asked them _______.
   a. how long they had been swimming there
   b. how long had they been sitting there
   c. how long they had been sitting there

3. He asked her _______.
   a. if was she eating when they called
   b. whether she was eating when they called
   c. if she had been reading when they called

4. She asked him _______.
   a. when was he going to repaint it
   b. when he was going to repaint it
   c. if he was going to repair it

5. He asked her _______.
   a. whether she was still sad
   b. if was she still mad
   c. if she was still mad

6. She asked him _______.
   a. when he was going to take a bath
   b. when he was going to study math
   c. if he had studied math

7. He asked me _______.
   a. were they too tall
   b. if they were too tall
   c. whether they were too small

8. She asked him _______.
   a. who had fixed the kitchen floor
   b. who had fixed the kitchen door
   c. who was going to fix the kitchen floor

I WHAT DID THEY ASK?

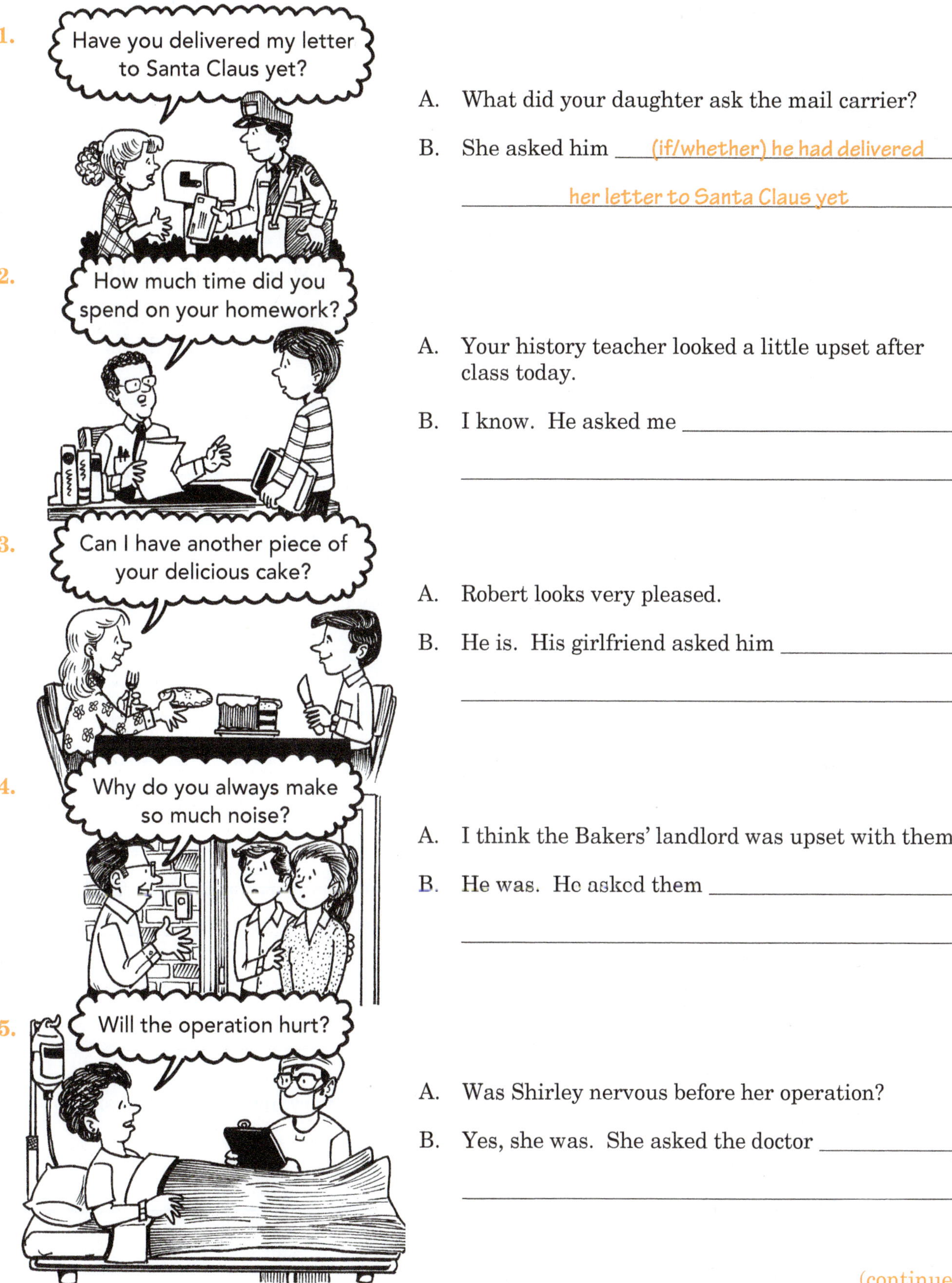

1. A. What did your daughter ask the mail carrier?

   B. She asked him (if/whether) he had delivered her letter to Santa Claus yet.

2. A. Your history teacher looked a little upset after class today.

   B. I know. He asked me ____________________________________.

3. A. Robert looks very pleased.

   B. He is. His girlfriend asked him ____________________________________.

4. A. I think the Bakers' landlord was upset with them.

   B. He was. He asked them ____________________________________.

5. A. Was Shirley nervous before her operation?

   B. Yes, she was. She asked the doctor ____________________________________.

(continued)

6.

A. George looks bored. What did he just ask his wife?

B. He asked her ______________________________

____.

7.

A. How did Alan feel when he bumped into his former girlfriend?

B. He was VERY surprised. She asked him ________

____.

8.

A. The students in your class look confused.

B. I know. They asked me ______________________

____.

9.

A. Your parents look very concerned. What did they ask you?

B. They asked me ______________________________

____.

10.

A. Your boss looks very upset. What did she ask you?

B. She asked me _______________________________

____.

J GrammarRap: *I Asked Her When She Had Learned to Ski* 

Listen. Then clap and practice.

When did you learn to ski?
I started when I was three.

I asked her when she had learned to ski.
She said she had started when she was three.

What are you going to do?
I'm planning to go to the zoo.

I asked him what he was going to do.
He said he was planning to go to the zoo.

Why did you fire Bob?
He's been doing a terrible job.

I asked her why she had fired Bob.
She said he'd been doing a terrible job.

How much did you pay for your pen?
It cost a dollar ten.

I asked him how much he had paid for his pen.
He said it had cost a dollar ten.

Do you want to swim?
I'm planning to go to the gym.

I asked him if he wanted to swim.
He said he was planning to go to the gym.

Will you be home at one?
I'll be home when my work is done.

I asked her whether she'd be home by one.
She said she'd be home when her work was done.

K WHAT DID THEY TELL YOU?

1. Speak confidently! — My teacher told me ___to speak confidently___.

2. Don't drive too fast! — My parents told me ______________________.

3. Work quickly! — My boss told me ______________________.

4. Don't eat too much candy! — My doctor told me ______________________.

5. Don't play loud music! — My neighbors told me ______________________.

L WHAT'S THE ANSWER?

1. We're getting worried about our son. We told him _______ by 11:00 P.M.
   a. to be home (circled)
   b. be home

2. Howard looks exhausted. I told him _______ so hard.
   a. not to work
   b. don't work

3. My doctor told me _______ exercising every day.
   a. start
   b. to start

4. The food at this restaurant is terrible! Now I know why my friends told me _______ here.
   a. not to eat
   b. don't eat

5. My supervisor told me _______ the report over because I had made a lot of mistakes.
   a. do
   b. to do

6. I'm really upset. My girlfriend told me _______ her anymore.
   a. to not call
   b. not to call

7. The teacher told us _______ Chapter 5, but I read Chapter 4.
   a. to read
   b. read

8. I'm in trouble! My father told me _______ his new car, but I did. And I got into an accident!
   a. not to drive
   b. to not drive

M EVERYBODY ALWAYS TELLS HIM WHAT TO DO

I'm tired of being told what to do. All day yesterday everybody told me what to do.

1. Hurry! Your breakfast is getting cold.

As soon as I woke up, my mother told me to hurry.

She said my breakfast was getting cold.

2. Don't forget your umbrella! It's going to rain later.

At breakfast my father told me ____________________ ____________________.

He said ____________________.

3. Don't walk so slowly! We'll be late for school.

On the way to school, my friend Jimmy told me ____________________ ____________________.

He said ____________________.

4. Be quiet! You're disturbing the class!

At school, Ms. Johnson told me ____________________ ____________________.

She said ____________________.

5. ....
....

When we were walking home from school, the police officer on the corner told me ____________________.

He said ____________________.

(continued)

6.

When I went to soccer practice, my coach told me

____.

He said ______________________________________.

7.

At my music lesson, my violin teacher told me

____.

She said _____________________________________.

8.

When I was helping my family wash the dinner dishes,

my mother told me ____________________________.

She said _____________________________________.

9.

....

........................! You'll fail
your math test if you
don't study.

I was hoping to watch TV after dinner, but my older

brother told me ______________________________.

He said ______________________________________

____.

10.

....

You have to get up early for
school.

I couldn't even choose my own bedtime. My parents

told me ______________________________________.

They said ____________________________________.

I can't wait until I grow up!
Then I can tell everybody else
what to do!

N TODAY AT SCHOOL

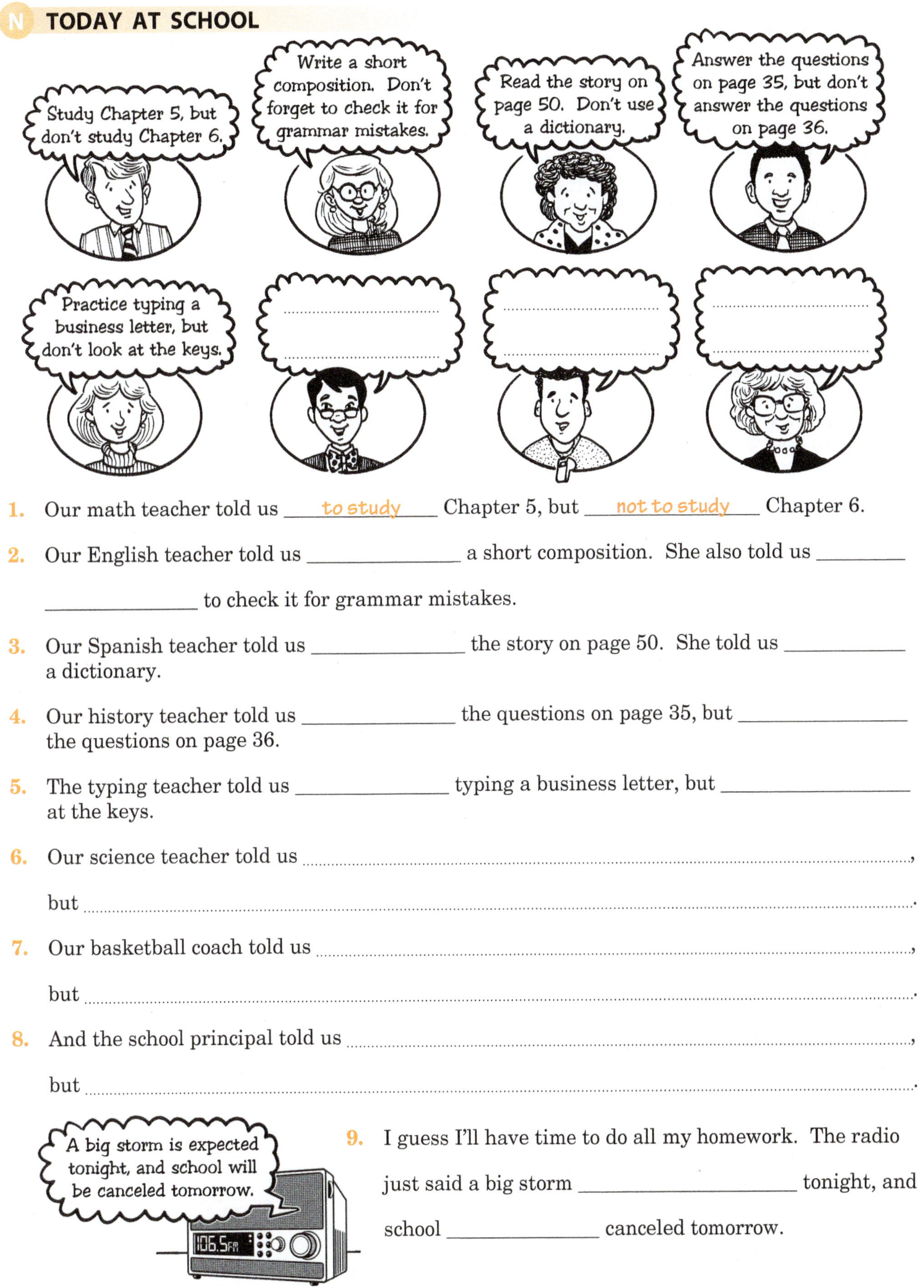

1. Our math teacher told us ___to study___ Chapter 5, but ___not to study___ Chapter 6.
2. Our English teacher told us ______________ a short composition. She also told us ______________ to check it for grammar mistakes.
3. Our Spanish teacher told us ______________ the story on page 50. She told us ______________ a dictionary.
4. Our history teacher told us ______________ the questions on page 35, but ______________ the questions on page 36.
5. The typing teacher told us ______________ typing a business letter, but ______________ at the keys.
6. Our science teacher told us ....,
   but ....
7. Our basketball coach told us ....,
   but ....
8. And the school principal told us ....,
   but ....
9. I guess I'll have time to do all my homework. The radio just said a big storm ______________ tonight, and school ______________ canceled tomorrow.

O GrammarRap: *He Told Me Not to Eat Candy* 

Listen. Then clap and practice.

Don't eat candy!
Don't eat cake!
Eat a lot of fish!
Don't eat steak!

He told me not to eat candy.
He told me not to eat cake.
He told me to eat a lot of fish.
He told me not to eat steak.

Clean your bedroom!
Pick up your toys!
Put your clothes away!
Don't make noise!

They told me to clean my bedroom.
They told me to pick up my toys.
They told me to put my clothes away.
They told me not to make noise.

Come to the meeting at ten!
Don't be late!
Get there early!
We won't wait!

She told me to come to the meeting at ten.
She told me not to be late.
She told me to get there early.
She told me they wouldn't wait.

Break up with Harry!
Break up with Ned!
Don't go out with Bob or
Barry or Larry or Fred!

They told me to break up with Harry.
They told me to break up with Ned.
They told me not to go out with Bob
Or Barry or Larry or Fred.

P CHOOSE THE RIGHT WORD

1. Have you heard the news? A lion has (erased **escaped**) from the zoo!
2. This (calculator casserole) tastes delicious! Who made it?
3. What's everybody so (talking anxious) about?
4. Please remember to (lock look) the door when you leave tonight.
5. My niece Nancy was the most beautiful (groom bride) I've ever seen!
6. I think I'm getting the (flu flew). I'd better call the doctor.
7. What can we do to (present prevent) robberies in our neighborhood?
8. I'm sorry. I don't (no know) how to do that, but I'll ask somebody.
9. This new (puddle poodle) is the cutest puppy I've ever seen.
10. My landlord told me not to pour (pipes grease) down the kitchen sink.
11. We felt very (reassured rearranged) after we spoke to the police.
12. Did you know that the president wanted to raise (taxis taxes)?
13. We can always depend on our parents to give us good (suggest advice).
14. I'll be (away way) from home all next week, but you can reach me by e-mail.
15. Did you hear that all the DVD players in the store are on (sail sale) this week?
16. My parents asked me when I was going to (brake break) up with my boyfriend.
17. I'm so excited! I just met a wonderful girl, and I think I'm (falling failing) in love with her.
18. Somebody broke (out of into) the house across the street and stole a lot of jewelry.
19. I'm a little (irritable annoyed) at my neighbors. They're noisy, and they aren't very friendly.
20. The interviewer asked me why I thought I was (qualified willing) for the position.
21. The teacher said we weren't allowed to use (examinations dictionaries) during the test.
22. My friend Bill asked me (whether weather) I wanted to go sailing, and I told him it was going to rain.
23. Michael and Sue got (engaged married) last month, and they're going to get (engaged married) in June.

Q LISTENING

Listen to each word and then say it.

1. stand
2. start
3. fantastic
4. rest

9. skate
10. ask
11. scare
12. discover

17. sports
18. spring
19. special
20. hospital

5. that's
6. patients
7. writes
8. tickets

13. works
14. thinks
15. likes
16. weeks

21. stops
22. skips
23. helps
24. escapes

R WHO IS THE BEST?

Fill in the missing letters and then read aloud.

Many pessimis_t_s don't trus_t_ dentis_t_s because they're s_c_ared the wors__ will happen. However, Dr. Wes__'s patien__s are all optimis__ic. They think Dr. Wes__ is the bes__ dentis__ in Bos__on.

1. S__uart li__es Dr. Wes__.

2. S__uar__'s sis__er also thin__s Dr. Wes__ is wonderful.

3. Mr. Jac__son can't s__and any other dentis__.

4. Be__sy always tal__s about Dr. Wes__.

5. Dr. Wes__'s S__anish-s__eaking patien__s are es__ecially pleased.

6. Margaret is very enthusias__ic about Dr. Wes__.

7. Patty thin__s Dr. Wes__ is the hardes__ working dentis__ she knows.

8. S__eve also li__es Dr. Wes__.

✓ CHECK-UP TEST: Chapters 6–8

A. Fill in the blanks.

1. George doesn't enjoy being a waiter. He wishes ________________ an actor.
2. Ann took violin lessons last year and didn't enjoy them. She wishes ____________________ guitar lessons.
3. Frank drives an old used car. He wishes ________________ a more reliable car.
4. By the time Jill got to the party, most of her friends had left. She wishes ________________ to the party earlier.
5. I don't speak English very well. I wish ________________ more fluently.
6. You ate all the ice cream in the refrigerator! I wish __________________________ it all!

B. Complete the sentences.

1. The Johnsons didn't enjoy their vacation because the weather wasn't warm.

   If the weather ______________ warm, they ____________________________ their vacation.

2. My doctor is concerned because I eat too many rich desserts.

   If I ___________________ so many rich desserts, my doctor ___________________ concerned.

3. Gloria arrived late because she missed the bus.

   If she ______________________ the bus, ______________________________________ late.

4. I'm frustrated because I can't type very fast.

   If ______________________ fast, ________________________ so frustrated.

5. You made a lot of mistakes because you weren't paying attention.

   If you ________________________ attention, you ____________________ so many mistakes.

6. Gary looks confused because he doesn't understand today's grammar.

   If he ________________ today's grammar, he ______________________________ so confused.

C. Complete the sentences.

Ex. *I'm feeling fine after my operation.*

Uncle Bill called. He said he ___was feeling___ fine after his operation.

1. *I got a big promotion.*

   My friend Betty called. She said ________________________ a big promotion.

2. *What's your name?*

The police officer asked me ____.

3. *Did you see me on TV last night?*

My friend Rita called. She asked me ____________________ on TV last night.

4. *I'm sorry I forgot your birthday.*

My sister-in-law called. She said ________________________________ my birthday.

5. *I won't be able to visit you this weekend.*

Grandpa called. He said __________________________________ us this weekend.

6. *Brush your teeth every day, and don't eat any candy.*

My dentist told me _____________ my teeth every day, and ____________________ any candy.

7. *When will I be old enough to drive?*

My son asked me ____________________ old enough to drive.

8. *Why are you leaving so early? Are you in a hurry to get somewhere?*

Aunt Martha asked me _________________________ so early. She wanted to know _________________________ to get somewhere.

D. Listening

Listen and complete the sentences.

Ex. (a.) I'd be able to see a movie.
b. I had seen a movie.

1. a. I wouldn't have had to stay home in bed.
b. I had to stay in bed.

2. a. I hadn't gotten depressed so often.
b. I wouldn't get depressed so often.

3. a. we had forgotten to pay our rent.
b. he'll call us back tonight.

4. a. when are we going to get married.
b. when we were going to get married.

5. a. if I had gone to college.
b. whether had I gone to college.

A POLISH UP YOUR INTERVIEW SKILLS!

SIDE by SIDE Gazette

STUDENT BOOK PAGES **125–128**

Read the article on student book page 125 and answer the questions.

1. The most important tip for a successful interview is to ______.
   a. be prepared
   b. brag about yourself
   c. write a thank-you note
   d. fill out an application

2. A good way to find out about a company is to ______.
   a. read job ads
   b. ask the interviewer
   c. look up the address
   d. use the Internet

3. During the interview, you should ______.
   a. tell about your family
   b. answer questions honestly
   c. ask about benefits
   d. ask about vacations

4. In paragraph 2, *dress appropriately* means ______.
   a. stand out from the crowd
   b. wear casual clothes
   c. dress neatly and in nice clothes
   d. dress in comfortable clothes

5. The interviewer will probably NOT ask about your ______.
   a. age
   b. education
   c. strengths
   d. plans for the future

6. You can expect an interviewer to ______.
   a. arrive late
   b. tell you about his or her background
   c. ask about your weaknesses
   d. ask you to come to a follow-up interview

7. *Get along with* in paragraph 3 means ______.
   a. supervise
   b. give instructions to
   c. do the same job as
   d. be friendly with

8. You can infer from the article that an interview ______.
   a. will probably last for an hour
   b. is an important way that companies evaluate job applicants
   c. is easy if you've never had one
   d. isn't challenging for most people

B POINTS IN A TEXT: Identifying Examples that Support the Author's Points

In the article about interview skills, the author makes points about good interview skills and gives examples to explain and support these points. Match the points and examples in the article.

____ 1. Learn about the company before the interview.

____ 2. Prepare for the questions you will be asked.

____ 3. Dress appropriately for the interview.

____ 4. Prepare questions to ask the interviewer.

____ 5. Follow up after the interview.

a. Don't wear casual clothes.

b. Be ready to explain why you want to leave your current job.

c. Write a thank-you letter to the interviewer.

d. Look at the company's website for information.

e. Ask about the job responsibilities.

C FACT FILE

Look at the Fact File on student book page 125 and answer the questions.

1. The second most common way to find a job is to ______.
   a. network
   b. go to an employment agency
   c. read the want ads
   d. write to or call the company yourself

2. More than one-third (1/3) of job applicants find their jobs by ______.
   a. reading the newspaper
   b. contacting an employer directly
   c. communicating with other people
   d. using an employment agency

D WHO GOT THE JOB?

Read the article on student book page 126 and answer the questions.

1. When asked about her experience, Sarah Jones ______.
   a. only talked about her education
   b. talked about her family
   c. gave a lot of information
   d. asked about the company

2. Sarah wants to leave her current job because ______.
   a. it isn't challenging enough
   b. it's too challenging
   c. she wants to travel more
   d. she has a lot of weaknesses

3. Sarah thinks she needs to ______ better.
   a. use computer software
   b. ask questions at an interview
   c. write follow-up notes
   d. write business letters

4. Bob wasn't familiar with the company's products because ______.
   a. he didn't need any software
   b. he hadn't prepared for the interview
   c. the interviewer didn't tell him
   d. he didn't have Internet access

5. Sarah made a better impression because ______.
   a. she asked about vacation days
   b. she wanted to work shorter hours
   c. she knew about the company
   d. she hadn't thought about her weaknesses

6. You can infer that Bob's interview ______.
   a. was longer than Sarah's
   b. was cancelled by the interviewer
   c. was successful
   d. was shorter than Sarah's

E AROUND THE WORLD

Read the article on student book page 126 and answer the questions.

1. In the U.S., interviewers do NOT usually ask about ______.
   a. language skills
   b. marital status
   c. educational background
   d. future plans

2. Eye contact is an example of ______.
   a. body language
   b. formality
   c. rudeness
   d. personality

3. A firm handshake is unusual in ______.
   a. Mexico
   b. Germany
   c. France
   d. the U.S.

4. The main idea of the article is that interviews ______ around the world.
   a. are similar
   b. are informal
   c. are formal
   d. are different

F INTERVIEW

Read the interview on student book page 127 and answer the questions.

1. Monica Salinas interviews _______.
   a. about 10 people a week
   b. about 50 people a day
   c. about 50 people a week
   d. about 100 people a year

2. She asks applicants about weekend activities because _______.
   a. she learns about applicants this way
   b. she's interested in hobbies
   c. they need to work weekends
   d. she's a friendly person

3. One applicant ate his sandwich during the interview because _______.
   a. he was nervous
   b. he was confident
   c. he wasn't prepared
   d. he was hungry

4. An employee from Brazil received a bonus check because _______.
   a. she sent money to her family
   b. she was a hard worker
   c. she was promoted
   d. she was given a raise

5. According to Monica Salinas, the best advice for interviews is to _______.
   a. reschedule them
   b. talk only about yourself
   c. be serious and honest
   d. be relaxed and be yourself

6. You can infer that Monica Salinas _______.
   a. works overtime
   b. will be promoted
   c. enjoys her job
   d. works in an international company

G YOU'RE THE INTERVIEWER!

Imagine you're a Human Resources manager. Interview a classmate for a job at your company. Write the answers below. Then role-play the interview for the class.

Tell me about your background and experience.	
How would a friend describe you? (Suggest at least four words that person might use.)	
What do you enjoy doing on the weekend? Do you have any hobbies?	
What would you be able to contribute to our company?	

H FUN WITH IDIOMS

Choose the best response.

1. Aunt Dorothy talks my head off.
   a. Did you call her back?
   b. I know. She never says much.
   c. Yes. She's a good speaker.
   d. It's true. She's never quiet.

2. Frank really put his foot in his mouth.
   a. I was surprised it fit.
   b. I think he should apologize.
   c. He was very prepared.
   d. It was a nice thing for him to say.

3. Our boss never beats around the bush.
   a. Yes. She always says what she's thinking.
   b. Is she a gardener?
   c. That can be confusing.
   d. Is it difficult to understand her?

4. I think Richard inflated his resume.
   a. That was a good idea.
   b. It's good to have a long resume.
   c. He should have been honest.
   d. I know. It's very short.

I WE'VE GOT MAIL!

Choose the words that best complete each sentence.

1. Marcy said she wouldn't be able to come to the party. She said she _______ sorry.
   a. is being c. will be
   b. had been d. was

2. We heard from Uncle Carl. He said he _______ visiting us this spring.
   a. has been c. wouldn't be
   b. can be d. had been

3. The tenants told the owner of the building they _______ upset with the superintendent.
   a. been c. will be
   b. were d. have been being

4. All the students in our class knew that Sacramento _______ the capital of California.
   a. is c. be
   b. being d. been

5. They asked me where yesterday's meeting _______ held.
   a. is c. had
   b. has been d. had been

6. Our teacher told us that making eye contact _______ considered rude.
   a. hasn't c. being
   b. isn't d. hasn't been being

Choose the sentence that is correct and complete.

7. a. She told me she was surprised.
   b. She told me she has surprised.
   c. She told me she had surprised.
   d. She told me she being surprised.

8. a. He said he hasn't going to be late.
   b. He said he wasn't going to be late.
   c. He said he hadn't going to be late.
   d. He said he not going to be late.

9. a. I knew that the Nile be in Egypt.
   b. I knew that the Nile being in Egypt.
   c. I knew that the Nile is in Egypt.
   d. I knew that the Nile been in Egypt.

10. a. He asked me where the bank be.
    b. He asked me where the bank was.
    c. He asked me where the bank being.
    d. He asked me where the bank been.

11. a. Nobody knew where she is.
    b. Nobody knew where she be.
    c. Nobody knew where she been.
    d. Nobody knew where she had been.

12. a. They said they could help us.
    b. They said they can help us.
    c. They said they helping us.
    d. They said they be helping us.

J "CAN-DO" REVIEW

Match the "can do" statement and the correct sentence.

_____ 1. I can express certainty.
_____ 2. I can express agreement.
_____ 3. I can ask for a reason.
_____ 4. I can make a deduction.
_____ 5. I can empathize.
_____ 6. I can express a wish about something in the present.
_____ 7. I can express a wish about something in the past.
_____ 8. I can report what people have said.
_____ 9. I can express surprise.
_____ 10. I can express feelings and emotions.

a. Why do you say that?
b. I can't believe it!
c. I know what you mean.
d. I wish I had studied more for yesterday's test.
e. I suppose you're right.
f. He said he wouldn't be able to come to work.
g. We're annoyed at our landlord.
h. I'm positive.
i. I wish we lived in a larger apartment.
j. He must have been driving too fast.

A WHAT ARE THEY SAYING?

9

STUDENT BOOK PAGES **129–144**

1.

2.

3. You live around the corner,

__________________?

BUS STOP

4. You brought the plane tickets,

__________________?

5.

6.

7.

8.

9.

10.

B WHAT'S THE TAG?

1. The computer is working, _______?
   a. isn't it (circled)
   b. doesn't it

2. We've eaten here before, _______?
   a. haven't we
   b. didn't we

3. I'm on time, _______?
   a. amn't I
   b. aren't I

4. He'll be in the office next week, _______?
   a. won't he
   b. isn't he

5. You finished your report, _______?
   a. don't you
   b. didn't you

6. They're going to leave soon, _______?
   a. won't they
   b. aren't they

7. She was at the meeting, _______?
   a. wasn't she
   b. isn't she

8. Timmy, this baby food tastes good, _______?
   a. isn't it
   b. doesn't it

C I THINK I KNOW YOU

A. Excuse me, but I think I know you. You're a student at City College, ___aren't you___[1]?

B. Yes, ________________[2].

A. That's what I thought. I was sure I had seen you there, but I've forgotten when. Now I remember! You've been in a lot of school plays, ________________[3]?

B. Yes, ________________[4].

A. That's what I thought. And you sang in the school chorus last year, ________________[5]?

B. Yes, as a matter of fact, ________________[6].

A. I thought so. And now that I think of it, I've also seen you on Winter Street. You live there, ________________[7]?

B. Yes, ________________[8].

A. Isn't this ridiculous? I can remember so much about you, but I still can't remember your name. Wait . . . Now I remember. Your name is Mandy, ________________[9]?

B. No, it ________________[10].

A. It isn't?! I was sure your name was Mandy.

B. That's what everybody thinks. I'm Sandy. Mandy is my twin sister.

D WHAT ARE THEY SAYING?

1. The post office hasn't closed yet, ___has it___?

2. You aren't allergic to nuts, ________?

3. You don't still go out with Larry, ________?

4. I didn't hit you, ________?

5. I'm not permitted to skateboard here, ________?

6. You won't forget to call, ________?

7. We haven't run out of milk, ________?

8. This apartment doesn't have cockroaches, ________?

9. Yesterday wasn't our anniversary, ________?

10. Today isn't your birthday, ________?

E THAT'S WHAT I THOUGHT

When I woke up yesterday morning, I knew right away it was going to be a terrible day. I knew that everything was going to go wrong all day and that I couldn't do ANYTHING about it. My problems started the minute I got up.

1. Breakfast isn't ready yet, ___is it___?
   No, ___it isn't___.
   That's what I thought.

2. I don't have time to take a shower, ____________?
   No, ____________.
   That's what I thought.

3. I lost my English book. You haven't seen it anywhere, ____________?
   No, ____________.
   That's what I thought.

4. There isn't any more orange juice, ____________?
   No, ____________.
   That's what I thought.

5. My shirt hasn't been ironed yet, ____________?
   No, ____________.
   That's what I thought.

6. I won't be able to finish my breakfast, ____________?
   No, ____________.
   That's what I thought.

I arrived an hour late for school. My problems continued there.

7.

8.
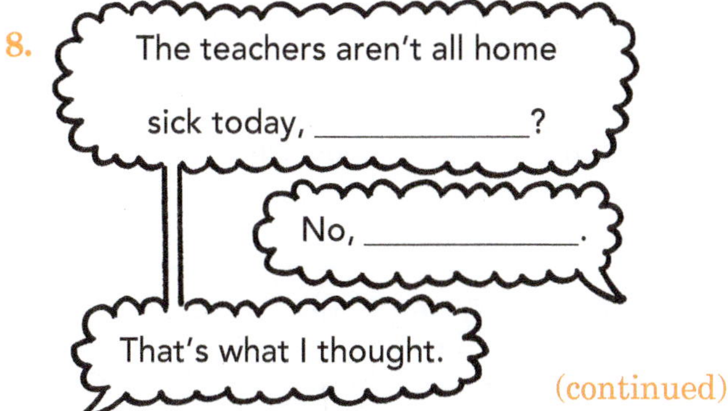

(continued)

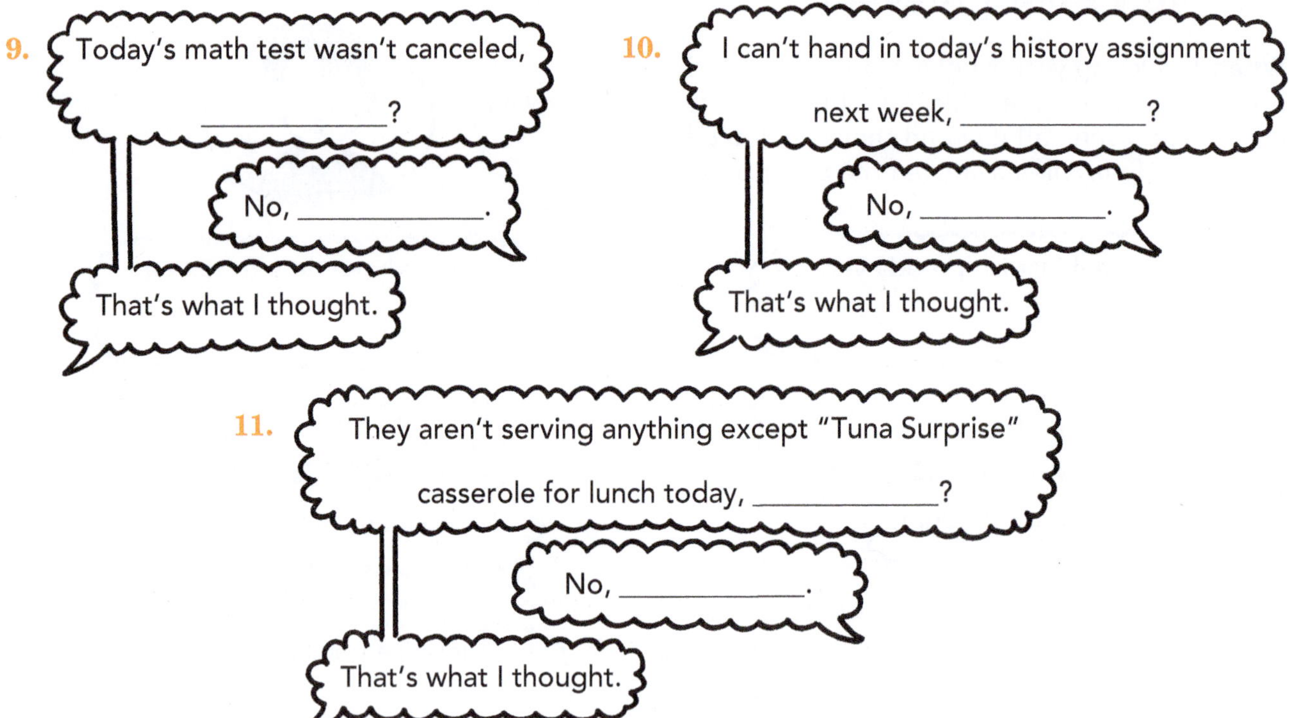

F WHAT'S THE TAG?

1. They aren't having problems, ______?
   a. are they
   b. aren't they

2. George was hired, ______?
   a. was he
   b. wasn't he

3. You didn't have to work overtime, ______?
   a. did you
   b. didn't you

4. You've done your homework, ______?
   a. have you
   b. haven't you

5. I'm not late, ______?
   a. aren't I
   b. am I

6. The bank will be open tomorrow, ______?
   a. will it
   b. won't it

7. He wants to marry you, ______?
   a. doesn't he
   b. is he

8. Your mother isn't upset, ______?
   a. isn't she
   b. is she

9. I can skate on this pond, ______?
   a. can I
   b. can't I

10. You received my letter, ______?
    a. didn't you
    b. did you

11. There wasn't a big storm, ______?
    a. was there
    b. wasn't there

12. I'm going to be promoted, ______?
    a. am I
    b. aren't I

13. Your son has been here before, ______?
    a. hasn't he
    b. has he

14. You won't be upset if I'm late, ______?
    a. won't you
    b. will you

G LISTENING

Listen and complete the sentences.

1. a. do you?
   (b.) don't you?
2. a. aren't you?
   b. are you?
3. a. do we?
   b. don't we?
4. a. did you?
   b. didn't you?
5. a. does she?
   b. doesn't he?
6. a. haven't you?
   b. have you?
7. a. was she?
   b. wasn't she?
8. a. hasn't he?
   b. has he?
9. a. won't we?
   b. will we?
10. a. can we?
    b. can't we?
11. a. is it?
    b. isn't it?
12. a. didn't I?
    b. did I?

H YOU DECIDE: *A Good Father*

I can't understand why I've been having so many problems with my son, Timmy. After all, I'm a good father, ____aren't I____[1]? I usually try to be patient, ________[2]? I'm not very strict, ________[3]? And I'm always nice to his friends, ________[4]? Also, I've always ....[5], ________[6]? I didn't ....[7], ________[8]? When he was little, I ....[9], ________[10]? And now that he's older, I ....[11], ________[12]? I'm not ....[13], ________[14]? I don't ....[15], ________[16]? And I'm always there when he needs me, ________[17]? So what could have gone wrong?

I GrammarRap: *She Drives to Work, Doesn't She?*

Listen. Then clap and practice.

She drives to work, doesn't she?
She was late, wasn't she?

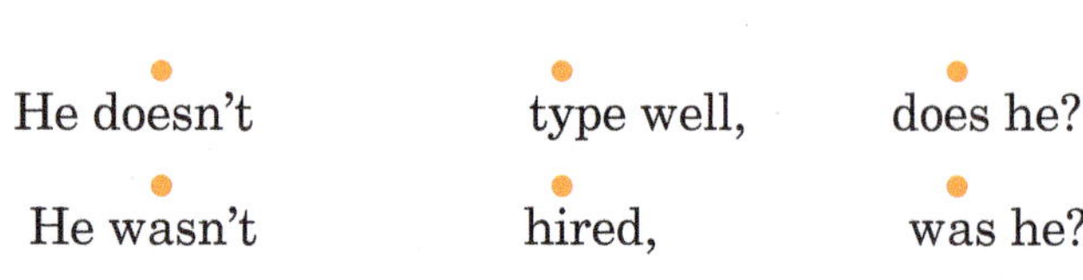

He doesn't type well, does he?
He wasn't hired, was he?

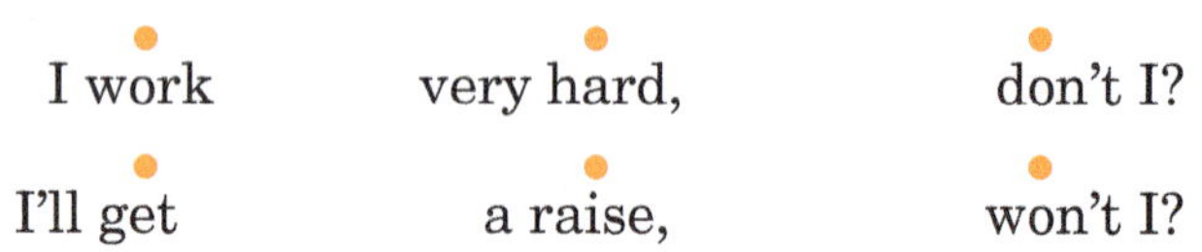

I work very hard, don't I?
I'll get a raise, won't I?

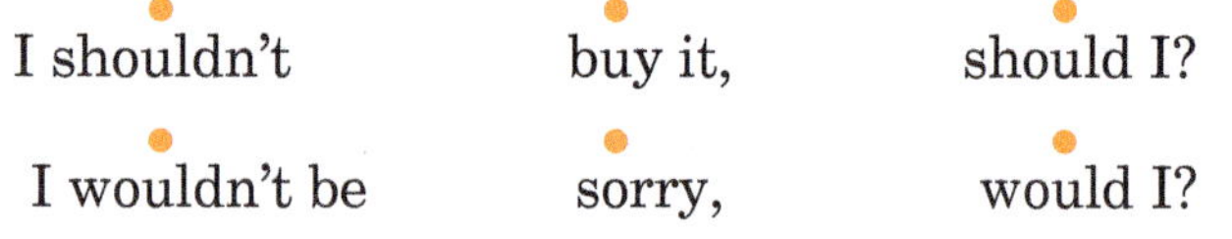

I shouldn't buy it, should I?
I wouldn't be sorry, would I?

You know them well, don't you?
You'll intro duce me, won't you?

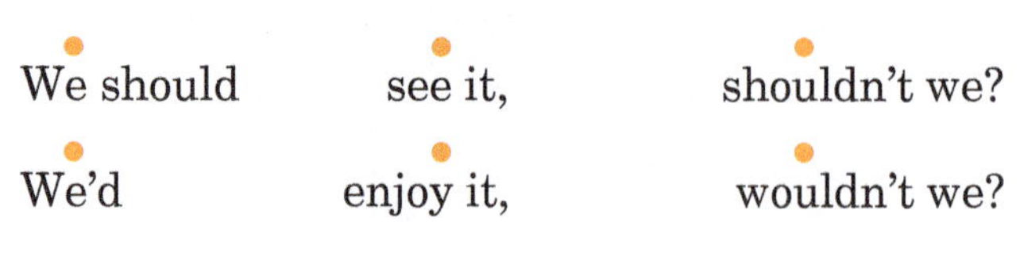

We should see it, shouldn't we?
We'd enjoy it, wouldn't we?

You love to dance, don't you?
You'll come to the party, won't you?

J SURPRISES

1. A. You haven't been standing in the rain long, ___have you___?

   B. I'm afraid ___I have___.

   A. ___You have___?! I'm really sorry. I had no idea it was so late.

2. A. Barbara is going to law school next year, ______________?

   B. No, ______________.

   A. ______________?! I thought she wanted to be a lawyer like her mother.

3. A. Alan won't be graduating from college this year, ______________?

   B. Yes, ______________.

   A. ______________?! I can't believe the time has gone by so fast.

4. A. Our spring vacation begins tomorrow, ______________?

   B. No, ______________.

   A. ______________?! I'm really surprised. I've been looking forward to tomorrow all month.

5. A. It's timc to cat. You brought the sandwiches, ______________?

   B. Sandwiches?! No, ______________.

   A. ______________?! How could you have forgotten? I was sure you were going to bring them.

6. A. Ricky doesn't drive yet, ______________?

   B. I know it's hard to believe, but ______________.

   A. ______________?! I can remember when he was just learning how to walk. Children grow up so quickly.

K WHAT ARE THEY SAYING?

1. A. You were expecting us, ___weren't you___?
   B. Actually, I wasn't.
   A. You weren't?! I'm really surprised! I was sure ___you had been expecting___ us.

2. A. You have medical insurance, ________?
   B. Actually, I don't.
   A. You don't?! That's very surprising! I was sure ________ medical insurance.

3. A. She's been here before, ________?
   B. Actually, she hasn't.
   A. She hasn't?! I'm surprised! I was sure ________ here before.

4. A. He isn't going to be transferred, ________?
   B. Actually, he is.
   A. He is?! I don't believe it! I was sure ________ transferred.

5. A. We can leave early today, ________?
   B. Actually, we can't.
   A. We can't?! I'm really surprised! I was sure ________ early.

6. A. This suit is on sale, ________?
   B. Actually, it isn't.
   A. It isn't?! I can't believe it! I was sure this suit ________ on sale.

7. A. I don't have to work overtime, ________?
   B. Actually, you do.
   A. I do?! I can't believe it! I was sure ________ have to work overtime.

8. A. You'll marry her someday, ________?
   B. Actually, I won't.
   A. You won't?! I'm surprised! I was sure ________ her someday.

L LISTENING

Listen and complete the conversations.

1. a. she had been a doctor.
   (b.) she was going to be a doctor.
2. a. you had sold your house.
   b. you didn't sell your house.
3. a. it had new brakes.
   b. it has new brakes.
4. a. you aren't angry with me.
   b. you weren't angry with me.
5. a. they would be arriving this weekend.
   b. they'll be arriving this weekend.
6. a. you got searched.
   b. you hadn't gotten searched.
7. a. children were allowed to see it.
   b. children weren't allowed to see it.
8. a. he still worked at the bank.
   b. he still works at the bank.
9. a. she had been hired by the Bay Company.
   b. she was hired by the Bay Company.
10. a. he can deliver babies.
    b. he could deliver babies.

M HIGH SCHOOL REUNION

1. A. Do you ever see our old friend Susan? She was one of the nicest people in our class.

   B. As a matter of fact, I see her all the time. I married her!

   A. ___You did___?! I don't believe it! You ___didn't___ really ___marry___ Susan, ___did you___?

   B. Yes, ___I did___.

2. A. Do you still go canoeing every weekend?

   B. Not anymore. I'm MUCH too busy. I have three small children at home.

   A. __________?! I never would have believed it! You __________ really __________ three children, __________?

   B. Yes, __________.

3. A. Do you still work for an insurance company?

   B. Not anymore. As a matter of fact, I'm the president of my own company.

   A. __________?! I don't believe it! You __________ really the president of your own company, __________?

   B. Yes, __________.

4. A. Do you keep in touch with Julie Montero?

   B. Yes. I see her all the time. As a matter of fact, she was just chosen "Employee of the Year" at her company.

   A. __________?! That's fantastic! She __________ really __________ "Employee of the Year," __________?

   B. Yes, __________.

(continued)

5. A. I wonder whatever happened to Margaret Wong.

B. Well, the last time I saw her she had just won a million dollars on a TV game show.

A. ____________?! That's unbelievable! She ____________ really ____________ a million dollars, ____________?

B. Yes, ____________.

6. A. Have you heard? Vincent Lewis quit his job and ....

B. ____________?! I can't believe it! He ____________ really do that, ____________?

A. Yes, ____________.

7. A. Tell me about your son, Billy. I hear he's a very special little boy.

B. You don't really want to hear about Billy, ____________?

A. Yes, of course. I'm very interested.

B. Well, Billy is only four years old, but he can .... and ....

A. ____________?! I don't believe it! He ____________ really do all those things, ____________?

B. Yes, ____________.

8. A. How's little Patty?

B. My daughter Patty isn't so little anymore. She's going to .... next month.

A. ____________?! I don't believe it! She ____________ really going to ____________ next month, ____________? She was just a baby the last time I saw her.

N WHAT ARE THEY SAYING?

1. A. You know . . . you've been a little "touchy" recently.

   B. I guess you're right. I ___have___ been a little "touchy" recently, ___haven't I___!

2. A. You know, we shouldn't be fishing here.

   B. I suppose you're right. We __________ be fishing here, __________!

3. A. I think our guests had a great time at our party.

   B. I agree. They __________ a great time, __________!

4. A. You know . . . the people in this neighborhood aren't very friendly.

   B. You're right. They __________ very friendly, __________!

5. A. Mr. Mudge is in a terrible mood today.

   B. I agree. He __________ in a terrible mood today, __________!

6. A. You know . . . this pizza tastes terrible!

   B. You're right. This pizza __________ terrible, __________!

7. A. You know, I hate to say it, but you were impolite to the boss.

   B. I guess you're right. I __________ impolite to the boss, __________!

8. A. You know . . . I think we'll have to work overtime this weekend.

   B. I'm afraid you're right. We __________ have to work overtime, __________!

9. A. You know . . . we haven't called Grandma in a long time.

   B. You're right. We __________ called her in a long time, __________!

10. A. I'm sorry to say it, but that tie looks terrible with that shirt!

    B. I guess you're right. It __________ terrible with this shirt, __________!

11.

O YOU DECIDE: *Why Shouldn't They Break Up?*

A. I'm thinking of breaking up with my boyfriend, Howard.

B. I don't believe it. Why do you want to break up with Howard? He's a wonderful person. He's kind and generous.

A. I guess he ___is___ 1 kind and generous, ___isn't he___ 2!

B. And he sends you flowers all the time.

A. Come to think of it, he ______ 3 ______ 4 me flowers all the time, ______ 5!

B. And he's .... 6.

A. I guess you're right. He ______ 7, ______ 8!

B. And remember last month. Howard gave you .... 9, and you were very happy.

A. Come to think of it, he ______ 10 ______ 11 me ______ 12 last month, ______ 13! And I ______ 14 very happy, ______ 15!

B. Yes. But I really wasn't surprised because he's always given you a lot of presents.

A. That's true. He ______ 16 always ______ 17 me a lot of presents, ______ 18!

B. Here's something else to think about. He doesn't .... 19.

A. You're right. He ______ 20, ______ 21!

B. Also, ... 22.

A. Come to think of it, that's true. ______ 23, ______ 24!

B. And how do you think Howard would feel? He'd be very upset if you broke up with him.

A. I'm afraid you're right. He ______ 25 be very upset, ______ 26! You know, I'm glad I talked to you. I guess I won't break up with Howard after all.

P LISTENING

Listen to each word and then say it.

1. boat
2. better
3. about
4. bought
5. bright

6. vote
7. vacation
8. avoid
9. oven
10. travel

11. won't
12. weather
13. away
14. window
15. worry

Q BEVERLY WILSON'S BROKEN KEYBOARD

Beverly Wilson's keyboard is broken. The b's, v's, and w's don't always work. Fill in the missing b's, v's, and w's, and then read Beverly's letters aloud.

1.

Dear _B_etty,

You'_v_e pro__a__ly heard from Bo__ a__out the terri__le ro____eries __e'__e __een ha__ing in our neighborhood. (There ha__e __een se__en ro____eries in fi__e __eeks!) Of course, e__ery__ody's __een __ery __orried __ecause they still ha__en't disco__ered who the ro____ers are.

Last __ednesday, my neigh__or's __icycle __as stolen from his __asement. The next e__ening, some__ody __roke into a __uilding on __righton __oule__ard and took se__eral sil__er __racelets, a __allet, and t__o __edding rings.

Then last __eekend, __elie__e it or not, the Relia__le __ank __as ro____ed. I'll al__ays remem__er the e__ening of the ro____ery. I __as taking a __ath, and my hus__and, __ill, __as reading his fa__orite no__el in __ed __hen Ro__er __egan __arking. He must ha__e heard the ro____ers dri__ing a__ay. __y the time I got out of the __athtu__, e__ery__ody in the neigh__orhood __as talking a__out the ro____ers' escape.

__ell, e__er since the __ank ro____ery last __eekend, __e'__e all __een __ery ner__ous. Some of the neigh__ors are so __orried that they're thinking a__out mo__ing a__ay. __ill and I ha__e __een __ondering __hat __e should do.

Lo__e,

__e__erly

(continued)

2.

Dear __etsy,

__e're ha__ing a __edding anni__ersary cele__ration on __ednesday for my __rother-in-law, __arry, and his wife, Ro__erta, and __e __ould lo__e it if you and your hus__and, __alter, __ere there. It __on't __e a __ery __ig cele__ration, just a few relati__es, __illiam, __incent, Eliza__eth, Ste__e, and of course my __rothers and their __i__es.

__e've heard that your __rother's little __oy __o____y is __isiting you this __eek. __hy don't you __ring him along __ith you __hen you come o__er on __ednesday?

Lo__e,

__e__erly

3.

Dear Al__ert,

__e're ha__ing a __onderful time on our __acation in __oston, __ut __e __ish you and your __ife __ere here __ith us. I'm positi__e __oth you and __ar__ara __ould lo__e it here. __ar__ara __ould lo__e the __oston Pu__lic Garden and the __oats on the Charles Ri__er. And you __ould ha__e a __onderful time __isiting the uni__ersities and the __oston Pu__lic Li__rary. __e're staying __ith __ill's relati__es __hile __e're in __oston. They li__e in a __ery modern high-rise __uilding __ith a __eautiful __iew of the ri__er. __e'__e __een __ery lucky. __ill's relati__es dri__e us e__ery__here.

The __eather in __oston __as __ery __arm __hen __e arri__ed, but now it's __indy. I __ish __e had __rought __armer clothes to __ear.

__y the __ay, __ill and I __ent to a li__ely __ase__all game last __ednesday, and __e'__e __een to the __allet t__ice. __e'__e also __een __ery __usy __uying presents for e__ery__ody at home and sou__enirs for oursel__es. (Unfortunately, __e __eren't a__le to __uy the __atch your __rother __alter __anted.)

Lo__e,

__e__erly

A WHAT'S THE ANSWER?

10

STUDENT BOOK PAGES **145–158**

1. I don't feel like _______.
   a. take a walk
   ⓑ taking a walk

2. I never get tired _______.
   a. of going on picnics
   b. to go on picnics

3. I'm not going to work out today. _______ at the gym yesterday.
   a. If I had worked out
   b. I worked out

4. My friends and I usually love _______ the mall.
   a. going to
   b. going

5. Thanks. _______ to have dinner with you.
   a. I'll like
   b. I'd like

6. _______ go sailing?
   a. Would you like
   b. Would you like to

7. I'd be happy _______ you to the airport.
   a. to take
   b. take

8. _______ a movie yesterday, I'd be happy to go with you today.
   a. If I hadn't seen
   b. If I saw

9. I won't be able to go to your son's wedding. I hope _______.
   a. you understand
   b. I understand

10. _______ you can't go bowling with us.
    a. I'd be disappointed
    b. I'm disappointed

B WHAT ARE THEY SAYING?

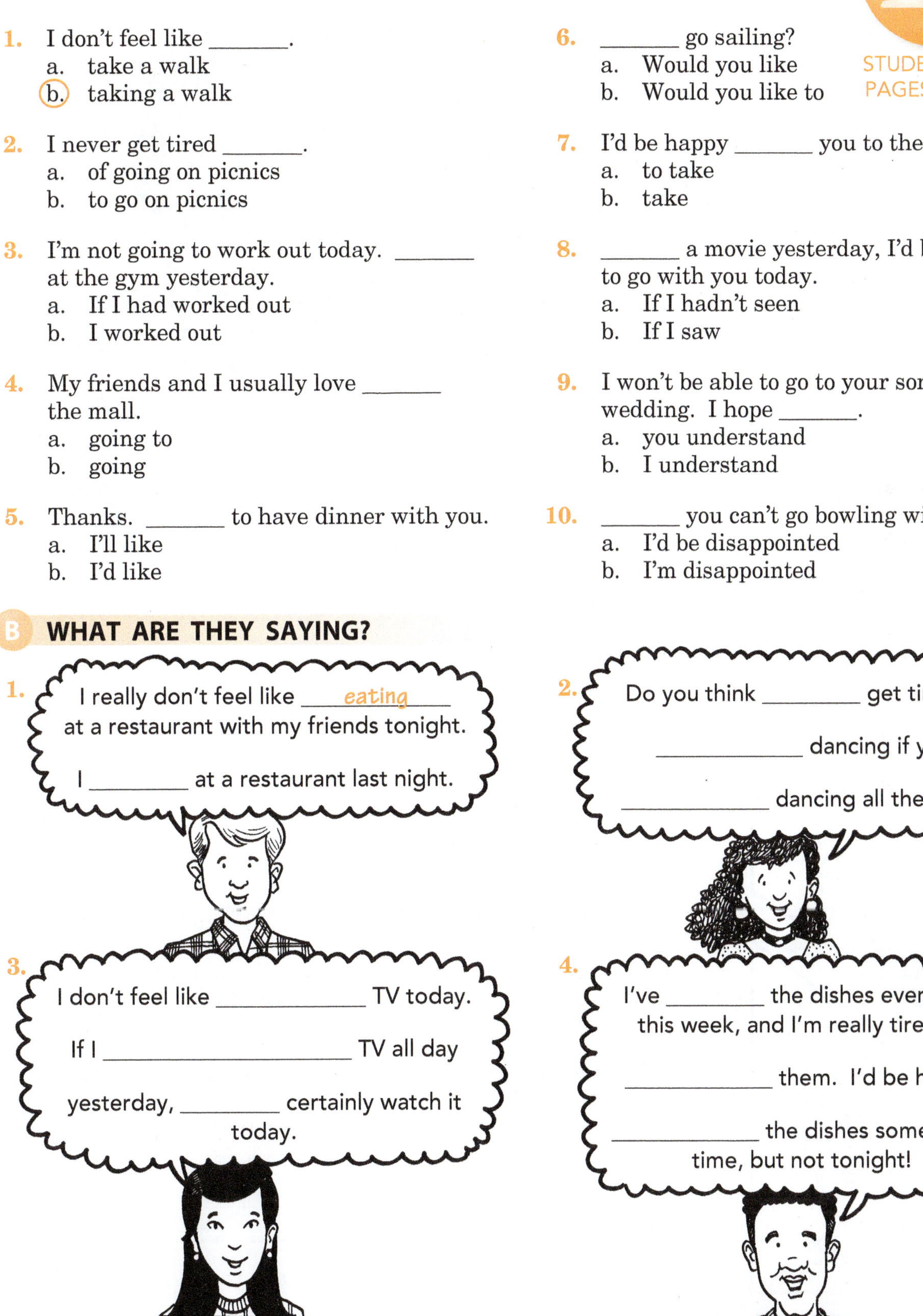

C WHAT ARE THEY SAYING?

see

A. Do you really want ___to see___[1] a movie again tonight? I know you enjoy ______[2] movies, but you've already ______[3] four movies this week, and you just ______[4] a movie this afternoon. Don't you EVER get tired of ______[5] movies? If I were you, I certainly ______[6] another movie tonight.

B. Maybe I'm a little crazy, but there's nothing I like more than ______[7] movies. I really DO feel like ______[8] a movie with you tonight, and believe it or not, I'm planning ______[9] another movie tomorrow!

go

A. We're ______[10] camping this weekend. Would you like to come with us?

B. I don't really feel like ______[11] camping this weekend. To be honest, I don't enjoy ______[12] camping.

A. You don't?! I thought you ______[13] camping all the time!

B. I do, but that's only because everybody else in my family loves ______[14] camping. If you really want to know the truth, I can't stand ______[15] camping! Ever since I first ______[16] camping years ago, I've hated it! If my family didn't enjoy ______[17] camping so much, I'd never ______[18] camping at all!

A. I'm sorry you feel that way. I'll never ask you ______[19] camping again!

D GrammarRap: *I Suppose You'd Get Tired* 

Listen. Then clap and practice.

I suppose you'd get tired of driving downtown
If you drove downtown every day.
You would also get tired of driving around
If you didn't know your way.

I suppose you'd get tired of eating cheese
If you ate it at every meal.
You'd probably get a bad stomachache
And complain about how you feel.

I suppose you'd get tired of typing reports
If you typed them without taking breaks.
If you didn't stop and rest for a while,
Your reports would be full of mistakes.

I suppose I'd get tired of having cake
If I had some each night for dinner.
If I had more fruit instead of cake
I'd probably be a lot thinner.

I suppose you'd get tired of watching TV
If you always watched the same shows.
If you listened to music or read a book,
You wouldn't be bored, I suppose.

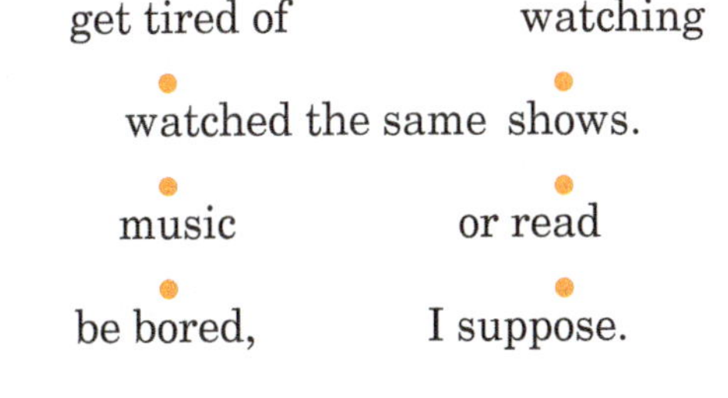

E THEY NEVER WOULD HAVE DONE THAT!

1. Emily hit the wrong key and deleted all her files.

   If ___she hadn't hit___ the wrong key,

   she never ___would have deleted___ all her files.

2. Henry drove into a tree because he was daydreaming.

   If ______________ daydreaming, he never

   ______________ into a tree.

3. I got a terrible score on my SAT because during the test I had my mind on something else.

   If ______________ my mind on something else,

   I never ______________ a terrible score.

4. My wife and I were an hour late to the party because we misunderstood the directions.

   If ______________ the directions,

   we never ______________ an hour late to the party.

5. Albert decided to take a bath, and he forgot to take his cake out of the oven.

   If ______________ to take a bath,

   he never ______________ to take his cake out of the oven.

6. Alice put salt in her coffee. She thought it was sugar.

   If ______________ it was sugar,

   she never ______________ salt in her coffee.

7. Mr. and Mrs. Jackson accidentally mixed up their video tapes, and they erased the video of their wedding.

   If ______________ their video tapes,

   they never ______________ the video of their wedding.

F GRAMMARRAP: *I Must Have* 

Listen. Then clap and practice.

I'm very sorry I took your CD.
I must have thought it belonged to me.

I'm sorry it's midnight, and now you're awake.
I must have called you by mistake.

The cake was bad, and it's all my fault.
I must have mixed up the sugar and salt.

I'm sorry I shouted. I know I was rude.
I must have been in a very bad mood.

G YOU DECIDE: *I'm Really Sorry*

1. You've been invited to a party. You arrive on the wrong day. Your friends are cleaning their house!

YOUR FRIENDS: What a nice surprise! As you can see, we're getting ready for tomorrow's party.

YOU: ....

YOUR FRIENDS: ....

YOU: ....

2. You've been stopped by a police officer because you went through a red light at the last intersection.

POLICE OFFICER: You just drove through a red light! Didn't you see it?

YOU: ....

POLICE OFFICER: ....

YOU: ....

H WHAT ARE THEY SAYING?

1. A. My husband is out of work.

   B. What a shame! How long ___has he been___ out of work?

   A. ___For___ more than two months.

2. A. My house has termites!

   B. That's terrible! How long ________ ________________________ termites?

   A. __________ last summer.

3. A. I'm having trouble concentrating on my work.

   B. That's too bad. How long ______ ______________________________ concentrating on your work?

   A. __________ I moved to Hawaii.

4. A. I've been feeling a little depressed recently.

   B. That's a shame How long __________ ________________________ depressed?

   A. __________ my girlfriend broke up with me.

5. A. My knees hurt!

   B. I'm sorry to hear that. How long ____________________________?

   A. __________ the past few weeks.

6. A. My car is at the repair shop.

   B. Oh, really? How long _________________ ____________________ at the repair shop?

   A. __________ last Monday.

7. A. My employees are on strike.

   B. They are? How long _________ ___________________ on strike?

   A. __________ more than a month.

8. A. My wife wants to buy a motorcycle.

   B. She does?! How long ____________ ____________________ a motorcycle?

   A. __________ her fortieth birthday.

I WHAT'S WRONG?

for	since

DOCTOR: How long have you been sick, Mr. Lawson?

PATIENT: I've been sick ___since___ 1 last Tuesday.

DOCTOR: I see. How long have you had a pain in your chest?

PATIENT: I've had a pain in my chest __________ 2 about three days.

And I've had a backache __________ 3 last week.

DOCTOR: You have a fever, too. Do you know how long you've had a fever?

PATIENT: __________ 4 the past week. Also, I've felt dizzy __________ 5 I got the fever.

DOCTOR: Tell me, Mr. Lawson, have you been working?

PATIENT: No, I've been at home __________ 6 April 2nd. And I've been

in bed __________ 7 about a week. I've been very tired.

I've been sleeping __________ 8 about 14 hours a day.

DOCTOR: I think you need to go to the hospital so we can do some tests.

How long has it been __________ 9 you had a physical examination?

PATIENT: I haven't seen a doctor __________ 10 more than a year.

DOCTOR: Well, you certainly need a complete examination. You really should take better care of yourself.

J LISTENING 

Listen and complete the sentences.

1. (a.) last week.
   b. two days.
2. a. last weekend.
   b. three days.
3. a. Monday morning.
   b. more than a week.
4. a. a long time.
   b. I returned from my trip.
5. a. many weeks.
   b. we got married.
6. a. over a week.
   b. I started calling him.
7. a. the past few months.
   b. we discovered termites.
8. a. two or three weeks.
   b. I bought it.
9. a. at least a week.
   b. the other day.

K WHAT'S THE ANSWER?

1. I can't _______ my new apartment until next week.
   (a.) move into
   b. move

2. My husband almost always _______ the children after school.
   a. picks out
   b. picks up

3. My cousin said she would come over and _______ my new curtains.
   a. put on
   b. put up

4. Please tell Ms. Lee I'm _______, and I'll be at the office soon.
   a. on my way
   b. in my way

5. My husband and I have to _______ a gift for his sister's new baby.
   a. pick out
   b. pick on

6. It's important to _______ the application completely.
   a. fill
   b. fill out

7. Our teacher wants us to _______ the math problems by ourselves.
   a. figure
   b. figure out

8. Can you send someone to _______ my new computer?
   a. hook up
   b. hook on

9. I need some help this afternoon. Can you possibly _______?
   a. give me a hand
   b. hand me

10. Before I can use it, I need to _______ my new cell phone.
   a. call
   b. program

L COMPLETE THE SENTENCES

1. I'm sorry I can't help you move tomorrow. I have to work.
If I __didn't have to__ work, I'd be glad to help you move.

2. It's a shame you're sick. If I had known you __________ sick, I wouldn't have bothered you.

3. I'm sorry you're having trouble ______________ up your satellite dish. If I ______________ busy all day, I'd be happy to help you.

4. I didn't realize you ____________ programmed your new cell phone. That's why I couldn't reach you.

5. If I ____________ on my way to an important job interview now, ______ be glad to help you hook up your new TV.

6. It's too bad you're having trouble ___________________ out the math problems. ________ come over and help you, but I've got a doctor's appointment.

7. If I __________ about ______ leave for a vacation, ______ be happy to help you move today.

8. I didn't know you __________________ trouble setting up your computer. If I ____________ you __________________ trouble, I ___________________ come over and helped you. Next time you have a problem, don't forget to call me.

M GrammarRap: *If I Had Known*

Listen. Then clap and practice.

If I had known you were packing for your trip to Japan,
I never would have called you to help me fix my van.

If I had known that your children were sick with the flu,
I never would have offered to take them to the zoo.

If I had known you were waiting for the carpenter to call,
I never would have asked you to help me paint my hall.

If I had known that your relatives were visiting from Spain,
I never would have called you to help me fix my drain.

If I had known that you were planning to give your dog a bath,
I never would have called you to help me with my math.

N WHAT'S THE WORD?

about	by	in	into	of	on	out	to	up	with

1. I can't stop sneezing. I think I'm allergic ___to___ something in this room!
2. Do you ________ any chance know when the movie begins?
3. Sylvia is being sent to London ________ business next month.
4. I got confused, and I mixed ________ the sugar and flour containers.
5. Jack got ________ a terrible argument, and I had to break up the fight.
6. If you drop ________ of school, I know you'll regret it.
7. What are you worried ______________? I'm sure you'll do well on the exam.
8. The elevator in our building has been out ________ order for several weeks!
9. They don't have anything ________ common. Do they get along ________ each other?

about	at	by	from	in	of	off	on	past	to	up	with

10. I'll be away for a few days. I'm sorry I won't be able to help you hook ________ your new computer.
11. Do you by any chance know who this beautiful building was designed ________?
12. I'm not sure whether your car is ready. Why don't you check ________ the mechanic?
13. I'm concerned ______________ Mrs. Wong. She was taken ________ the hospital last night.
14. The Blakes love their new apartment. It has a beautiful view ________ the river.
15. You've been complaining all day. You're ________ a terrible mood, aren't you!
16. I think you just drove ________ my house. We'll have to turn around.
17. Let's meet at Dave's Diner for lunch ________ around noon.
18. I should have turned ________ the TV and gone to sleep!
19. We ate lunch at a restaurant far ________ our office.
20. Careful! Don't step ________ that wet floor!

O WHAT'S THE WORD?

1. My father is wearing a cast on his leg. He lost his ______balance______ and fell off a ladder.
2. Don't forget to take your ________________ with you when you leave the country.
3. The painter says we need new ________________ in our living room.
4. The police finally arrested the ________________ in all the robberies in our neighborhood.
5. My son is growing up. Last week he learned how to ____________ his shoes.
6. I'm sorry I missed your barbecue last week. It completely ________________ my mind.
7. Edward couldn't finish making his cake. He ran out of ________________.
8. Many people need to have their ________________ teeth removed.
9. It's difficult for parents to adjust when their children grow up and ________________ on their own.
10. The McDonalds had to get rid of their cat because Mr. McDonald was ______________ to it.
11. It isn't a good idea to ________________ your job if the economy isn't good.
12. My friends and I did our homework incorrectly. We must have __________________________ the directions.
13. Our ________________ got out of its cage and made a big ________________ in the kitchen.
14. Here. You can use this. It's just a piece of ________________ paper.
15. I hope I find a job soon. I hate being ____________________.
16. Cindy is a talented athlete. She won the school tennis ________________ again.
17. Do you ________________ what you just did?!
18. Be careful! Don't hit the wrong key and ____________ all the ____________ on your computer.

P LISTENING

Read the questions. Listen to each passage. Then answer the questions.

Jeff's Problem

1. Jeff's friend advised him _______.
   a. not to talk to his boss
   (b.) to talk to his boss

2. Jeff told his boss _______.
   a. why he didn't like his job
   b. why he was satisfied with his work

3. Jeff's boss said _______.
   a. she complained too much
   b. she wasn't pleased with his work

4. Jeff wishes _______.
   a. he had listened to his friend
   b. he weren't unemployed

Amy and Tom

5. Amy's parents told her _______.
   a. to marry Tom
   b. not to marry Tom

6. Amy's parents thought Tom was _______.
   a. lazy
   b. successful

7. Amy is happy because _______.
   a. she followed her parents' advice
   b. Tom has been a wonderful husband

8. Amy isn't concerned because her sons _______.
   a. aren't like their father
   b. are just like her husband

Q OUT OF PLACE

1.	cut	bite	(date)	hurt	destroy
2.	superintendent	politician	mail carrier	snowman	librarian
3.	CD	DVD	disk	mural	keyboard
4.	astronomy	chemistry	apology	history	philosophy
5.	lake	pond	ocean	poodle	river
6.	teacher	baker	customer	professor	instructor
7.	depressed	discovered	disappointed	upset	sick and tired
8.	hamster	cockroach	cactus	dolphin	puppy
9.	usher	prime minister	mayor	senator	governor
10.	unemployed	fired	retired	promoted	out of work
11.	assemble	delete	disconnect	erase	lose
12.	amazing	fascinating	magnificent	aggressive	impressive
13.	rewrite	register	replace	reopen	repaint
14.	tires	accident	headlight	bumper	battery
15.	annoyed	irritable	angry	mad	confused

R LISTENING 

Listen to each word and then say it.

1. blush—brush
2. light—right
3. long—wrong
4. vote—boat
5. chop—shop
6. she's—cheese
7. watch—wash
8. heard—hurt
9. ride—write
10. ridden—written
11. someday—Sunday
12. mice—nice
13. send—sent
14. wide—white
15. run—rung

S HAVE YOU HEARD? 

Listen and complete the sentences.

watch	wash

1. a. . . . TV?
   (b.) . . . my shirt? It's dirty.

light	right

2. a. . . . I agree with you.
   b. . . . just went out. It's dark in here.

Someday	Sunday

3. a. . . . is my favorite day of the week.
   b. . . . I'll be rich and famous.

long	wrong

4. a. . . . It's more than 3 pages.
   b. . . . , but I can't find my mistake.

light	right

5. a. . . . I can lift it easily.
   b. . . . Your answer is fine.

watch	wash

6. a. . . . the dishes now.
   b. . . . my favorite TV program.

hurt	heard

7. a. . . . about Jane?
   b. . . . your arm?

chopping	shopping

8. a. . . . onions.
   b. . . . at the supermarket.

boys	voice

9. a. . . . are my nephews.
   b. . . . is better than mine.

heard	hurt

10. a. . . . my ankle.
    b. . . . from Jack recently.

ridden	written

11. a. . . . to your cousins?
    b. . . . your bicycle recently?

blushes	brushes

12. a. . . . when he makes a mistake.
    b. . . . his teeth every morning.

✓ CHECK-UP TEST: Chapters 9–10

A. Complete the sentences.

Ex. Betty was in the office yesterday, ___wasn't she___?

1. The plane hasn't arrived yet, ________________?
2. You fed the hamster, ________________?
3. There weren't any cell phones when you were young, ________________?
4. We don't need a new toaster, ________________?
5. Your son plays on the school baseball team, ________________?
6. Your parents won't be home this afternoon, ________________?
7. You didn't forget to drop off the clothes at the cleaners, ________________?
8. You can come to my party this weekend, ________________?
9. I'm a good husband, ________________?
10. You'll be finished soon, ________________?

B. Respond with an emphatic sentence.

Ex. A. Howard is a hard worker.

B. You're right. ___He is a hard worker___, ___isn't he___!

1. A. Aunt Fran hasn't called in a long time.

   B. You're right. ________________________________, ________________!

2. A. That was a boring movie.

   B. I agree. ________________________________, ________________!

3. A. Carol works very hard.

   B. You're right. ________________________________, ________________!

4. A. Your son will be a fine doctor someday.

   B. I agree. ________________________________, ________________!

5. A. Those cookies taste wonderful.

   B. You're right. ________________________________, ________________!

C. Write the question.

Ex. I've decided to quit my job. ____What have you decided to do____?

1. We'll be staying at the Ritz Hotel. ________________?
2. We got engaged a few days ago. ________________?
3. We spent fifty dollars. ________________?
4. My father has been cooking all day. ________________?
5. She mentioned you six times. ________________?
6. I was assembling my new bookcases. ________________?
7. He goes to the gym because he wants to lose weight. ________________?

D. Fill in the blanks.

see

I don't really feel like ________[1] a movie again tonight. I usually enjoy ________[2] movies, but I've already ________[3] three movies this week, and I just ________[4] a very boring movie last night. If I ________[5] so many movies this week, I'd be happy ________[6] a movie with you tonight.

E. Listening 

Listen and complete the sentences.

Ex. a. I never drive past your house.
(b.) I never would have driven past your house.

1. a. I'd be happy to take a walk with you today.
   b. I'll be happy to take a walk with your today.
2. a. I wouldn't delete all my files.
   b. I wouldn't have deleted all my files.
3. a. if you go dancing all the time.
   b. if you went dancing all the time.
4. a. I wouldn't have called you.
   b. I won't call you.
5. a. I'll be glad to help you put in your air conditioner.
   b. I'd be glad to help you put in your air conditioner.

A TECHNOLOGY IN OUR LIVES

SIDE by SIDE Gazette

STUDENT BOOK PAGES 159–162

Read the article on student book page 159 and answer the questions.

1. In general, the article states that technology has _______ our lives.
   a. limited
   b. improved
   c. increased
   d. protected

2. The most changes in technology have come in the past _______.
   a. year
   b. 10 years
   c. 100 years
   d. 200 years

3. The first telephones didn't have any _______.
   a. receivers
   b. operators
   c. calls
   d. dials

4. Doctors use _______ to help people in remote areas.
   a. satellite communication
   b. scanners
   c. ATMs
   d. "smart highways"

5. Nowadays, a cashier can _______ to enter the price of an item.
   a. pay by credit card
   b. scan a bar code
   c. use a cell phone
   d. take a picture

6. Currently, people are NOT able to _______.
   a. use a "smart highway"
   b. send digital photos by e-mail
   c. do banking online
   d. use a store scanner without a cashier

7. The author's *structure* in paragraph 2 _______.
   a. compares current and future technology in our lives
   b. describes technology problems and solutions
   c. describes historical events in sequence (order)
   d. compares old and new technology in our lives

8. *Smart homes* in paragraph 3 means homes where computers _______.
   a. clean rooms
   b. destroy privacy
   c. control home appliances
   d. enter and leave rooms

9. In the last paragraph, *technology has its price* means _______.
   a. technology is expensive
   b. technology presents problems
   c. technology makes things cheaper
   d. technology for ATMs and banking is most important

10. You can infer from the last paragraph that the author's *point of view* is that _______.
    a. technology is always good
    b. lonely people like technology
    c. technology protects personal information
    d. protecting the privacy of information is important

B FACT FILE

Look at the Fact File on student book page 159 and answer the questions.

1. There were approximately _______ Internet users in 1996.
   a. 50
   b. 50,000
   c. 5,000,000
   d. 50,000,000

2. The number of Internet users increased by about _______ between 1995 and 2000.
   a. 40 million
   b. 200 million
   c. 280 million
   d. 320 million

C AROUND THE WORLD

Read the article on student book page 160 and answer the questions.

1. Many people use _______ to communicate with family members who live far away.
   a. video conferences
   b. scanners
   c. telemedicine
   d. e-mail

2. _______ are used to provide electricity in Sudan.
   a. Satellite dishes
   b. Solar batteries
   c. Utilities
   d. Scanners

3. In Japan, eye-scanning technology is used to _______ a person's identity.
   a. name
   b. ask about
   c. verify
   d. take a photo of

4. In many _______, scanners are used to screen luggage.
   a. airports
   b. hospitals
   c. homes
   d. stores

5. Telemedicine allows a doctor to _______ a patient.
   a. only talk with
   b. see and talk with
   c. talk with and touch
   d. do a blood test on

6. Many cars have _______ that allow drivers to see a map.
   a. video cameras
   b. keyboards
   c. computers
   d. scanners

7. In some remote areas, television service is received by a _______.
   a. DVD
   b. satellite dish
   c. cable system
   d. solar battery

8. Businesspeople from different locations can have a meeting using _______.
   a. a video conference
   b. a tape recorder
   c. telemedicine
   d. a meeting room

9. New technology is used _______.
   a. mostly by businesspeople
   b. only by residents in remote areas
   c. only for personal enjoyment
   d. by businesses and individuals

10. You can infer that technology makes distances between people seem _______.
    a. more important
    b. shorter
    c. longer
    d. more difficult

D YOU'RE THE INTERVIEWER!

Read the interviews on student book page 161. Then interview a classmate, a neighbor, or a friend. Use the chart below to record the person's answers. Share what you learned with the class.

How much time do you spend each day on a computer? a phone? a tablet or other device?	
Which technology do you use to keep in touch with your friends?	
What is your favorite type of technology? Why?	
How has technology changed your life in the last five years?	

E FUN WITH IDIOMS

Choose the best response.

1. Our computer must be out of memory.
   a. Yes. I forgot it.
   b. Let's turn it off.
   c. Yes. We have too much information on it.
   d. That's okay. We can telecommute.

2. Oh, no! My computer is frozen!
   a. Since nothing is happening, you should restart it.
   b. You can't use it when it's so cold.
   c. That's okay. It will just work slowly.
   d. My software doesn't work either.

3. Do you think my computer has a virus?
   a. Yes. You should call a doctor.
   b. Yes. None of the programs are working correctly.
   c. Yes. You need a new computer.
   d. Yes. It feels very warm.

4. I think this software has a bug.
   a. Look carefully. Can you see it?
   b. That software often has problems.
   c. It must be very old.
   d. That's because it doesn't have enough memory.

F WE'VE GOT MAIL!

Read the letters on student book page 162 and choose the correct answer.

1. It's a good idea to ______ English after finishing the *Side by Side* program.
   a. take a break from studying
   b. keep studying
   c. stop studying
   d. only study

2. Most students ______ grammar.
   a. should stop studying
   b. don't need to learn more
   c. should forget about
   d. should keep studying

3. Watching movies is a good way to ______.
   a. improve your English
   b. enjoy your classes
   c. communicate with people
   d. learn grammar rules

4. Studying in class and using English outside the classroom ______.
   a. have to be done with a teacher
   b. will confuse you
   c. are both important
   d. are very similar

G "CAN-DO" REVIEW

Match the "can do" statement and the correct sentence.

_____ 1. I can verify information.	a.	You know . . .
_____ 2. I can congratulate someone.	b.	Would you like to have lunch with me?
_____ 3. I can initiate a topic of conversation.	c.	I must have pressed the wrong button.
_____ 4. I can ask for a reason.	d.	Do you realize what you just did?
_____ 5. I can invite someone to do something.	e.	Congratulations!
_____ 6. I can express feelings and emotions.	f.	I'm sorry.
_____ 7. I can call attention to a person's actions.	g.	You seem upset. Is anything wrong?
_____ 8. I can apologize.	h.	What makes you think I'm nervous?
_____ 9. I can make a deduction.	i.	It's going to rain today, isn't it?
_____ 10. I can express concern about someone.	j.	I'm disappointed.

A NOTES TO SCHOOL

Match the sentence beginnings and endings.

____ 1. I give permission for my daughter
____ 2. My son has to leave school early today
____ 3. My daughter was absent yesterday
____ 4. I can't attend the parent-teacher conference
____ 5. My daughter will be late to school tomorrow
____ 6. My son is afraid to go to school
____ 7. I give permission for my son
____ 8. My son was absent yesterday
____ 9. My son has been having trouble with his homework

a. because she had a bad cold.
b. because she has a doctor's appointment in the morning.
c. because children are teasing him.
d. because he has a doctor's appointment this afternoon.
e. because he doesn't understand the directions.
f. because he had a high fever.
g. to go to the zoo with her class.
h. because I have to work.
i. to go home with his friend Mark today.

1

STUDENT BOOK PAGES **14a–14d**

B QUESTIONS ABOUT READING

Textbooks and tests have many different types of questions after a reading. Match the questions that have the same (or similar) meaning.

____ 1. What is the main idea of the reading?
____ 2. Why did the author write this?
____ 3. What key information supports the main idea?
____ 4. What is the sequence of information the author provides?
____ 5. What is the author's opinion?
____ 6. How do you feel about what you have read?
____ 7. What unusual words and phrases does the author use use?

a. In what order do the details appear?
b. What's your opinion about the reading?
c. What was the author's purpose?
d. What does the writer think about the topic?
e. What special vocabulary did you notice in the reading?
f. What are the important supporting details?
g. What is the central theme?

C INFORMATIONAL READING: Parenting

Read the article on student book page 14c and answer the questions.

1. What is the main purpose of the article?
   a. To teach children how to succeed in school
   b. To tell teachers how to encourage children
   c. To help parents help their children succeed
   d. To encourage children to read

2. Which advice DOESN'T support the main idea of the article?
   a. Attend parent-teacher conferences.
   b. Children need a quiet place to do homework.
   c. Take your children to the library.
   d. Children should watch TV at least ten hours a week.

3. In paragraph 3, to show that you *value learning* means you show that ______.
   a. education is expensive
   b. learning is important to you
   c. you enjoy school activities
   d. you like to follow recipes

4. What ISN'T an example of a good question to ask to find out about a child's day at school?
   a. Did you do any special activities today?
   b. What was your favorite class today?
   c. How was your day?
   d. Did your teacher ask about the news today?

5. In paragraph 7, what is the meaning of *Look for signs of trouble at school?*
   a. Notice any problems a child is having at school.
   b. Ask a child specific questions about school.
   c. Pay attention to school signs.
   d. Express concerns to teachers.

6. What can you infer from the article?
   a. The author is a teacher.
   b. The author is a parent.
   c. The author doesn't watch TV.
   d. The author cares about children's success.

D CHECKLIST: Helping Children Succeed in School

Use the article on student book page 14c as a reference. Check (✓) the suggestions that help children succeed in school according to the article.

____ 1. Take your children to the library.

____ 2. Limit TV watching to five hours a day.

____ 3. Ask specific questions about your child's school day.

____ 4. Read to your children when they are very young.

____ 5. Give your children a breakfast high in sugar and low in protein.

____ 6. Make sure your children go to bed late.

____ 7. Participate in school events and activities.

____ 8. Give your child a quiet place with good lighting to do homework.

____ 9. Encourage your child to talk to friends while doing homework.

____ 10. Contact your child's teacher if your child is unable to concentrate.

____ 11. Spend a lot of money on your children.

____ 12. Limit the number of books and magazines you have in your home.

____ 13. Contact your child's teacher if your child is having trouble with homework.

____ 14. Attend parent-teacher conferences.

A TRAIN SCHEDULE

2

STUDENT BOOK PAGES **30a–30d**

Look at the train schedule. Answer the questions.

PACIFIC SURFLINER SOUTHBOUND

Los Angeles • Irvine • Oceanside • San Diego

Train Number ▶			564	566	572	578	582
Days of Operation ▶			Daily	Daily	Daily	Daily	Daily
	Mile						
Los Angeles	222	Dp	7:20A	8:30A	11:10A	**2:00P**	**4:10P**
Fullerton	248		7:50A	9:00A	11:40A	**2:30P**	**4:40P**
Anaheim	253		7:59A	9:09A	11:49A	**2:39P**	**4:49P**
Orange	255			9:13A		**2:43P**	
Santa Ana	258		8:08A	9:20A	11:58A	**2:50P**	**4:58P**
Irvine	268		8:22A	9:31A	**12:11P**	**3:01P**	**5:09P**
Laguna Niguel/Mission	277			9:41A		**3:11P**	
San Juan Capistrano	280		8:40A	9:48A	**12:25P**	**3:18P**	**5:23P**
San Clemente Pier	288			10:00A			
Oceanside	309		9:13A	10:23A	**12:59P**	**3:48P**	**5:55P**
Solana Beach	325		9:29A	10:39A	**1:19P**	**4:08P**	**6:18P**
San Diego (Old Town)	347		9:58A	11:08A			
San Diego (Tijuana)	350	Ar	10:10A	11:20A	**1:55P**	**4:50P**	**7:00P**

1. How many stops does Train 572 make after Los Angeles? __________
2. How long does it take for Train 564 to get from Los Angeles to Irvine? __________
3. How long does it take for Train 566 to get from Los Angeles to Solana Beach? __________
4. How many miles is it from Orange to San Diego (Tijuana)? __________
5. If you leave from Anaheim at 9:09 in the morning, what time will you arrive at Oceanside? __________
6. If you want to arrive in San Juan Capistrano at around noon, which train should you get from Los Angeles? __________
7. If you want to arrive in Laguna Niguel in the morning, which train should you get from Fullerton? __________

B INFORMATIONAL READING: Parts of a Newspaper Article

Look at student book page 30c. Match the parts of the newspaper article with their examples.

____ 1. caption — a. What to Do If a Police Officer Pulls You Over

____ 2. byline — b. Linville, March 15

____ 3. sidebar — c. Police Department Starts New Community Outreach Program

____ 4. dateline — d. Juan Mendoza and Officer Hannon at City Hall.

____ 5. headline — e. By Lisa Evans

C WRITING: A Driver's License Application

Complete the form.

APPLICATION FOR DRIVER'S LICENSE OR IDENTIFICATION CARD — Use black ink only.

DRIVER'S LICENSE ☐ IDENTIFICATION CARD ☐

NAME ______________ ______________ ______________
FIRST MIDDLE LAST

ADDRESS ______________________________ ________
NUMBER STREET APT. #

______________ ________ ________
CITY STATE ZIP CODE

HOME PHONE ______________ BUSINESS PHONE ______________

SSN ____–____–____ DATE OF BIRTH ______________ PLACE OF BIRTH ______________

PERSONAL INFORMATION	SEX ☐M ☐F	EYE COLOR	HAIR COLOR	RACE	HEIGHT FT. IN.	WEIGHT LBS.

REQUIRED INFORMATION FROM ALL APPLICANTS:

YES NO

1. ( ) ( ) Have you ever had an identification card from this state?
   Number ______________ When? ______________
2. ( ) ( ) Have you ever had a license or instruction permit in this state?
   Number ______________ When? ______________
3. ( ) ( ) Have you ever had a license or instruction permit in any other state? State(s) ________
   Number(s) ______________ When? ______________
4. ( ) ( ) Are you a citizen of the United States?
5. ( ) ( ) Would you like to complete a voter registration application form today? You must be eligible.
6. ( ) ( ) Do you have a health condition that may impede communication with a police officer? If yes, please list:
   ____

REQUIRED INFORMATION FROM DRIVER'S LICENSE APPLICANTS:

YES NO **DRIVING HISTORY INFORMATION**

7. ( ) ( ) Are you enrolled in or have you completed a driver education course?
8. ( ) ( ) Is your driver's license currently suspended, revoked, canceled, denied, or disqualified in **ANY** state?
   Where? ________ When? ________ Why? ________
9. ( ) ( ) Has your driver's license or driving privilege ever been suspended, revoked, canceled, denied, or disqualified in **ANY** state?
   Where? ________ When? ________ Why? ________
10. ( ) ( ) Are you currently placed out of service for operating a commercial motor vehicle?
    Why? ______________________________

SIGNATURE OF APPLICANT (APPLICATION NOT COMPLETE WITHOUT SIGNATURE)

I have reviewed the Application Form and swear, under the penalties of perjury, that the information I have provided is true and complete.

Signature: ______________________ Date: ______________

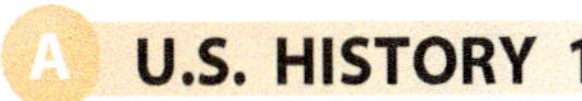

A U.S. HISTORY 1

STUDENT BOOK PAGES **46a–46d**

Complete the history facts.

Allies	New Deal	Social Security
Great Depression	Pearl Harbor	World War II

1. ______________________ started in 1939 and ended in 1945.
2. England, Russia, and France were the ______________________ in World War II.
3. In the ______________________, hundreds of banks closed and many people in the United States lost most of their money.
4. In the ______________________ during the 1930s, the U.S. government gave unemployed people jobs to build roads, parks, bridges, and buildings.
5. The ______________________ system was established to give people unemployment, health, and welfare benefits.
6. The U.S. entered World War II when the Japanese bombed ______________________.

B U.S. HISTORY 2

Complete the history facts.

Cold War	Martin Luther King, Jr.	United Nations
Korean War	superpowers	Vietnam War

1. The ______________________ is an international organization established to keep peace among countries around the world.
2. Between 1945 and 1991, the world's two ______________________ were the Soviet Union and the United States.
3. In the ______________________, the Soviet Union and the United States competed economically and politically.
4. In the ______________________, the Communist North fought against the non-Communist South from 1950 to 1953.
5. In the ______________________, the Communist North fought against the non-Communist South from 1964 to 1973.
6. ______________________ was the most famous leader of the civil rights movement in the United States.

C U.S. HISTORY 3

Complete the history facts.

Afghanistan	George W. Bush	Pentagon	Saddam Hussein

1. ______________________ was the dictator of Iraq from 1979 to 2003.
2. ______________________ was the president of the United States from 2000 to 2008.
3. The United States sent troops to ______________________ in 2001.
4. The ______________________ is the headquarters of the U.S. military.

D U.S. HISTORY 4: *Timeline*

Match the years and the events in U.S. history.

____ 1. 1917 a. The United States entered World War II.
____ 2. 1929 b. Franklin D. Roosevelt became President of the United States.
____ 3. 1932 c. Terrorists attacked the United States.
____ 4. 1941 d. World War II ended.
____ 5. 1945 e. The United States entered World War I.
____ 6. 1963 f. Martin Luther King, Jr. gave his famous "I Have a Dream" speech.
____ 7. 2001 g. The U.S. stock market collapsed

E YOUR TIMELINE

Think about important events in your life such as the following:

When were you born?
When did you start school?
When did you graduate from school?
When did you take your first English class?
When did you have your first job?
When did you get a pay raise or a job promotion?
When did you move to the United States?
When did you meet your spouse?

Write a timeline of important dates and events in your life.

Month/Year	Event

Now make a timeline like the one on student book page 46c. Write each event in your life and its year on the timeline.

A NUMERACY: Estimating Costs

Read the ad and answer the questions.

STUDENT BOOK
PAGES **64a–64d**

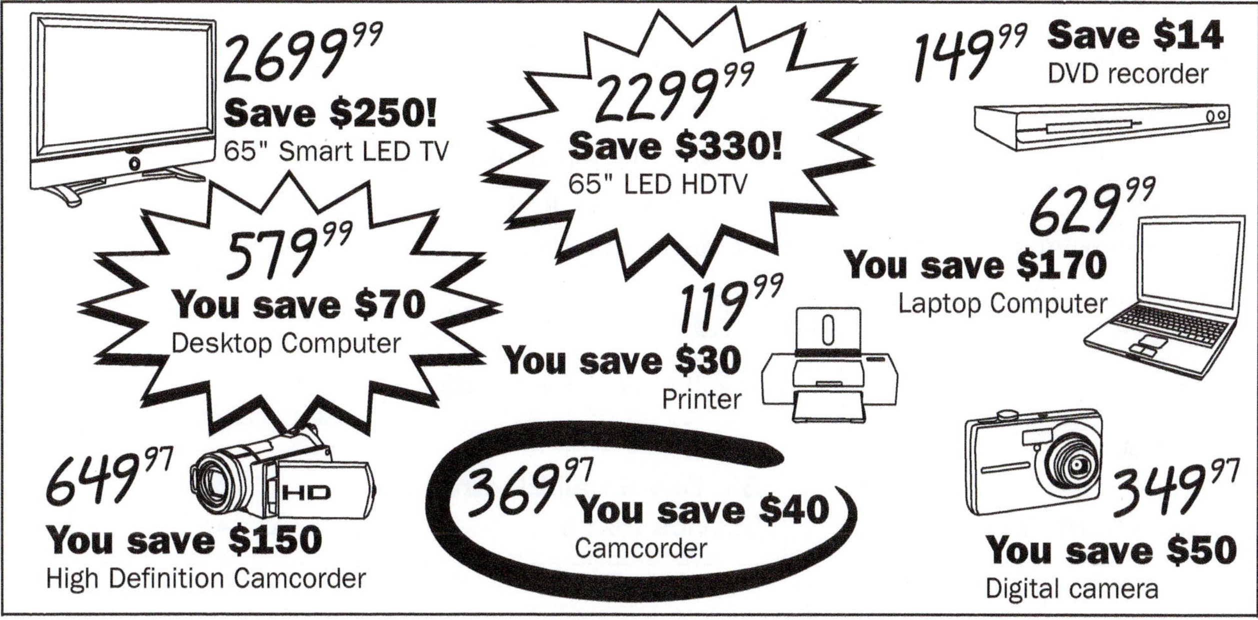

1. The Rodriguez family wants to buy the 65-inch LED TV and the DVD recorder. How much will their purchases cost?
   a. about $2450
   b. about $2550
   c. about $2850

2. Steve wants to buy the laptop computer and the printer. How much will his purchases cost?
   a. about $650
   b. about $750
   c. about $775

3. Linda wants to buy the desktop computer and the printer. How much will her purchases cost?
   a. about $680
   b. about $690
   c. about $700

4. The Chan family wants to buy the digital camera and the printer. How much will their purchases cost?
   a. about $450
   b. about $470
   c. about $490

5. The Batiste family wants to buy the 65-inch Smart LED TV and the high definition camcorder. How much will their purchases cost?
   a. about $2950
   b. about $3070
   c. about $3350

6. Sue and Bill want to buy the camcorder and the desktop computer. How much will their purchases cost?
   a. about $950
   b. about $1150
   c. about $1550

B WARRANTIES: Understanding Vocabulary from Context

Look at the warranties on student book page 64b. You might not know all the words, but you can probably understand many new words from their context. Match the warranty words with their meanings.

____	1. bill of sale	a. a problem with the product
____	2. defect	b. person who sells a certain kind of product
____	3. disposable	c. to promise
____	4. purchaser	d. can be thrown away
____	5. to ship	e. quality of work
____	6. workmanship	f. to send something in the mail
____	7. dealer	g. person who buys the product
____	8. to guarantee	h. a receipt for the purchase

C NUMERACY: Interpreting Charts and Prices

Read the store repair and replacement plans and answer the questions.

Big Buy Small Electronics Replacement Plans

Purchase Price	1-Year Plan
$\$0$–$\$49^{99}$	$\$4^{99}$
$\$50^{00}$–$\$99^{99}$	$\$9^{99}$
$\$100^{00}$–$\$149^{99}$	$\$14^{99}$
$\$150^{00}$–$\$199^{99}$	$\$19^{99}$
$\$200^{00}$–$\$249^{99}$	$\$29^{99}$
$\$250^{00}$–$\$299^{99}$	$\$39^{99}$

Big Buy Small Electronics Service Plans

Purchase Price	2-Year Plan	4-Year Plan
$\$300^{99}$–$\$399^{99}$	$\$49^{99}$	$\$99^{99}$
$\$400^{99}$–$\$499^{99}$	$\$59^{99}$	$\$139^{99}$
$\$500^{99}$–$\$799^{99}$	$\$99^{99}$	$\$169^{99}$
$\$800^{99}$–$\$899^{99}$	$\$149^{99}$	$\$199^{99}$
$\$1{,}000^{99}$–$\$1{,}999^{99}$	$\$229^{99}$	$\$299^{99}$
$\$2{,}000^{99}$–$\$4{,}999^{99}$	$\$279^{99}$	$\$349^{99}$

- The plan begins upon expiration of manufacturer's labor warranty. During the manufacturer's warranty period, any parts or labor are the sole responsibility of the manufacturer.
- Product replacements only for failed products under $300.

The Hanson family bought a $\$159^{00}$ DVD player with a 90-day manufacturer's warranty. They also bought a replacement plan.

1. How much did they pay for the replacement plan?
   a. $\$9^{99}$ b. $\$14^{99}$ c. $\$19^{99}$

2. If their DVD player doesn't work two months later, which warranty will take care of the problem?
   a. The manufacturer's warranty
   b. The Big Buy Service Plan
   c. The Big Buy Replacement Plan

The Yamamoto family bought a $\$1199^{97}$ camera with a 1-year manufacturer's warranty. They also bought a 4-year service plan.

3. How much did they pay for the service plan?
   a. $\$229^{99}$ b. $\$299^{99}$ c. $\$349^{99}$

4. If the camera doesn't work 16 months later, what can they do?
   a. Repair it with the Big Buy Service Plan
   b. Repair it with the manufacturer's warranty
   c. Replace it with the Big Buy Service Plan

A THE HEIMLICH MANEUVER 1

5

STUDENT BOOK PAGES **78a–78d**

Read the information on student book page 78a. Decide if each statement is True (T) or False (F).

____ 1. The Heimlich maneuver is for emergency use only.

____ 2. If a person is coughing, you should perform the Heimlich maneuver.

____ 3. If a person isn't breathing, he or she can't speak or cough.

____ 4. If a person can't breathe for four seconds, he or she will have brain damage.

____ 5. The Heimlich maneuver pushes food out of a person's stomach.

____ 6. The Heimlich maneuver can injure a person.

____ 7. The Heimlich maneuver can save a person's life.

B THE HEIMLICH MANEUVER 2

Number the steps of the Heimlich maneuver from 1–6.

____ Grab your fist with your other hand.

____ Make a fist with one hand.

____ Press into the person's abdomen with four quick inward and upward thrusts.

____ Put the thumb side of your fist below the person's rib cage.

____ Repeat until the object comes out.

__1__ Stand behind the person.

C YOUR HOME FIRE SAFETY CHECKLIST

Read the safety poster on student book page 78b. Do you practice fire safety in your home? Answer Yes (Y) or No (N). (All of these are important!)

____ 1. Do you have a fire extinguisher in your kitchen?

____ 2. Do you have smoke detectors in your home?

____ 3. Do you change the batteries in your smoke detectors every six months?

____ 4. Do you store flammable products away from heat?

____ 5. Do you keep space heaters away from flammable materials?

____ 6. Do you have an escape route plan?

____ 7. Do you have a meeting place in case of fire?

____ 8. Do you have a first-aid kit?

____ 9. Do you practice your escape plan twice a year?

____ 10. Do you know how to shut off your utilities?

D A SMOKE DETECTOR DIAGRAM

Read the diagram and answer the questions.

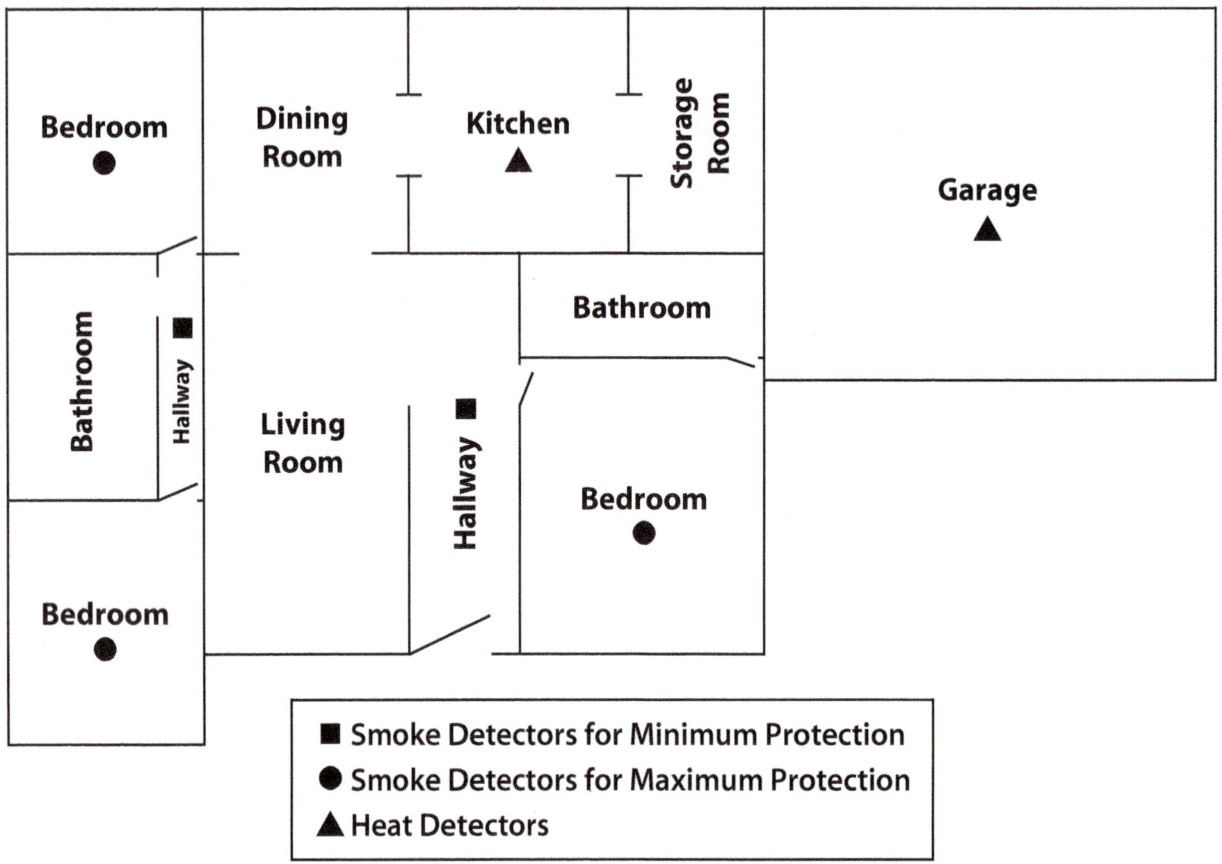

1. Which areas should have smoke detectors for minimum protection?
   a. The bedrooms
   b. The hallways
   c. The kitchen and garage

2. Which areas should have smoke detectors for maximum protection?
   a. The kitchen and garage
   b. The bathrooms
   c. The bedrooms

3. Which areas should have heat detectors?
   a. The bedrooms
   b. The kitchen and garage
   c. The hallways

4. Which areas of the home don't need smoke detector protection?
   a. The dining room and living room
   b. The storage room
   c. a and b

5. According to the diagram, how many smoke detectors are needed for minimum protection?
   a. One
   b. Two
   c. Three

E APARTMENT AD ABBREVIATIONS

Write the correct word next to each abbreviation.

air conditioning	bedroom	elevator	included	parking
available	building	heat	large	transportation
basement	dining room	hot water	living room	utilities
bathroom	eat-in kitchen	immediately	near	washer and dryer

1. BR ___bedroom___
2. W/D ______
3. A/C ______
4. EIK ______
5. DR ______
6. LR ______
7. BA ______
8. elev. ______
9. bldg. ______
10. pkg. ______
11. trans. ______
12. ht. ______
13. incl. ______
14. hw ______
15. immed. ______
16. nr. ______
17. bsmt. ______
18. lg. ______
19. avail. ______
20. util. ______

F READING APARTMENT ADS

Look at the apartment ads. Read the sentences. Write the letter of the correct apartment next to each sentence.

A	B	C
CHELSEA Avail. now. Lg. 3 BR apt. 1 BA, LR, EIK, W/D, A/C, $1600 plus util. Pkg. Call Rick 413-555-2948.	SUMMERHILL 1 BR apt. 1.5 BA, elev. in bldg. A/C, W/D in bsmt. $850. Util. incl. Nr. trans. Avail. 6/10. Call 312-555-0295.	WESTVILLE 2 BR, 1 BA apt. Lg. kit. LR, DR, nr. shopping. $1200. Ht. hw. incl. Avail. immed. Call owner 971-555-1352.

____ 1. It has two bedrooms.

____ 2. It has an eat-in kitchen.

____ 3. It's not available now.

____ 4. It has parking.

____ 5. Utilities are not included.

____ 6. It has one and a half bathrooms.

____ 7. Heat and hot water are included.

____ 8. It's near public transportation.

____ 9. There's an elevator in the building.

____ 10. It doesn't have air conditioning.

A NUMERACY: Word Problems about Money

STUDENT BOOK PAGES **94a–94d**

Solve the word problems.

Maria is at the bank.

1. She has $1,325 in her savings account. She makes a deposit of $850.00. Now how much is in her account? ____________

2. The next day, Maria makes a withdrawal of $280 from her savings account. Now how much is in her savings account? ____________

Ivan is at the bank.

3. He has $1,185 in his checking account. He makes a withdrawal of $540 to send overseas. Now how much is in his account? ____________

4. He orders more checks. The bank charges him $5.60 for the checks. They make the withdrawal from his checking account. Now how much money does Ivan have in his account? ____________

5. Ivan makes a deposit of $230 in his checking account. Now how much money does he have in his account? ____________

Eliza is at a clothing store.

6. She has $80 in her wallet. She wants to buy the following items: a blouse for $24.00, socks for $5.50, a skirt for $29.00, and a pair of pants for $15.00. Does she have enough cash to buy all the items? ____________

7. There are no taxes on clothes in her state. How much change does Eliza get back? ____________

Kenji is at a gift store.

8. He is buying a $15.99 clock. The sales tax is an additional $.96. What is the total cost of the clock? ____________

9. He gives the cashier a $50 bill for the clock. What is his change? ____________

Julia is at the supermarket.

10. The total cost of Julia's groceries is $63.54. She gives the cashier $70.00. He gives her $7.44 in change. Is that the correct change? ____________

11. The cashier notices his mistake. How much does Julia have to return to him? ____________

B TYPES OF BANK ACCOUNTS: Understanding Vocabulary from Context

Look at the bank brochure on student book page 94b. You might not know all the words, but you can probably understand many new words from their context. Match the banking words with their meanings.

_____ 1. daily balance
_____ 2. monthly fee
_____ 3. opening deposit
_____ 4. record keeping
_____ 5. interest
_____ 6. minimum balance
_____ 7. online banking
_____ 8. waive a fee
_____ 9. safe deposit box
_____ 10. passbook

a. bank services a customer can use on the Internet
b. writing down the information about what goes in and out of an account
c. the money a bank customer earns by leaving his or her money in a bank account
d. a small booklet that records all the money coming in and going out of a savings account
e. the amount of money in an account at the end of one day
f. a small storage unit in a bank to keep valuable items such as jewelry or legal documents
g. a required amount of money a customer must keep in a bank account
h. the first amount of money a customer puts in a new account
i. money a customer pays a bank 12 times a year to have an account
j. to allow a customer *not* to pay a bank charge

C A BANK ACCOUNT APPLICATION

Fill out the form to open a bank account.

Midtown Bank Account Application (Single Account Owner)

For a Personal Checking Account

Which account do you wish to open?

☐ Basic Checking ☐ Regular Checking ☐ Checking Plus

For a Personal Savings Account

Which account do you wish to open?

☐ Statement Savings ☐ Passbook Savings ☐ Money Market Savings

APPLICANT

Last Name ____________________ First Name ____________________ MI ______

Social Security Number ____________________ Date of Birth __ __ / __ __ / __ __ __ __

Home Address ____
STREET CITY STATE ZIP CODE

Home Phone No. ____________________ Work Phone No. ____________________

Cell Phone No. ____________________ E-mail Address ____________________

I certify that the above information is correct.

Applicant Signature ______________________________ Date ______________

D A MONTHLY BUDGET

Read the article about budget-planning strategies on student book page 94c. Then think about your own monthly expenses. Complete the budgeting worksheet.

	Monthly Payments	
Housing Expenses		
Rent or Mortgage	$________	
Utilities	$________	
Insurance	$________	
Repairs	$________	
Taxes	$________	
= Total		$________
Car/Travel Expenses		
Loan Payment(s)	$________	
Gas	$________	
Insurance	$________	
Maintenance & Repairs	$________	
Public Transportation	$________	
= Total		$________
Debts		
#1 ________ Balance ________	$________	
#2 ________ Balance ________	$________	
= Total		$________
Miscellaneous Expenses		
Groceries, Lunches, Meals Out	$________	
Childcare	$________	
School Fees/Supplies	$________	
Medical Care	$________	
Prescription Medicines	$________	
Entertainment, Cable, Internet	$________	
Clothing	$________	
Gifts	$________	
(Other): ____________	$________	
(Other): ____________	$________	
= Total		$________
Monthly Expense Totals		
Housing	$________	
Car	$________	
Debts	$________	
Miscellaneous	$________	
= Total Expenses		$________
Total Take-Home Income – Total Expenses =		$________

E NUMERACY: A Cell Phone Bill

Read the bill and answer the questions.

Mobile Talk
P.O. Box 926653
Cincinnati, OH 45724

Statement for: **Cathy Lin**
Account Number: 9925364
Amount Due by 6/27/18 $86.28

Phone Accounts	Monthly Charges	Taxes and Surcharges	Total Current Charges
312-555-2435	69.94	4.65	$ 74.59
773-555-7243	9.99	1.70	$ 11.69
Total	**79.93**	**6.35**	**$ 86.28**

Account Service Detail

Monthly Phone Account Charges		**$ 79.93**
Family Plan	49.99	
Unlimited Instant Messages	19.95	
Added Line	9.99	
Taxes, Fees, and Surcharges		**$ 6.35**
Federal Universal Service Fund	1.00	
State Sales tax	3.55	
State 911	.60	
Regulator Programs Fee	1.20	
Total Charges		**$ 86.28**

1. Cathy Lin has a total cell phone bill of ____________.

2. She has to pay her bill on or before ____________.

3. She has to pay a total of ____________ in Monthly Phone Account Charges.

4. The phone number account of 312-555-2435 has two detail charges. One charge is $____________ for the Family Plan and the other charge is $____________ for Unlimited Messaging.

5. Cathy thinks there's a mistake on her cell phone bill. She's going to call Customer Assistance and ask about two new charges that she hasn't seen before—the Federal Universal Service Fund and the Regulator Programs Fee. Together these add $____________ to her phone bill.

STUDENT BOOK
PAGES **108a–108f**

A SYMPTOMS AND MEDICAL ADVICE

Write the correct word to complete each sentence.

bump	knee	muscle
exercise	low-fat	swollen

1. I think I pulled a ________________.
2. It hurts when I bend my ________________.
3. I have a big ________________ on my head.
4. My wrist is ________________ because I fell on it while I was playing soccer.
5. You need to eat ________________ dairy products.
6. You need to ________________ regularly.

B NUMERACY: Nutrition Amounts on a Food Label

Write the correct word to complete each sentence.

Countryside Plain Non-Fat Yogurt

Nutrition Facts	
Serving Size: 1 cup	
Servings Per Container: 1	
Calories 110	Calories from Fat 0
	% Daily Value
Total Fat 0g	0%
Saturated Fat 0g	0%
Trans Fat 0g	
Cholesterol 3mg	1%
Sodium 160mg	7%
Total Carbohydrate 15g	5%
Dietary Fiber 0g	
Sugars 0g	
Protein 13g	
Vitamin A 0%	Vitamin C 4%
Calcium 45%	Vitamin D 0%

1. How many servings are there in this container?

____

2. How many calories are there in a serving?

____

3. How many calories are there in half a cup of this yogurt?

____

4. How much protein is there in a serving?

____

5. How much fiber is there in a serving?

____

C INFORMATIONAL READING: Using Medicine Carefully

Read the article on student book page 108d and answer the questions.

1. What is the main purpose of the article?
   a. To describe ingredients and side effects of medications
   b. To warn teenagers about drug abuse
   c. To recommend medications for different symptoms and ailments
   d. To show that reading medicine labels carefully is important

2. In paragraph 1, to *ignore* directions means ______.
   a. to follow them
   b. to not follow them
   c. to agree with them
   d. to check them

3. According to the article, you should call a doctor when ______.
   a. your over-the-counter medication expires
   b. you don't understand the ingredients on a medicine label
   c. you have bad side effects from a drug
   d. you don't have a dosage cup or measuring spoon for medicine

4. What type of over-the-counter medication is NOT mentioned in the article?
   a. Vitamins
   b. Cold medicine
   c. Antacids
   d. Cough medicine

D READING A MEDICINE LABEL

Read the label. Decide if the statements are True (T) or False (F).

Extra-Strength Pain Reliever

Active Ingredient: Acetaminophen 500 mg

Uses: Temporarily relieves the aches and pains due to
- headache
- backache
- the common cold
- toothache
- arthritis
- reduces fever

Directions
- Adults and children 12 years and over: Take 2 caplets every 6 hours.
- Do not take more than 8 caplets in 24 hours.
- Children under 12: Do not use this Extra-Strength product.

Alcohol Warning
If you consume 3 or more alcoholic drinks a day, ask your doctor if you should take acetaminophen. It may cause liver damage.

Stop Use If
- redness and swelling is present.
- fever gets worse or lasts for more than 3 days.
- pain gets worse or lasts for more than 10 days.

Inactive Ingredients: carnauba wax, croscarmellose sodium, starch, stearic acid **Expiration date:** 11/2021

____ 1. Take this medicine if you have a fever.

____ 2. Take this medicine if you have a stomachache.

____ 3. Don't take this medicine if you drink three alcoholic drinks a day.

____ 4. Children under 12 should not take this medicine.

____ 5. Ten caplets in 24 hours is an overdose.

____ 6. If the pain gets worse, stop taking this medicine.

____ 7. Starch and stearic acid are active ingredients.

____ 8. You should throw this medicine out in December 2021.

____ 9. If you have a fever for three or more days, you should take three caplets every 6 hours.

E WORKPLACE SAFETY

Write the correct words under the safety signs.

biohazard	first-aid kit	no drinks allowed	safety glasses
combustible materials	flammable materials	no food allowed	safety gloves
corrosive materials	helmet	poison	
fire extinguisher	high voltage	respirator	

1. ______________________

2. ______________________

3. ______________________

4. ______________________

5. ______________________

6. ______________________

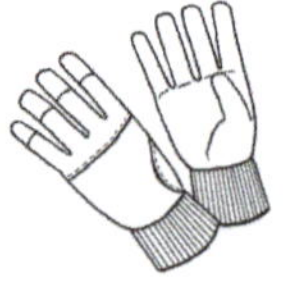

7. ______________________

8. ______________________

9. ______________________

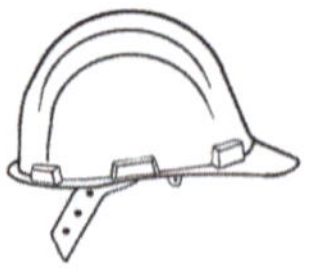

10. ______________________

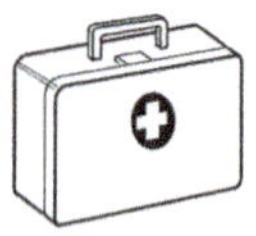

11. ______________________

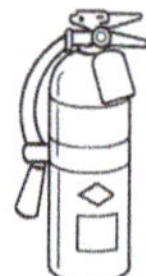

12. ______________________

13. ______________________

14. ______________________

F MAP READING: An Evacuation Map

This is an evacuation map for Miami-Dade County in Florida. If there is a hurricane, residents might need to evacuate their homes and go to a shelter. Evacuation orders depend on the intensity (category) of the hurricane and the location (zone) of the home. Look at the map and decide: Do these people need to evacuate? Answer Yes (Y) or No (N).

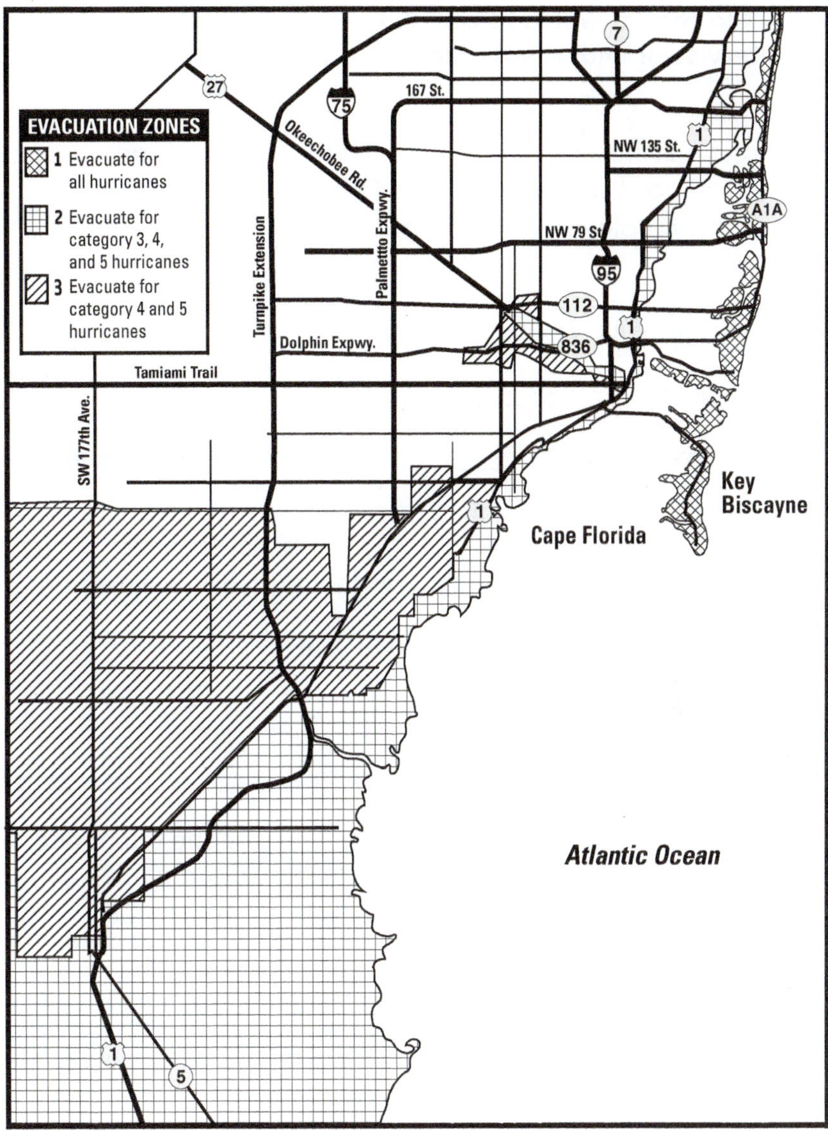

_____ 1. Eric lives in Zone 3. A category 2 hurricane is coming.

_____ 2. Amanda lives in Zone 1. A category 1 hurricane is coming.

_____ 3. The Johnsons live in Zone 2. A category 4 hurricane is coming.

_____ 4. The Garcias live on Key Biscayne. A category 3 hurricane is coming.

_____ 5. Lisa and Rick live in Zone 2. A category 2 hurricane is coming.

_____ 6. The Lees live in Zone 3. A category 5 hurricane is coming.

A JOB INTERVIEW VOCABULARY

8

STUDENT BOOK PAGES **124a–124d**

Write the correct words to complete the conversation between a job interviewer and an applicant.

attitude	familiar	position	skills
communicator	get along	promotion	specific
employed	goals		

A. What are your greatest strengths?

B. I'm a good ________________ 1, and I ________________ 2 well with people. I have a positive ________________ 3, and I try to improve my ________________ 4.

A. Do you know what we do here?

B. Yes. I'm ________________ 5 with your work because my friend Ruth Gomez has been ________________ 6 here for two years.

A. Do you have any questions for me?

B. Yes. Can you tell me more about the ________________ 7 job responsibilities?

A. Certainly. You will greet patients, answer the telephone, schedule appointments, find medical records, and communicate with insurance companies.

B. Are there opportunities for ________________ 8 and advancement?

A. Yes. You can move up to the position of office supervisor. What are your long-term ________________ 9?

B. I would like to become a medical office administrator.

A. I see.

B. When do you plan to fill the ________________ 10?

A. The job starts October 4th.

B DIFFICULT JOB INTERVIEW QUESTIONS

What do you consider your greatest strengths and your greatest weaknesses? Make two lists.

My Strengths	My Weaknesses
________________	________________
________________	________________
________________	________________

C JOB AD ABBREVIATIONS

Write the correct word next to each abbreviation.

assistant	certified	driver's license	experience	previous
available	company	equivalent	office	references
benefits	diploma	excellent	opportunity	required

1. excel. ______________________
2. asst. ______________________
3. co. ______________________
4. refs. ______________________
5. driv. lic. ______________________
6. exp. ______________________
7. req'd ______________________
8. cert. ______________________
9. ofc. ______________________
10. bnfts. ______________________
11. equiv. ______________________
12. avail. ______________________
13. dipl. ______________________
14. oppt. ______________________
15. prev. ______________________

D HELP WANTED ADS

Read the help wanted ads. Choose the correct answer.

Secretary

Ofc. asst. 2 years. prev. exp. req'd. High School dipl. or equiv. Excel bnfts. Oppt. for promotion. Fax resume to 209-555-3656.

Home Health Aide

Need cert. home aides. Co. car avail. Must have driv. lic., refs. 1 year prev. exper. Weekend and evening hours. Call Maxim at 209-555-7412.

1. Both positions require ______.
   a. a driver's license
   b. a high school diploma
   c. references
   d. previous experience

2. Neither ad includes information on ______.
   a. the benefits
   b. the name of the person to call
   c. the pay
   d. the work days

3. The home health aide must ______.
   a. drive
   b. work weekends
   c. provide references
   d. do all the above

4. The secretary job doesn't require ______.
   a. a high school diploma
   b. a promotion
   c. experience
   d. a resume

E YOUR WORK AND EDUCATION EXPERIENCE TIMELINE

Get ready to list your work experience and skills. Think about your answers to these questions.

When and where did you go to school when you were young? Did you graduate?

When did you start working? What was your first job? What were your job duties?

When did you get your second job? What was the job? What were your job duties?

Have you ever received a pay raise or a job promotion? When?

Have you ever taken an interesting class or learned a special skill in a training program? What was it? Where? When?

When did you start studying English?

Now write a timeline of your important work and education experiences and their dates. Start with your most recent experience.

Month / Year	Work or Education Experience

F YOUR RESUME

Write your own resume.

____
(Name)

____
(Address)

____
(Phone Number or E-mail)

WORK EXPERIENCE (LIST MOST RECENT FIRST)

Dates
FROM:
TO:

____
(Position, Place of Employment)

____
(City, State)

____
(Description of job duties)

Dates
FROM:
TO:

____
(Position, Place of Employment)

____
(City, State)

____
(Description of job duties)

Dates
FROM:
TO:

____
(Position, Place of Employment)

____
(City, State)

____
(Description of job duties)

EDUCATION HISTORY

Dates
FROM:
TO:

____
(Degree or certification)

____
(School, City, State)

Dates
FROM:
TO:

____
(Degree or certification)

____
(School, City, State)

SKILLS

(List special skills here, for example: languages you speak, typing or computer skills, machine operating skills, any special license you have to drive or operate equipment, etc.)

____

____

____

____

____

____

A INFORMATIONAL READING: Employee Benefits

9

STUDENT BOOK PAGES **144a–144d**

Read the employee benefits information on student book page 144b. Decide if each statement is True (T) or False (F).

_____ 1. Part-time employees get health insurance.

_____ 2. Employees help pay the health insurance premium.

_____ 3. The health insurance plan covers eyeglasses.

_____ 4. Full-time employees can have free check-ups with their dentist.

_____ 5. Only full-time employees are eligible for nine paid holidays a year.

_____ 6. For every dollar an employee saves in the 401(k) retirement plan, the company saves a dollar for the employee, too.

_____ 7. If an employee doesn't use all four personal days, the employee can save them for the following year.

_____ 8. Employees can get free counseling.

_____ 9. Employees can take their nine holidays any time they want to.

_____ 10. The company pays for its full-time employees' life insurance plan.

_____ 11. Money in a 401(k) plan is not taxed until a person has retired.

_____ 12. Employees get two weeks of sick days every year.

_____ 13. Employees can save up as many vacation days as they wish and use them in the future.

B NUMERACY: Reading a Pay Stub

Look at the pay stub and complete the statements on the next page.

Shelby Company		Erin Taylor Employee No. 2132		Pay Period Ending 04/02/18
Earnings	**Rate**	**Hours**	**This Period**	**Year to Date**
Regular	12.00	32	384.00	5,928.00
Overtime	18.00	5	90.00	990.00
Holiday	12.00	8	96.00	192.00
		Gross Pay	570.00	7,110.00
Leave	**Earned**	**Used**	**Used–Year to Date**	**Accrued–Year to Date**
Vacation	1.6	0.0	8.0	16.8 hours
Sick Time	.75	0.0	0.0	9.75 hours
Taxes & Deductions			**This Period**	**Year to Date**
Federal Tax			58.00	735.00
State Tax			27.00	350.00
FICA/Medicare			45.00	550.00
Health Plan			40.00	520.00
401(k) (co. match 100%)			40.00	520.00
Total			210.00	2,675.00
Net Pay			360.00	4,435.00

1. Erin worked a total of __________ regular and overtime hours during this pay period.

2. __________ was deducted from Erin's paycheck this pay period.

3. Erin took home __________ this pay period.

4. Before deductions, Erin has earned __________ this year.

5. She has taken home __________ in paychecks.

6. She paid __________ for state and federal taxes in this pay period.

7. Erin has paid __________ for state and federal taxes this calendar year.

8. Erin contributed __________ to her retirement plan this pay period.

9. The company contributed __________ to her retirement plan this pay period.

10. Erin has contributed __________ to her retirement plan this calendar year.

11. Erin's health plan costs __________ each pay period.

12. Erin has accrued __________ hours of sick time this year.

13. Erin has used __________ vacation hours this calendar year.

C DESCRIBING YOUR QUALITIES

The article on student book page 144c describes the personal qualities of five people who are "moving up" at their workplaces. Choose five of these adjectives that describe you. Write a sentence for each adjective to give an example of this personal quality.

adaptable	dedicated	flexible	helpful	industrious
considerate	dependable	friendly	honest	punctual
cooperative	efficient	hardworking		

____

____

____

____

____

Now choose two of these statements that describe you. Write a sentence to give an example of each personal quality.

I'm a good communicator.	I'm a problem solver.
I'm a team player.	I focus on the big picture.
I'm a leader.	I try to improve all the time.

____

____

A CIVICS VOCABULARY

STUDENT BOOK PAGES **158a–158d**

Look at the civics lesson on student book pages 158a–b. You might not know all the words, but you can probably understand many new words from their context. Match the words with their meanings.

____ 1. income tax	a.	a person who moves to the United States and then becomes a citizen
____ 2. jury	b.	the military—for example, the army, navy, and air force
____ 3. national defense	c.	duties
____ 4. natural-born citizen	d.	a special right or advantage a person has
____ 5. naturalized citizen	e.	the tax a person pays the government for the things he or she owns (for example, a house, a car, a boat)
____ 6. permanent resident	f.	the decision a jury makes about whether a person is guilty or innocent
____ 7. privilege	g.	a person who legally lives in the United States but is not a citizen
____ 8. property tax	h.	a group of 12 citizens in a court who decide if a person is guilty or innocent
____ 9. responsibilities	i.	a person who was born in the United States
____ 10. criminal or civil offense	j.	the tax an employee pays the government for the money that person makes
____ 11. verdict	k.	a procedure in court to decide if someone is guilty or innocent
____ 12. trial	l.	when a person is accused of breaking the law

B COMMUNITY LEGAL SERVICES

Look at the community legal services brochure on student book page 158c. For each sentence, write the letter of the office that the person should contact.

A Family Law	**C** Tenant Rights
B Domestic Violence	**D** Immigration Services

____ 1. Magda has received an eviction letter from her landlord.

____ 2. Kenji's visa is going to expire.

____ 3. Janice wants to get a divorce.

____ 4. Tomas wants to become naturalized.

____ 5. Kate's husband hurts her and the children.

____ 6. The superintendent still hasn't fixed the lock on the apartment door.

____ 7. Lydia's ex-husband wants to see the children more often.

____ 8. Alicia needs to get a work permit.

Listening Scripts

Page 3 Exercise C

Listen and decide what is being talked about.

1. A. Have they sung them yet?
   B. Yes, they have. They sang them a little while ago.
2. A. Has she written it yet?
   B. Yes, she has. She wrote it a little while ago.
3. A. I've spoken it for a long time.
   B. Oh. I didn't know that.
4. A. Have you swum there?
   B. Yes. We've swum there for a long time.
5. A. Have you ridden it yet?
   B. Yes. I rode it a little while ago.
6. A. I've drawn them for many years.
   B. I didn't know that.
7. A. Have you taken it?
   B. Yes, we have. We took it a little while ago.
8. A. Have you driven it yet?
   B. Yes. I drove it a little while ago.
9. A. She's grown them for many years.
   B. Yes. I knew that.

Page 6 Exercise G

Listen and complete the sentences.

1. A. How long have you played the violin?
   B. I've played the violin for . . .
2. A. How long has Peter known Monica?
   B. He's known her since . . .
3. A. How long have Mr. and Mrs. Johnson had that car?
   B. They've had it since . . .
4. A. How long have we been married?
   B. We've been married for . . .
5. A. How long has your sister had the flu?
   B. She's had the flu for . . .
6. A. How long have you wanted to be an actor?
   B. I've wanted to be an actor since . . .
7. A. How long has Debbie sung in the church choir?
   B. She's sung in the church choir since . . .
8. A. How long have you been a teacher?
   B. I've been a teacher for . . .
9. A. How long has Kevin had a Boston accent?
   B. He's had a Boston accent for . . .

Page 8 Exercise K

Listen and choose the correct answer.

1. I'm really frustrated. I've been having problems with my TV for the past few weeks, and I can't find anyone who can fix it.
2. I think I'll start looking for another job. I've been working here at the State Street Bank since I graduated from college.
3. We've been sitting here for more than a half hour, and no one has taken our order yet.
4. Do you think Peter and Jane will get married someday? After all, they've been going out since they were in high school.
5. We've been complaining to our landlord about the ceiling in our bedroom, but he hasn't done anything about it. We don't know what to do. It's been leaking for the past two weeks.
6. I'm exhausted. We've been riding around town all day. Let's stop somewhere and rest for a while.

Page 29 Exercise M

Listen and choose the correct answer.

1. Billy fell asleep in school today.
2. Alice called her friends at midnight and woke them up.
3. I wonder why Gary didn't come to the meeting this morning.
4. We sat at the football game in the rain all afternoon.
5. Roger was hoping to get a promotion this year, but he didn't get one.
6. The play was terrible. The actors couldn't remember their lines!
7. I called my cousin Betty all week, but she didn't answer the phone.
8. Grandpa moved the refrigerator by himself!

Page 31 Exercise P: *Have You Heard?*

Listen and complete the sentences.

1. How do you feel . . .
2. Do you still . . .
3. Does he like these . . .
4. She needed . . .
5. They live . . .
6. We're leaving . . .
7. Alan is sleeping late because he's . . .
8. I'm sorry you didn't like the salad. It . . .
9. I'll try to finish this . . .
10. This week . . .
11. Will you still want to see your old friends when you're rich . . .
12. You should fill . . .
13. They don't feed . . .
14. I'm glad you like the chocolate cake. Eat . . .
15. I don't think those boys steal . . .
16. George is very glad his . . .

Page 35 Exercise E

Listen and decide what is being talked about.

1. They've already been made.
2. It was directed by Fellini.
3. It was sent last week.
4. It was worn by her grandmother.
5. They've already been given out.
6. They've already been written.
7. It's already been sung.
8. They've already been fed.
9. It's already been set up.

Page 39 Exercise L

Listen and choose the correct answer.

1. Hello. This is Mrs. Riley. I'm calling about my VCR. Is it ready?
2. Is the meeting room ready?
3. This is a beautiful photograph of your children.
4. I can't wait to hear those songs.
5. Why is Robert so upset?
6. We've been waiting all morning for the courier from your company.
7. Have you heard the good news about Nancy's raise?
8. Why is Roberta so pleased?
9. Where are the new pictures we bought last weekend?
10. Is the birthday cake ready?
11. I'm really looking forward to hearing the Mozart sonata.
12. Why is Aunt Helen so happy?

Page 43 Exercise R

Listen and choose the correct answer.

1. This magnificent mural is being painted by students in our school.
2. Mrs. Allen, your watch has been repaired.
3. The beds will be done soon.
4. All the paychecks have been given out.

(continued)

5. The meeting room is ready now.
6. Mr. Winter, your car is being repaired.
7. All the cookies have been baked.
8. The babies are being fed.

Page 45 Exercise D

Listen and choose the correct answer.

Ex: It's already been painted.

1. All the photographs have been taken.
2. The holiday decorations are being hung up.
3. The beds on the third floor are ready now.
4. The report is being rewritten right now.
5. Mr. Williams, your VCR has been repaired.

Page 49 Exercise E

Listen and decide what is being talked about.

1. I'm sorry. I don't know what time it arrives. Check with the ticket agent.
2. I have no idea what this means.
3. Do you have any idea when this was taken?
4. I have no idea what the problem is with the engine. Check with the mechanic.
5. I have no idea what time it begins. You should look in the newspaper.
6. I'm sorry. I don't know how much this costs. You should ask that salesperson over there.
7. Do you know when they were sent?
8. Do you have any idea when they were fed?

Page 53 Exercise J

Listen and decide where these people are.

1. Can you tell me if surfing is allowed here?
2. Do you by any chance know whether these shirts are on sale?
3. Do you know whether the play has begun yet?
4. Do you remember if our car is on the third floor or on the fourth?
5. Do you have any idea if it'll be arriving soon?
6. Could you tell me whether there's a lot of pepper in the stew?
7. Do you know whether swimming is allowed here?
8. Could you possibly tell me if lettuce is on sale this week?
9. Do you by any chance know if the monkeys are sleeping?

Page 58 Exercise D

Listen and complete the sentences.

1. If it rains this weekend, . . .
2. I'll skip dessert if . . .
3. We'll be late for work if . . .
4. If they finish their homework soon, . . .
5. If our car doesn't start tomorrow morning, . . .
6. If you don't come to class next Monday, . . .
7. I know I'll fall asleep in class if . . .
8. I'll send your package by overnight mail if . . .
9. If Charlie doesn't get a raise soon, . . .
10. Please call me if . . .
11. Janet will pick up her husband at the airport if . . .
12. If the children don't feel any better, . . .
13. We won't go on vacation if . . .
14. She'll regret it if . . .

Page 63 Exercise J

Listen and choose the polite response.

1. Do you think it will snow soon so we can go skiing?
2. Do you think you'll lose your job?
3. Will the teacher yell at us if we make a mistake?
4. Do you think the baby will cry all night?
5. Will Jane go out with me if I ask her?
6. Am I going to regret taking this job?
7. Am I going to have trouble on my history exam?
8. Will you graduate soon?
9. Will the movie be exciting?
10. Will there be pickpockets in the crowd?
11. Do you think John will apologize to his sister?
12. Will YOUR children give their colds to MY children?

Page 66 Exercise N

Listen and choose the correct answer based on what you hear.

1. You know, George, if you took more vacations, you'd feel more energetic.
2. I would enjoy listening to the orchestra if the musicians were more talented.
3. If you were more aggressive, you'd be a much better used car salesman.
4. Bob's car would be in better condition if he tuned it up more often.
5. If they had more in common, they'd get along with each other.
6. If Mona were a good teacher, she'd care more about her students.
7. We would be able to use the Internet if our school had more computers.
8. If these cookies had more sugar, they'd be sweeter.

Page 77 Exercise D

Listen and complete the sentences.

Ex. If the weather is nice this weekend, . . .

1. If I miss the bus, . . .
2. If I were more careful, . . .
3. You'll regret it if . . .
4. If I didn't have to work overtime, . . .
5. If she weren't busy this weekend, . . .

Page 80 Exercise E

Listen and complete the sentences.

1. I wouldn't grow a beard if I were you. If you grew a beard, . . .
2. I'm not feeling well today, but if I feel better tomorrow, . . .
3. You know, I wouldn't ride in that old car if I were you. If you rode in that old car, . . .
4. If I have some time this weekend, . . .
5. I wouldn't show this political cartoon to the president. If you showed it to him, . . .
6. To be honest, I wouldn't go to Alaska in February. If you went there in February, . . .
7. If I have to spend a lot of money on car repairs this year, . . .
8. If I were you, I wouldn't buy a used computer. If you bought a used computer, . . .
9. If you skip today's meeting, I know . . .
10. To be honest with you, I wouldn't start an Internet company if I were you. If you did, . . .
11. If you keep on parking your car in my parking space, . . .
12. To tell the truth, I wouldn't marry George if I were you. If you married him, . . .

Page 83 Exercise I

Listen and complete the conversations.

1. A. Do you think the weather in London is sunny and warm at this time of year?
   B. No, I don't. But I wish . . .
2. A. Are you unhappy when I talk too much?
   B. Yes, I am. I wish . . .
3. A. Does your daughter enjoy her English class?
   B. Yes, she does. But she wishes . . .
4. A. Do you think Michael daydreams too much in class?
   B. Yes, I do. I wish . . .
5. A. Do you like scary movies?
   B. Yes. As a matter of fact, I usually wish . . .

6. A. Are you annoyed when I sing loudly in the shower?
   B. The truth is, I wish . . .
7. A. Do you like your cell phone?
   B. Yes, I do. But I wish . . .
8. A. Are you tired of getting stuck in traffic?
   B. Of course, I am. I wish . . .
9. A. Do you like being single?
   B. It's okay. But the truth is, I wish . . .
10. A. Are you enjoying living in your new apartment?
    B. It's fine, but it's a little too small. I wish . . .
11. A. Is Harry upset about being laid off?
    B. He certainly is. He wishes . . .
12. A. Are you worried when I don't call you?
    B. Yes, I am. I wish . . .

Page 86 Exercise N

Listen and decide what the person is talking about.

1. If your pronunciation were better, I'd be able to understand you.
2. If I planted them now, I could eat them in three months.
3. If I took driver's ed, I could get it soon.
4. If I skipped it, my mother would be angry.
5. If I saved enough, I'd probably be able to visit you.
6. If I didn't concentrate, I could make a mistake.

Page 93 Exercise E

Listen and choose the statement that is true based on what you hear.

1. If she had spoken more confidently at her job interview, she would have gotten the job.
2. If he hadn't been late for work every day, he wouldn't have gotten fired.
3. If it had rained, we would have had to cancel the picnic.
4. If you hadn't been in a hurry, you wouldn't have made so many careless mistakes on your homework.
5. If I had remembered their phone number, I would have called them.
6. If the play hadn't been so boring, the audience wouldn't have fallen asleep.
7. If we had been in the mood to go swimming, we would have gone to the beach with you.
8. If he hadn't been speeding, he wouldn't have gotten a ticket.
9. If I had written legibly, they would have been able to read my letter.
10. If I hadn't forgotten about the meeting, I definitely would have been there.

Page 102 Exercise R

Listen and complete the sentences.

1. I wish I didn't have an exam tomorrow. If I didn't have an exam, . . .
2. I hope we're having spaghetti for dinner tonight. If we're having spaghetti for dinner, . . .
3. I wish my brother weren't in a bad mood all the time. If he weren't in a bad mood all the time, . . .
4. I wish my daughter had taken her umbrella to school. If she had taken her umbrella, . . .
5. I hope Jim is at the party Saturday night. If he's at the party, . . .
6. I wish I lived near a bus stop. If I lived near a bus stop, . . .

Page 102 Exercise S: Hopes and Wishes

Listen and complete the sentences.

1. My son isn't feeling very well. I wish . . .
2. I was confused about yesterday's English lesson. I hope . . .
3. My best friend just moved away. I wish . . .
4. Alice hates working at Paul's Pizza Shop. She hopes . . .
5. I sometimes feel lonely. I wish . . .
6. I'll try not to step on your feet. I wish . . .
7. The school play is this weekend. We hope . . .
8. My daughter lost her notebook. I wish . . .
9. I'm making chocolate chip cookies for dessert. I hope . . .
10. This cactus looks terrible. I wish . . .
11. Our fax machine is broken. I hope . . .
12. Vicky's used car has been giving her a lot of trouble. She wishes . . .
13. I don't have any eggs. I hope . . .
14. I sometimes forget people's names. I wish . . .

Page 103 Exercise U: *Have You Heard?*

Listen and complete the sentences.

1. This morning I met . . .
2. They fell . . .
3. A tailor . . .
4. There isn't enough pepper . . .
5. Are you afraid . . .
6. Have they made . . .
7. The men . . .
8. We're going to shake . . .
9. My daughter's wedding . . .
10. Nancy's neighbor . . .
11. Barbara paid . . .
12. I'll check . . .
13. I don't want to go to school because I fail . . .
14. We have to hurry because Tom's waiting . . .
15. Roger's never . . .
16. I'm Fred . . .

Page 108 Exercise E

What did they say? Listen and choose the correct answer.

1. I have some good news. I can fix your car next week.
2. My daughter is going to have a baby in July.
3. I have an important announcement. Tomorrow's meeting has been canceled.
4. My wife was just promoted to manager of her department.
5. I don't believe it! The bus drivers are going on strike!
6. I love Melanie, and she loves me!
7. You won't believe it! The monkeys have escaped from the zoo!
8. I'm nervous about my interview tomorrow.
9. My parents sold their house and moved into a condominium.
10. I'm going to do something I've always want to do. I'm going to quit my job and move to Hollywood!

Page 110 Exercise H

Listen and choose the correct answer.

1. Patty, did you break up with Gary?
2. How long have you been sitting here?
3. Were you reading when they called?
4. When are you going to repaint it?
5. Are you still mad?
6. When are you going to study math?
7. Are they too small?
8. Who fixed the kitchen floor?

Page 123 Exercise D

Listen and complete the sentences.

Ex: I wish I didn't have to study tonight. If I didn't have to study tonight, . . .

1. I wish I hadn't been sick last weekend. If I hadn't been sick, . . .
2. I wish I were an optimist. If I were an optimist, . . .
3. The landlord called this morning. He said . . .

(continued)

4. You won't believe what my girlfriend asked me! She asked me . . .
5. You won't believe what one of my students asked me! He asked me . . .

Page 129 Exercise G

Listen and complete the sentences.

1. You live at the corner of Broadway and Main, . . .
2. You aren't thinking of quitting, . . .
3. We don't need any more onions, . . .
4. You returned your library books, . . .
5. Nancy doesn't go out with Peter any more, . . .
6. You've done your assignment, . . .
7. Your sister was invited to the wedding, . . .
8. He's been a good employee, . . .
9. We won't we leaving soon, . . .
10. My brother and I can swim at this beach, . . .
11. This isn't your parking space, . . .
12. I didn't forget to call my mother last weekend, . . .

Page 132 Exercise L

Listen and complete the conversations.

1. A. Ruth is going to be a doctor, isn't she?
   B. Actually, she isn't.
   A. She isn't?! That's surprising! I was sure . . .
2. A. You sold your house, didn't you?
   B. Actually, I didn't.
   A. You didn't?! I'm surprised. I was sure . . .
3. A. This car has new brakes, doesn't it?
   B. No, it doesn't.
   A. It doesn't?! I was sure . . .
4. A. You aren't angry with me, are you?
   B. Actually, I am.
   A. You are?! I'm disappointed. I was sure . . .
5. A. Your cousins from Chicago will be arriving this weekend, won't they?
   B. Actually, they won't be arriving until next month.
   A. Oh. I was sure . . .
6. A. You didn't get searched at the airport, did you?
   B. Actually, I did.
   A. You did?! I'm surprised. I was sure . . .
7. A. Children aren't allowed to see this movie, are they?
   B. Actually, they are.
   A. They are?! That's very surprising! I was sure . . .
8. A. Albert still works at the bank, doesn't he?
   B. Actually, he doesn't.
   A. He doesn't?! I didn't know that. I was sure . . .
9. A. Cynthia was hired by the Bay Company, wasn't she?
   B. Actually, she wasn't.
   A. She wasn't?! That's too bad. I was sure . . .
10. A. Dr. Miller can deliver babies, can't he?
    B. Actually, he can't. He's a dentist.
    A. Oh. I didn't know that. I was sure . . .

Page 145 Exercise J

Listen and complete the sentences.

1. My fax machine has been broken since . . .
2. My son has had chicken pox for . . .
3. Our elevator has been out of order since . . .
4. My passport has been missing since . . .
5. We've been having trouble communicating for . . .
6. He's refused to fix our shower for . . .
7. We've wanted to sell our house since . . .
8. I've been having problems with my VCR for . . .
9. My wisdom teeth have hurt since . . .

Page 150 Exercise P

Read the questions. Listen to each passage. Then answer the questions.

Jeff's Problem

When I was unhappy with my job last month, my friend told me not to complain to him. He said I should tell my boss how I felt. So I decided to take my friend's advice. I made an appointment with my boss and told her why I didn't like my job. My boss listened quietly for a while, and then she told me why she wasn't satisfied with my work. She said I worked much too slowly, I made too many mistakes, and I complained too much. She told me she thought we'd both be happier if I worked someplace else. I'm very sorry I listened to my friend's advice. If I hadn't listened to his advice, I wouldn't have been fired and I wouldn't be out of work right now.

Amy and Tom

I started going out with Tom when I was a teenager. We fell in love with each other when we were in high school. When I was 25 years old, Tom asked me to marry him, and I accepted. My parents urged me not to marry Tom. They told me if I married Tom, I'd always regret it. They said he didn't work hard enough, he wasn't serious enough, and he would never be successful. Well, I'm glad I didn't follow my parents' advice, and so are they. Tom and I have been married for 20 years, and we've been very happy. Tom has a good job, and he's a wonderful husband and father. Our sons are teenagers now, and my parents are a little concerned about them because they aren't serious enough. But I'm not worried about my sons at all. They're just like their father used to be.

Page 151 Exercise S: *Have You Heard?*

Listen and complete the sentences.

1. When are you going to wash . . .
2. You're right.
3. Someday . . .
4. My answer is long.
5. That's light.
6. It's time to watch . . .
7. Have you hurt . . .
8. I hate chopping . . .
9. My brother's voice . . .
10. I've heard . . .
11. Why haven't you written . . .
12. Alexander brushes . . .

Page 153 Exercise E

Listen and complete the sentences.

Ex. I'm sorry I drove past your house. I must have had my mind on something else. If I hadn't had my mind on something else, . . .

1. If I hadn't taken a walk yesterday, . . .
2. I can't believe I deleted all my files. I must have hit the wrong key. If I hadn't hit the wrong key, . . .
3. I'm sure you'd get tired of going dancing . . .
4. If I had known your relatives were visiting, . . .
5. If I weren't on my way to a concert, . . .

ACTIVITY WORKBOOK 4 ANSWER KEY: Pages 2–153c

UNIT 1

WORKBOOK PAGE 2

A. For Many Years

1. swims
   He's swum
2. takes
   She's taken
3. drives
   He's driven
4. speak
   I've spoken
5. sing
   We've sung
6. writes
   He's written
7. rides
   She's ridden
8. draws
   He's drawn
9. flies
   She's flown
10. grows
    He's grown

WORKBOOK PAGE 3

B. A Little While Ago

1. Have, gone
   they have, They went
2. Has, taken
   she has, She took
3. Have, done
   I have, I did
4. Have, eaten
   we have, We ate
5. Has, given
   he has, He gave
6. Has, written
   she has, She wrote
7. Have, fed
   I have, I fed
8. Has, seen
   he has, He saw

C. Listening

1. a
2. b
3. a
4. b
5. b
6. a
7. b
8. a
9. b

WORKBOOK PAGE 4

D. In a Long Time

1. Have, taken
   we haven't, We haven't taken
2. Has, written
   she hasn't, She hasn't written
3. Has, gotten
   he hasn't, He hasn't gotten
4. Have, gone
   I haven't, I haven't gone
5. Have, swum
   they haven't, They haven't swum
6. Has, been
   it hasn't, It hasn't been
7. Have, seen
   we haven't, We haven't seen
8. Has, ridden
   she hasn't, She hasn't ridden
9. Have, eaten
   I haven't, I haven't eaten
10. Has, done
    he hasn't, He hasn't done
11. Have, given
    you haven't, You haven't given

WORKBOOK PAGE 6

F. What Are They Saying?

1. has, known
   He's known, for
2. has, had
   She's had, since
3. have, played
   I've played, for
4. have, owned
   They've owned, for
5. has, liked
   He's liked, since
6. has, wanted
   She's wanted, since
7. have, worked
   We've worked, for
8. have, been
   We've been, for

G. Listening

1. a
2. b
3. a
4. b
5. b
6. a
7. a
8. b
9. b

WORKBOOK PAGE 7

H. What's the Question?

1. How long have, had a toothache
2. How long has, wanted to be a teacher
3. How long has, been in the hospital
4. How long have, known how to swim
5. How long have, owned your own home

WORKBOOK PAGE 8

J. How Long?

1. He's been waiting for a taxi for
2. She's been practicing the piano since
3. I've been feeling sick for
4. You've been talking for
5. They've been going out since
6. It's been making strange noises for
7. I've been doing sit-ups for
8. He's been snoring since

K. Listening

1. b
2. b
3. a
4. b
5. a
6. b

WORKBOOK PAGES 9–10

L. What Are They Saying?

1. has she been crying
   She's been crying
2. has it been leaking
   It's been leaking

(continued)

3. has he been fighting
He's been fighting
4. has it been making
It's been making
5. has it been raining
It's been raining
6. have they been barking
They've been barking

WORKBOOK PAGE 11

M. What Are They Saying?

1. I've been giving
I've given
2. I've been baking
I've, baked
3. We've been selling
We've, sold
4. They've been building
They've, built
5. I've been taking
I've, taken
6. She's been seeing
she's seen
7. You've been writing
You've, written
8. I've been making
I've, made
9. You've been doing
You've, done

WORKBOOK PAGE 12

N. They've Been Working Very Hard

1. has been washing, He's, washed
2. He's, been vacuuming, He's, vacuumed
3. has been hanging up, She's, hung up
4. She's, been making, She's, made
5. has been planting, He's, planted
6. He's, been throwing out, He's, thrown out
7. has been baking, She's, baked
8. She's, been writing, She's, written
9. has been singing, They've, sung
10. They've been looking, looked

WORKBOOK PAGE 13

O. They Had Done That Before

1. had put
had eaten
2. had snored
3. had been
4. had gone
5. had left
6. had, assembled
7. had had
8. had given
9. had seen
10. had spent
11. had worn
12. had taken
13. had made

WORKBOOK PAGE 14

P. By the Time

1. got, had, closed
2. did, had, gone
3. arrived, had, gotten
4. drove, had, sailed
5. brought, had, borrowed
6. called, had, taken
7. saw, had been
8. found, had, begun
9. dropped, had, left
10. stopped, had fallen

WORKBOOK PAGE 15

Q. What Had They Been Doing?

1. had been planning
2. had been going out
3. had been training
4. had been living
5. had been rehearsing
6. had been preparing
7. had been having
8. had been working
9. had been coming,
had been falling
10. had been looking
11. had been practicing

WORKBOOK PAGE 17

T. What Are They Saying?

A. My brother Theodore doesn't think he can go to the theater with us tomorrow because he has a sore throat.

B. Another sore throat? That's terrible! Didn't he just get over one last Thursday?

A. That's right. Believe it or not, this is the third sore throat he's had this month. My poor brother always gets sick when the weather is very cold.

B. I hope it isn't serious this time.

A. I don't think so. Theodore says his sore throat isn't bothering him too much, but both my mother and father say he'll have to rest in bed for at least a few days. They're worried because he isn't eating anything, and they don't think he looks very healthy.

B. Then I guess he won't be going to the Sunday concert either.

A. Probably not. And he's very disappointed. He really loves classical music.

B. Well, I'm sorry our plans fell through. Please tell Theodore I hope he feels better soon. Oh, I almost forgot. My little sister Martha is having a small birthday celebration today at three thirty. Would you like to come?

A. Yes, of course. Thank you very much.

WORKBOOK PAGE 18

A. What Should They Have Done?

1. should have gotten
2. should have taken
3. should have studied
4. should have had
5. should have gone
6. should have seen
7. should have spoken
8. should have sat
9. should have kept
10. should have bought

WORKBOOK PAGE 19

B. Good Advice

1. b
2. b
3. a
4. a
5. b
6. b

WORKBOOK PAGE 21

D. What Might Have Happened?

1. might have missed
2. may have eaten
3. may have broken
4. might have gone
5. may have been
6. might have forgotten
7. might have lost

E. What's the Answer?

1. a
2. b
3. a
4. a
5. b
6. a

WORKBOOK PAGE 22

F. I Don't Understand It!

1. could have watched
2. could have worn
3. could have married
4. could have ridden
5. could have become
6. could have skated
7. could have taken
8. could have been
9. could have made
10. could have named
11. could have painted
12. could have eaten
13. could have gone
14. could have written

WORKBOOK PAGE 24

H. What Happened?

1. must have gotten up
2. must have eaten
3. must have met
4. must have left
5. must have spoken
6. must have been
7. must have broken up
8. must have bought
9. must have had
10. must have cost
11. must have done

WORKBOOK PAGE 29

L. What's the Word?

1. should have
2. must have
3. couldn't have
4. might have, might have
5. could have
6. must have
7. couldn't have
8. should have
9. might have
10. shouldn't have, could have
11. must have

M. Listening

1. a
2. b
3. b
4. a
5. b
6. a
7. b
8. a

WORKBOOK PAGE 30

N. What Does It Mean?

1. a
2. c
3. c
4. b
5. c
6. b
7. b
8. a
9. a
10. c
11. c
12. a
13. b
14. a
15. c
16. b

WORKBOOK PAGE 31

P. Have You Heard?

1. a
2. b
3. a
4. b
5. a
6. b
7. a
8. b
9. b
10. a
11. b
12. a
13. a
14. b
15. b
16. a

UNIT 3

WORKBOOK PAGE 32

A. Who Did It?

1. was painted
2. were built
3. was served
4. was composed
5. was discovered
6. was written
7. was worn
8. was directed
9. was taken
10. was baked

WORKBOOK PAGES 33–34

B. You Decide: *At the Museum*

1. was owned
   ....
   was made
   ....
   ....
2. was flown
   ....
   ....
   was designed
   ....
3. was worn
   ....
   was given
   ....
   was left
4. were found
   ....
   ....
   were forgotten
5. was written
   ....
   ....
   was, sent
   was discovered
6. was built
   ....
   was begun
   wasn't finished
7. ....
   was composed
   ....
   was sung
   ....

WORKBOOK PAGE 35

D. It's Too Late

1. they've, been done
2. it's, been set
3. they've, been ironed
4. it's, been made
5. They've, been taken down
6. it's, been swept
7. they've, been bought
8. It's, been hung up

E. Listening

1. a
2. b
3. b
4. a
5. a
6. b
7. a
8. b
9. a

WORKBOOK PAGE 36

F. Nothing Is Ready!

1. haven't been made
2. hasn't been swept
3. hasn't been prepared
4. hasn't been fed
5. haven't been put

G. At the Hospital

1. Has
2. been taken
3. has
4. been given
5. Has
6. been done
7. was done
8. Has
9. been told
10. He's
11. been sent

WORKBOOK PAGE 37

H. Can We Leave Soon?

1. has been stopped
2. have been turned off
3. Has
4. been set
5. has
6. been taken out

I. Crossword

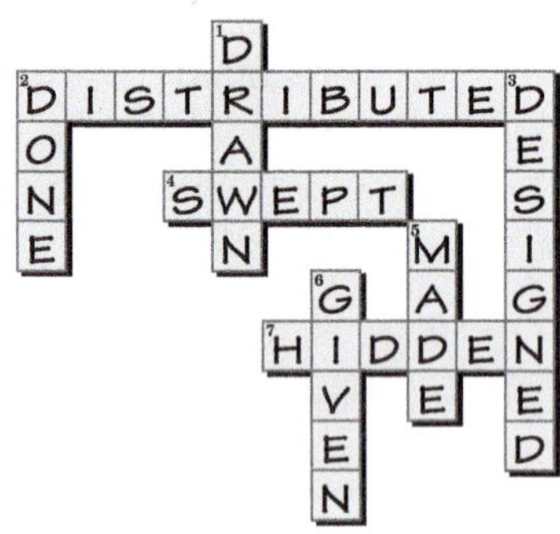

WORKBOOK PAGE 38

J. Ernest Hemingway

1. a
2. c
3. b
4. a
5. b
6. c

WORKBOOK PAGE 39

K. A Robbery

1. were
2. robbed
3. was
4. stolen
5. was
6. left
7. wasn't
8. taken
9. given
10. was
11. seen
12. was
13. arrested
14. was
15. sent
16. were
17. returned
18. been
19. ripped

L. Listening

1. a
2. b
3. b
4. a
5. a
6. b
7. b
8. a
9. a
10. a
11. b
12. b

WORKBOOK PAGE 40

M. You Decide: *A Famous Composer*

1. ....
2. have
3. been
4. performed
5. ....
6. heard
7. ....
8. ....
9. was
10. given
11. ....
12. were
13. rejected
14. ....
15. were
16. recorded
17. ....
18. ....
19. was
20. appreciated
21. was
22. considered
23. was
24. understood
25. ....
26. respected
27. ....
28. was
29. used
30. have
31. been
32. played
33. ....
34. was
35. hurt
36. ....
37. was
38. chosen
39. was
40. invited

WORKBOOK PAGE 41

N. What Are They Saying?

1. It's being rewritten
2. It's, being repaired
3. It's, being baked
4. They're, being taken in
5. she's being promoted
6. It's, being set up
7. It's being washed
8. is being clipped

WORKBOOK PAGE 42

P. A Factory Tour

1. is
2. made
3. is
4. taken
5. is
6. put
7. is
8. mixed
9. is
10. poured
11. are
12. prepared
13. are
14. being
15. chopped
16. are
17. being
18. sliced
19. are
20. added
21. was
22. invented
23. is
24. kept
25. is
26. sent
27. be
28. enjoyed

WORKBOOK PAGE 43

Q. What Does It Mean?

1. a
2. c
3. a
4. b
5. b
6. a
7. c
8. b
9. a
10. c
11. c
12. b
13. c
14. b

R. Listening

1. a
2. b
3. b
4. a
5. b
6. a
7. b
8. a

WORKBOOK PAGES 44–45

CHECK-UP TEST: Units 1–3

A.

1. I've spoken
2. has ridden
3. haven't taken
4. haven't eaten
5. haven't written, wrote
6. have, been
7. has been
8. had seen
9. had, taken
10. had been going

B.

1. must have practiced
2. should have done
3. might have left, might have left
4. could have built
5. must have studied
6. shouldn't have worn
7. should have fed
8. could have fallen
9. might have spent, might have spent

C.

1. was drawn
2. It's, being repaired
3. has been given
4. be taught
5. They've, been done
6. They're, being taken in
7. was chosen
8. be made
9. hasn't been sent

D.

1. b
2. a
3. b
4. b
5. a

GAZETTE

WORKBOOK PAGES 45a–d

A. Inventions That Changed the World

1. c
2. b
3. d
4. a
5. b
6. d
7. a
8. c

B. Fact File

1. c
2. a
3. d
4. b

C. Around the World

1. b
2. c
3. d
4. b
5. d
6. c
7. b
8. c
9. a
10. d
11. a
12. b

E. Interview

1. d
2. c
3. b
4. d
5. c
6. a

G. Fun with Idioms

1. b
2. a
3. c
4. d

H. We've Got Mail!

1. c
2. a
3. b
4. d
5. c
6. d
7. d
8. c
9. a
10. b
11. d
12. c

I. "Can-Do" Review

1. e
2. h
3. a
4. j
5. b
6. d
7. i
8. f
9. c
10. g

UNIT 4

WORKBOOK PAGE 46

A. They Didn't Say

1. where they're living now
2. where Janet is working
3. how their children are
4. when he'll be starting his new job
5. when they're going to come to New York
6. when their new house will be finished
7. what they've been doing
8. why they haven't e-mailed us
9. what their telephone number is

WORKBOOK PAGE 47

B. I'm Not the Person to Ask

1. what this painting means
2. why Robert always gets to school so early
3. when the ice cream truck came by
4. where Margaret works
5. how Sam broke his arm
6. why Alice rewrote her novel
7. when the concert begins
8. when the bank opens tomorrow
9. what we did in French class yesterday
10. where Mom and Dad went
11. how much a quart of milk costs

WORKBOOK PAGE 48

C. Too Many Questions!

1. when I learned to drive
2. why Grandma doesn't drive
3. why the sky is blue
4. how birds learn to fly
5. why clouds are white
6. what time the zoo opens tomorrow
7. where that mouse is now
8. ....
9. ....
10. ....
11. ....

WORKBOOK PAGE 49

D. What Are They Saying?

1. a	5. b	9. a
2. b	6. a	10. b
3. b	7. b	
4. a	8. b	

E. Listening

1. a	4. b	7. a
2. a	5. a	8. b
3. b	6. b	

WORKBOOK PAGES 50–51

G. You Decide: *What Are They Saying?*

1. how much this bicycle costs
   ....
2. where the nearest clinic is
   ....
3. whose cell phone this is
   ....
4. why you've been late to work all week
   ....
5. when my dog will be ready
   ....
6. how long we've been driving
   ....
7. why Johnny is sitting in a puddle
   ....
8. when the post office opens
   ....
9. what's in the "Chicken Surprise Casserole"
   ....
10. when you'll be getting out of here
   ....

WORKBOOK PAGE 53

I. What Are They Saying?

1. a	5. a	9. a
2. b	6. a	10. a
3. a	7. a	
4. b	8. b	

J. Listening

1. a	4. a	7. b
2. a	5. a	8. b
3. b	6. b	9. a

WORKBOOK PAGE 54

L. Renting an Apartment

1. if it's been rented yet
2. if there's an elevator in the building
3. if the kitchen has a microwave
4. if pets are allowed
5. if there's a bus stop nearby
6. if the landlord lives in the building
7. if the apartment has an Internet connection
8. ....
9. if I can see the apartment today.

WORKBOOK PAGES 55–56

M. You Decide: *The College Visit*

1. how many students go to your school
2. if I have to take any special examinations
3. how I get an application form
4. if the classes are difficult
5. if the dormitories are noisy
6. what kind of food you serve in the cafeteria
7. what students do on weekends
8. how much your school costs
9. ....
10. ....

UNIT 5

WORKBOOK PAGE 57

A. If

1. b	5. a	9. a
2. a	6. a	10. b
3. b	7. b	
4. b	8. b	

B. Scrambled Sentences

1. If Barbara has a lot to do, she'll work late at the office tonight.
2. If Tom feels energetic, he'll clean his attic this weekend.
3. If I decide to forget about my diet, I'll have cake for dessert.
4. If the weather isn't nice tomorrow, I'll stay home and fill out my income tax forms.
5. If I still have a cold tomorrow, I'll go to the clinic and see Dr. Lopez.

WORKBOOK PAGE 58

D. Listening

1. b	6. b	11. a
2. a	7. a	12. b
3. a	8. a	13. a
4. b	9. b	14. a
5. b	10. b	

WORKBOOK PAGES 60–61

F. They Might

1. a	4. a	7. a
2. b	5. b	8. b
3. a	6. b	

G. You Decide: *What Might Happen?*

1. you drink, . . .
2. you put, . . .
3. we send, . . .
4. you skip, . . .
5. you practice, . . .
6. you stay, . . .
7. you go hiking, . . .
8. you get married, . . .

WORKBOOK PAGE 63

I. What's the Polite Answer?

1. b	4. b	7. b
2. b	5. b	
3. a	6. a	

J. Listening

1. a	5. a	9. a
2. b	6. b	10. b
3. b	7. b	11. a
4. b	8. a	12. b

WORKBOOK PAGE 64

K. Hopes

1. it rains
   we have to cancel
   it doesn't rain
2. it's cold
   doesn't start
   it isn't cold
3. it's
   is
   it isn't
4. is
   we don't have
   it isn't

WORKBOOK PAGE 65

L. The Exam

1. you
   I'll
2. it's
   I do
   will be
3. isn't
   is
   she'll
4. I
   I
   I'll
   I'm
   I'll

WORKBOOK PAGE 66

M. What If?

1. b	5. b	9. a
2. a	6. a	10. a
3. b	7. b	11. a
4. a	8. b	12. b

N. Listening

1. b	4. a	7. a
2. a	5. b	8. a
3. b	6. b	

WORKBOOK PAGE 69

Q. Matching

1. d	5. h	9. f
2. j	6. e	10. c
3. g	7. b	11. i
4. a	8. k	

WORKBOOK PAGES 71–72

S. If

1. she didn't want to get
   wouldn't work overtime
2. he weren't afraid
   wouldn't be hiding
3. she didn't want to win
   wouldn't run
4. he didn't love
   wouldn't wear
5. she weren't careless
   wouldn't make
6. he didn't want to lose
   wouldn't go
7. he didn't have
   wouldn't be
8. there weren't
   wouldn't be driving

WORKBOOK PAGES 74–75

X. Norman's Broken Keyboard

1.

Dear Amy,

I really enjoyed visiting you in your new apartment. It's one of the nicest apartments I've ever seen. I liked everything about it: the modern kitchen and bathroom, the elegant living room and dining room, and the sunny bedrooms. I can't believe there's even a garden with lemon and orange trees in front of the building. I think you'll be very happy in your new neighborhood. It's certainly very convenient to be so near a supermarket, a movie theater, and a train station.

I'm looking forward to seeing you again and meeting your new neighbors.

Sincerely,
Norman

2.

To Whom It May Concern:

I am writing to recommend Max Miller for the job of computer programmer at the ABC Computer Company. During the nine years I've known him, he's been an excellent employee and a kind and honest friend. He's never missed a day's work at our company, and he's always been on time. But most important, Max Miller really understands what makes a good computer programmer.

Sincerely,
Norman Brown
Manager
XYZ Computer Company

3.

Dear Brian,

I just finished reading your most recent poems, and in my opinion, they're amazing. The poem about the environment is very original, but my favorite ones are "Missing My Mother" and "Under My Umbrella."

According to my wife and friends, you're becoming famous in many foreign countries, and your poems are being translated into Russian, Chinese, German, Spanish, and Japanese. I think that's fantastic!

Have you begun writing your new novel yet? I wonder when we'll be hearing more about it.

Norman

4.

Dear Michael,

Remember when you explained to me how to make your mother's famous chicken and mushroom casserole? Well, I made some for dinner last night, and I'm afraid something must have gone wrong. I might have burnt the chicken, or maybe I didn't put in enough onions and mushrooms. I don't know what happened, but I know I must have made some mistakes because nobody enjoyed it very much. Tom and Nancy didn't complain, but they said yours was much more delicious.

Do you think you could send your mother's recipe to me by e-mail so I can try it again? When you explained it to me, I should have written it down.

Norman

WORKBOOK PAGES 76–77

CHECK-UP TEST: Units 4–5

A.

1. when the next train will be leaving
2. if/whether Michael was at work yesterday
3. how much this suit costs
4. if/whether there's a laundromat nearby
5. why David got up so early
6. if/whether Martha took her medicine this morning
7. how long we've been waiting

B.

1. have
2. he'd be
3. she wouldn't go
4. don't get
5. you won't
6. it doesn't
7. wins
8. will be
9. fed

C.

1. didn't work, she wouldn't be
2. studied, he'd get
3. had, they'd get along
4. weren't, she wouldn't make

D.

1. b
2. a
3. b
4. a
5. b

GAZETTE

WORKBOOK PAGES 77a–d

A. The Music of Wishes and Hopes

1. c
2. a
3. b
4. d
5. a
6. c
7. d
8. b

B. Music Lyrics and Metaphors

1. d
2. c
3. c
4. b

C. Fact File

1. c
2. b

D. Around the World

1. b
2. d
3. c
4. b
5. d
6. c
7. d
8. a
9. c
10. d

E. Interview

1. d
2. a
3. b
4. b
5. a
6. c

G. Fun With Idioms

1. b
2. a
3. d
4. c

H. We've Got Mail!

1. b
2. d
3. c
4. a
5. b
6. c
7. b
8. c
9. d
10. a
11. c
12. d

I. "Can-Do" Review

1. c
2. i
3. g
4. a
5. h
6. d
7. e
8. j
9. f
10. b

UNIT 6

WORKBOOK PAGE 78

A. What's the Word?

1. b
2. a
3. b
4. b
5. a
6. a
7. b
8. a
9. a
10. b

B. If

1. were
2. went out
3. got lost
4. had
5. ate
6. lost
7. quit
8. sold

WORKBOOK PAGE 79

C. You Decide: *If*

1. ....
   she would, She'd be
2. ....
   he would, He'd be
3. ....
   he/she would, He'd/She'd be
4. ....
   they would, They'd be
5. ....
   he/she would, He'd/She'd be
6. ....
   she would, She'd be

WORKBOOK PAGE 80

D. What's the Word?

1. b
2. a
3. b
4. b
5. a
6. b
7. a
8. b
9. b
10. a
11. b
12. b

E. Listening

1. b
2. a
3. b
4. a
5. b
6. b
7. a
8. b
9. a
10. b
11. b
12. a

WORKBOOK PAGES 81–82

F. Personal Opinions

1. went, you'd, fall
2. I'd, He'd, tune it up
3. went, you'd, have
4. you painted, it would
5. wouldn't drive, you drove, you'd
6. wouldn't have, you had, would be
7. wouldn't see, you saw, you'd
8. were, you bought, it would
9. ....

WORKBOOK PAGE 83

H. What Do They Wish?

1. b
2. a
3. a
4. b
5. a
6. a
7. b
8. b
9. a
10. b

I. Listening

1. b
2. b
3. a
4. b
5. b
6. a
7. b
8. a
9. b
10. a
11. b
12. a

WORKBOOK PAGE 84

J. I Wish

1. I wish I felt
2. I wish, were 5:00
3. I wish I sang
4. I wish I taught
5. I wish, gave
6. I wish I had a dog.

WORKBOOK PAGE 85

L. Looking for a Job

1. I could
2. you could
3. you'd be
4. you could repair DVD players
5. would be
6. I could/I were able to
7. ....
8. ....
9. ....
10. you could ....
11. would be
12. could/were able to
13. you could/you were able to be
14. you wouldn't have
15. ....
16. ....
17. I'd
18. ....
19. I could/I were able to

WORKBOOK PAGE 86

M. Choose

1. a	5. a	9. a
2. b	6. c	10. c
3. c	7. a	
4. b	8. b	

N. Listening

1. a	3. a	5. b
2. b	4. b	6. a

WORKBOOK PAGE 88

Q. What Does It Mean?

1. a	7. c	13. c
2. b	8. b	14. b
3. c	9. b	15. a
4. b	10. a	16. c
5. c	11. b	
6. a	12. a	

WORKBOOK PAGE 89

R. Sound It Out!

1. gets
2. take
3. Ted
4. paid
5. vacation
6. Spain
7. when
8. friend
9. When my friend Ted gets paid, he'll take a vacation in Spain.

10. play
11. eight
12. tennis
13. let's
14. next
15. Wednesday
16. Fred
17. Let's play tennis with Fred next Wednesday at eight o'clock.

UNIT 7

WORKBOOK PAGES 90–91

A. What's the Answer?

1. a	5. a	9. a
2. a	6. b	10. a
3. b	7. a	
4. b	8. b	

B. Complete the Sentences

1. had been approved, would have been able
2. had rung, would have arrived
3. had won, would have been
4. had known, would have gotten
5. had practiced, would have learned
6. had taken, would have been
7. had noticed, would have stopped
8. had bought, would have had

WORKBOOK PAGE 93

D. What's the Answer?

1. a	5. a	9. b
2. b	6. b	10. b
3. a	7. b	
4. b	8. a	

E. Listening

1. b	5. a	9. a
2. a	6. b	10. b
3. b	7. a	
4. b	8. b	

WORKBOOK PAGE 94

F. How I Became a Basketball Player

1. hadn't taken me
2. hadn't bought me
3. hadn't sent me
4. hadn't played
5. hadn't gone
6. wouldn't have become

G. I'm Really Glad

1. I hadn't gone
2. wouldn't have
3. hadn't learned
4. wouldn't have gotten
5. hadn't gotten
6. wouldn't have been
7. hadn't been
8. wouldn't have
9. hadn't met
10. wouldn't have been

WORKBOOK PAGE 95

H. Why Didn't You Tell Me?

1. you had told
2. wouldn't have gone
3. hadn't gone
4. would have been
5. I had been
6. would have been
7. had been
8. would have
9. had fixed
10. had told
11. made/prepared
12. had made/ had prepared
13. there had been
14. wouldn't have gone
15. hadn't gone
16. wouldn't have gotten
17. hadn't gotten
18. wouldn't have
19. hadn't had
20. would have been
21. have done
22. had done
23. wouldn't have been

WORKBOOK PAGE 97

K. What's the Answer?

1. b
2. a
3. b
4. a
5. a
6. b
7. b
8. a

L. Complete the Sentences

1. I had taken
2. she had studied
3. he worked
4. I had had
5. I knew
6. I had seen
7. we didn't have to

WORKBOOK PAGE 98

M. Patty's Party

1. hadn't gone, had done
2. hadn't been, would have been
3. hadn't sung, played, hadn't sung, played, wouldn't have had
4. didn't, had remembered/hadn't forgotten, had, wouldn't have
5. had known, had known, wouldn't have been, wouldn't have felt

WORKBOOK PAGE 100

O. Hopes and Wishes

1. could tell, can tell
2. worked, get
3. had sung, sings
4. had studied, spoke
5. didn't, have, were
6. weren't, lose

WORKBOOK PAGE 101

Q. Wish or Hope?

1. wish
2. wishes
3. hope
4. wishes
5. hopes
6. wish
7. hope
8. wishes
9. wishes

WORKBOOK PAGE 102

R. Listening

1. a
2. a
3. b
4. a
5. b
6. b

S. Listening: *Hopes and Wishes*

1. b
2. a
3. b
4. b
5. a
6. b
7. a
8. a
9. b
10. a
11. b
12. a
13. b
14. a

WORKBOOK PAGE 103

U. Have You Heard?

1. b
2. a
3. b
4. b
5. a
6. a
7. b
8. a
9. b
10. a
11. a
12. b
13. a
14. a
15. b
16. b

UNIT 8

WORKBOOK PAGE 104

A. What Did They Say?

1. he was having
2. they couldn't come
3. she would visit
4. he had forgotten
5. she was planning
6. he hadn't written
7. she was, she had
8. was, could pick
9. had seen, hadn't seen
10. she would be, she wouldn't
11. she had been working, needed

WORKBOOK PAGES 105–107

B. Messages

1. she had gotten an "A" on her biology test
2. he was home from the hospital and he was feeling much better
3. they had seen the Colosseum, but they hadn't gone to the Vatican yet
4. he hoped I could visit him when I came to Japan this summer
5. she was sorry, but I wasn't the right person for the job
6. he was very busy, and he couldn't repair our dishwasher this week
7. they loved Hawaii, and they were thinking of buying a condominium
8. he had been hoping to send me more money for college, but he wouldn't be able to because he was having financial problems
9. ....
10. ....
11. ....

WORKBOOK PAGE 108

D. What's the Answer?

1. b	**4.** a	**7.** a
2. a	**5.** b	**8.** a
3. b	**6.** b	

E. Listening

1. b	**5.** a	**9.** b
2. a	**6.** b	**10.** a
3. a	**7.** a	
4. b	**8.** a	

WORKBOOK PAGE 109

F. You Decide: *What Happened While Paula Wilson Was Away?*

1. he had gotten married	**7.** ....
2. she was in the hospital	**8.** ....
3. she had been	**9.** ....
4. had had	**10.** ....
5. had been	**11.** ....
6. was going to become	**12.** ....

WORKBOOK PAGE 110

G. You Won't Believe It!

1. b	**5.** a	**9.** b
2. a	**6.** a	**10.** a
3. a	**7.** b	
4. b	**8.** a	

H. Listening

1. b	**4.** b	**7.** c
2. c	**5.** c	**8.** a
3. c	**6.** b	

WORKBOOK PAGES 111–112

I. What Did They Ask?

1. if/whether he had delivered her letter to Santa Claus yet
2. how much time I had spent on my homework
3. if/whether she could have another piece of his delicious cake
4. why they always made so much noise
5. if/whether the operation would hurt
6. when the lecture was going to end
7. if he still loved her
8. why there were so many grammar rules in English
9. ....
10. ....

WORKBOOK PAGE 114

K. What Did They Tell You?

1. to speak confidently
2. not to drive too fast
3. to work quickly
4. not to eat too much candy
5. not to play loud music

L. What's the Answer?

1. a	**4.** a	**7.** a
2. a	**5.** b	**8.** a
3. b	**6.** b	

WORKBOOK PAGES 115–116

M. Everybody Always Tells Him What to Do

1. to hurry
my breakfast was getting cold
2. not to forget my umbrella
it was going to rain later
3. not to walk so slowly
we would be late for school
4. to be quiet
I was disturbing the class
5. ....
....
6. ....
....
7. ....
....
8. ....
....
9. ....
I would fail my math test if I didn't study
10. ....
I had to get up early for school

WORKBOOK PAGE 117

N. Today at School

1. to study, not to study
2. to write, not to forget
3. to read, not to use
4. to answer, not to answer
5. to practice, not to look
6. ....
....
7. ....
....
8. ....
....
9. was expected, would be

WORKBOOK PAGE 119

P. Choose the Right Word

1. escaped
2. casserole
3. anxious
4. lock
5. bride
6. flu
7. prevent
8. know
9. poodle
10. grease
11. reassured
12. taxes
13. advice
14. away
15. sale
16. break
17. falling
18. into
19. annoyed
20. qualified
21. dictionaries
22. whether
23. engaged, married

WORKBOOK PAGES 120–121

R. Who Is the Best?

Many pessimists don't trust dentists because they're scared the worst will happen. However, Dr. West's patients are all optimistic. They think Dr. West is the best dentist in Boston.

1. Stuart likes Dr. West.

   Not only is he honest, but he's the cheapest and the most reliable dentist in Boston.

2. Stuart's sister also thinks Dr. West is wonderful.

   Dr. West works very fast and never makes mistakes. He's the best dentist on State Street.

3. Mr. Jackson can't stand any other dentist.

   I go to Dr. West because I almost never feel any pain when I'm in his special dentist's chair. I could stay and rest there all day.

4. Betsy always talks about Dr. West.

   What I like most about Dr. West is that he doesn't ask a lot of questions when a patient's mouth is full of dental instruments.

5. Dr. West's Spanish-speaking patients are especially pleased.

   Dr. West studies Spanish in his spare time. We won't see any specialist but Dr. West.

6. Margaret is very enthusiastic about Dr. West.

   One day I got the hiccups in his office. Dr. West just stopped and stood there waiting patiently. He didn't make me feel stupid at all!

7. Patty thinks Dr. West is the hardest working dentist she knows.

   Dr. West never quits working all day. He even skips his lunch!

8. Steve also likes Dr. West.

   When I broke my leg playing basketball last spring, I missed two appointments. Dr. West wasn't upset at all. He even visited me in the hospital. We discussed politics and sports. That's when I discovered that Dr. West likes to ski and skate.

WORKBOOK PAGES 122–123

CHECK-UP TEST: Units 6–8

A.

1. he were
2. she had taken
3. he drove
4. she had gotten
5. I spoke
6. you hadn't eaten

B.

1. had been, would have enjoyed
2. didn't eat, wouldn't be
3. hadn't missed, she wouldn't have arrived
4. I could type, I wouldn't be
5. had been paying, wouldn't have made
6. understood, wouldn't look

C.

1. she had gotten
2. what my name was
3. if/whether I had seen her
4. she was sorry she had forgotten
5. he wouldn't be able to visit
6. to brush, not to eat
7. when he would be
8. why I was leaving, if/whether I was in a hurry

D.

1. a
2. b
3. a
4. b
5. a

GAZETTE

WORKBOOK PAGES 123a–d

A. Polish Up Your Interview Skills!

1. a	**4.** c	**7.** d
2. d	**5.** a	**8.** b
3. b	**6.** c	

B. Points in a Text

1. d	**3.** a	**5.** c
2. b	**4.** e	

C. Fact File

1. d	**2.** c

D. Who Got the Job?

1. c	**3.** d	**5.** c
2. a	**4.** b	**6.** d

E. Around the World

1. b	**3.** c
2. a	**4.** d

F. Interview

1. c	**3.** d	**5.** d
2. a	**4.** b	**6.** c

H. Fun with Idioms

1. d	**3.** a
2. b	**4.** c

I. We've Got Mail!

1. d	**5.** d	**9.** c
2. c	**6.** b	**10.** b
3. b	**7.** a	**11.** d
4. a	**8.** b	**12.** a

J. "Can-Do" Review

1. h	**5.** c	**9.** b
2. e	**6.** i	**10.** g
3. a	**7.** d	
4. j	**8.** f	

UNIT 9

WORKBOOK PAGE 124

A. What Are They Saying?

1. won't she	**6.** haven't we
2. can't I	**7.** won't he
3. don't you	**8.** weren't you
4. didn't you	**9.** isn't it
5. aren't I	**10.** aren't you

WORKBOOK PAGE 125

B. What's the Tag?

1. a	**4.** a	**7.** a
2. a	**5.** b	**8.** b
3. b	**6.** b	

C. I Think I Know You

1. aren't you	**6.** I did
2. I am	**7.** don't you
3. haven't you	**8.** I do
4. I have	**9.** isn't it
5. didn't you	**10.** isn't

WORKBOOK PAGE 126

D. What Are They Saying?

1. has it	**6.** will you
2. are you	**7.** have we
3. do you	**8.** does it
4. did I	**9.** was it
5. am I	**10.** is it

WORKBOOK PAGES 127–128

E. That's What I Thought

1. is it it isn't	**7.** did it it didn't
2. do I you don't	**8.** are they they aren't
3. have you I haven't	**9.** was it it wasn't
4. is there there isn't	**10.** can I you can't
5. has it it hasn't	**11.** are they they aren't
6. will I you won't	

F. What's the Tag?

1. a	**6.** b	**11.** a
2. b	**7.** a	**12.** b
3. a	**8.** b	**13.** a
4. b	**9.** b	**14.** b
5. b	**10.** a	

WORKBOOK PAGE 129

G. Listening

1. b	**5.** a	**9.** b
2. b	**6.** a	**10.** b
3. a	**7.** b	**11.** a
4. b	**8.** a	**12.** b

H. You Decide: ***A Good Father***

1. aren't I	**4.** aren't I
2. don't I	**5.–16.** ....
3. am I	**17.** aren't I

WORKBOOK PAGE 131

J. Surprises

1. have you
   I have
   You have
2. isn't she
   she isn't
   She isn't
3. will he
   he will
   He will
4. doesn't it
   it doesn't
   It doesn't
5. didn't you
   I didn't
   You didn't
6. does he
   he does
   He does

WORKBOOK PAGE 132

K. What Are They Saying?

1. weren't you
   you had been expecting
2. don't you
   you had
3. hasn't she
   she had been
4. is he
   he wasn't going to be
5. can't we
   we could leave
6. isn't it
   was
7. do I
   I didn't
8. won't you
   you would marry

L. Listening

1. b
2. a
3. a
4. b
5. a
6. b
7. b
8. a
9. a
10. b

WORKBOOK PAGES 133–134

M. High School Reunion

1. You did, didn't
   marry, did you
   I did
2. You do
   don't, have
   do you
   I do
3. You are, aren't
   are you
   I am
4. She was, wasn't
   chosen, was she
   she was
5. She did, didn't
   win, did she
   she did
6. ....
   He did, didn't
   did he
   he did
7. do you
   ....
   ....
   He can, can't
   can he
   he can
8. ....
   She is, isn't
   ...., is she

WORKBOOK PAGE 135

N. What Are They Saying?

1. have, haven't I
2. shouldn't, should we
3. did have, didn't they
4. aren't, are they
5. is, isn't he
6. does taste, doesn't it
7. was, wasn't I
8. will, won't we
9. haven't, have we
10. does look, doesn't it
11. did drive, didn't I

WORKBOOK PAGE 136

O. You Decide: *Why Shouldn't They Break Up?*

1. is
2. isn't he
3. does
4. send
5. doesn't he
6. ....
7. ....
8. isn't he
9. ....
10. did
11. ....
12. ....
13. didn't he
14. was
15. wasn't I
16. has
17. given
18. hasn't he
19. ....
20. ....
21. does he
22. ....
23. ....
24. ....
25. would
26. wouldn't he

WORKBOOK PAGES 137–138

Q. Beverly Wilson's Broken Keyboard

1.

Dear Betty,

You've probably heard from Bob about the terrible robberies we've been having in our neighborhood. (There have been seven robberies in five weeks!) Of course, everybody's been very worried because they still haven't discovered who the robbers are.

Last Wednesday, my neighbor's bicycle was stolen from his basement. The next evening, somebody broke into a building on Brighton Boulevard and took several silver bracelets, a wallet, and two wedding rings.

Then last weekend, believe it or not, the Reliable Bank was robbed. I'll always remember the evening of the robbery. I was taking a bath, and my husband, Bill, was reading his favorite novel in bed when Rover began barking. He must have heard the robbers driving away. By the time I got out of the bathtub, everybody in the neighborhood was talking about the robbers' escape.

Well, ever since the bank robbery last weekend, we've all been very nervous. Some of the neighbors are so worried that they're thinking about moving away. Bill and I have been wondering what we should do.

Love,

Beverly

(continued)

2.

Dear Betsy,

We're having a wedding anniversary celebration on Wednesday for my brother-in-law, Barry, and his wife, Roberta, and we would love it if you and your husband, Walter, were there. It won't be a very big celebration, just a few relatives, William, Vincent, Elizabeth, Steve, and of course my brothers and their wives.

We've heard that your brother's little boy Bobby is visiting you this week. Why don't you bring him along with you when you come over on Wednesday?

Love,

Beverly

3.

Dear Albert,

We're having a wonderful time on our vacation in Boston, but we wish you and your wife were here with us. I'm positive both you and Barbara would love it here. Barbara would love the Boston Public Garden and the boats on the Charles River. And you would have a wonderful time visiting the universities and the Boston Public Library. We're staying with Bill's relatives while we're in Boston. They live in a very modern high-rise building with a beautiful view of the river. We've been very lucky. Bill's relatives drive us everywhere.

The weather in Boston was very warm when we arrived, but now it's windy. I wish we had brought warmer clothes to wear.

By the way, Bill and I went to a lively baseball game last Wednesday, and we've been to the ballet twice. We've also been very busy buying presents for everybody at home and souvenirs for ourselves. (Unfortunately, we weren't able to buy the watch your brother Walter wanted.)

Love,

Beverly

UNIT 10

WORKBOOK PAGE 139

A. What's the Answer?

1. b
2. a
3. b
4. a
5. b
6. b
7. a
8. a
9. a
10. b

B. What Are They Saying?

1. eating, ate
2. you'd, going, went
3. watching, hadn't watched, I'd
4. done/washed, doing/washing, to do/to wash

WORKBOOK PAGE 140

C. What Are They Saying?

1. to see
2. seeing
3. seen
4. saw
5. seeing
6. wouldn't see
7. seeing
8. seeing
9. to see
10. going
11. going
12. going
13. went
14. to go/going
15. to go/going
16. went
17. going
18. go
19. to go

WORKBOOK PAGE 142

E. They Never Would Have Done That!

1. she hadn't hit
would have deleted
2. he hadn't been
would have driven
3. I hadn't had
would have gotten
4. we hadn't misunderstood
would have been
5. he hadn't decided
would have forgotten
6. she hadn't thought
would have put
7. they hadn't mixed up
would have erased

WORKBOOK PAGE 144

H. What Are They Saying?

1. has he been
For
2. has it had
Since
3. have you been having trouble
Since
4. have you been feeling
Since
5. have they hurt
For
6. has it been
Since
7. have they been
For
8. has she wanted to buy
Since

WORKBOOK PAGE 145

I. What's Wrong?

1. since
2. for
3. since
4. For
5. since
6. since
7. for
8. for
9. since
10. for

J. Listening

1. a
2. b
3. a
4. b
5. a
6. a
7. b
8. a
9. b

WORKBOOK PAGE 146

K. What's the Answer?

1. a
2. b
3. b
4. a
5. a
6. b
7. b
8. a
9. a
10. b

L. Complete the Sentences

1. didn't have to
2. were
3. putting, weren't
4. hadn't
5. weren't, I'd
6. figuring, I'd
7. weren't, to, I'd
8. were having, had known, were having, would have

WORKBOOK PAGE 148

N. What's the Word?

1. to
2. by
3. on
4. up
5. into
6. out
7. about
8. of
9. in, with
10. up
11. by
12. with
13. about, to
14. of
15. in
16. past
17. at
18. off
19. from
20. on

WORKBOOK PAGE 149

O. What's the Word?

1. balance
2. passport
3. wallpaper
4. suspect
5. tie
6. slipped
7. ingredients
8. wisdom
9. move out
10. allergic
11. quit
12. misunderstood
13. hamster, mess
14. scrap
15. unemployed
16. tournament
17. realize
18. delete, files

WORKBOOK PAGE 150

P. Listening

1. b
2. a
3. b
4. b
5. b
6. a
7. b
8. b

Q. Out of Place

1. date
2. snowman
3. mural
4. apology
5. poodle
6. customer
7. discovered
8. cactus
9. usher
10. promoted
11. assemble
12. aggressive
13. register
14. accident
15. confused

WORKBOOK PAGE 151

S. Have You Heard?

1. b
2. a
3. b
4. a
5. a
6. b
7. b
8. a
9. b
10. b
11. a
12. b

WORKBOOK PAGES 152–153

CHECK-UP TEST: Units 9–10

A.

1. has it
2. didn't you
3. were there
4. do we
5. doesn't he
6. will they
7. did you
8. can't you
9. aren't I
10. won't you

B.

1. She hasn't called in a long time, has she!
2. That was a boring movie, wasn't it!
3. You're right. She does work hard, doesn't she!
4. He will be a fine doctor someday, won't he!
5. They do taste wonderful, don't they!

C.

1. Where will you be staying?
2. When did you get engaged?
3. How much did you spend?
4. How long has he been cooking?
5. How many times did she mention me?
6. What were you assembling?
7. Why does he go to the gym?

D.

1. seeing
2. seeing
3. seen
4. saw
5. hadn't seen
6. to see

E.

1. a
2. b
3. b
4. a
5. b

GAZETTE

WORKBOOK PAGES 153a–c

A. Technology in Our Lives

1. b	**5.** b	**9.** b
2. c	**6.** a	**10.** d
3. d	**7.** d	
4. a	**8.** c	

B. Fact File

1. d **2.** c

C. Around the World

1. d	**5.** b	**9.** d
2. b	**6.** c	**10.** b
3. c	**7.** b	
4. a	**8.** a	

E. Fun with Idioms

1. c	**3.** b
2. a	**4.** b

F. We've Got Mail!

1. b	**3.** a
2. d	**4.** c

G. "Can-Do" Review

1. i	**5.** b	**9.** c
2. e	**6.** j	**10.** g
3. a	**7.** d	
4. h	**8.** f	

ACTIVITY WORKBOOK 4 ANSWER KEY: Pages 155–180

UNIT 1: Workbook Pages 155–156

A. Notes to School

1. g　**4.** h　**7.** i
2. d　**5.** b　**8.** f
3. a　**6.** c　**9.** e

B. Questions about Reading

1. g　**4.** a　**7.** e
2. c　**5.** d
3. f　**6.** b

C. Informational Reading: *Parenting*

1. c　**3.** b　**5.** a
2. d　**4.** c　**6.** d

D. Checklist: *Helping Children Succeed in School*

1. ✓　**8.** ✓
2. ___　**9.** ___
3. ✓　**10.** ✓
4. ✓　**11.** ___
5. ___　**12.** ___
6. ___　**13.** ✓
7. ✓　**14.** ✓

UNIT 2: Workbook Pages 157–158

A. A Train Schedule

1. 8
2. 1 hour and 2 minutes
3. 2 hours and 9 minutes
4. 95
5. 10:23 A.M.
6. Train 572 / the 11:10 A.M. train
7. Train 566 / the 9:00 A.M. train

B. Informational Reading: *Parts of a Newspaper Article*

1. d　**3.** a　**5.** c
2. e　**4.** b

UNIT 3: Workbook Pages 159–160

A. U.S. History 1

1. World War II
2. Allies
3. Great Depression
4. New Deal
5. Social Security
6. Pearl Harbor

B. U.S. History 2

1. United Nations
2. superpowers
3. Cold War
4. Korean War
5. Vietnam War
6. Martin Luther King, Jr.

C. U.S. History 3

1. Saddam Hussein
2. George W. Bush
3. Afghanistan
4. Pentagon

D. U.S. History 4: *Timeline*

1. e　**4.** a　**7.** c
2. g　**5.** d
3. b　**6.** f

UNIT 4: Workbook Pages 161–162

A. Numeracy: *Estimating Costs*

1. a　**3.** c　**5.** c
2. b　**4.** b　**6.** a

B. Warranties: *Understanding Vocabulary from Context*

1. h　**4.** g　**7.** b
2. a　**5.** f　**8.** c
3. d　**6.** e

C. Numeracy: *Interpreting Charts and Prices*

1. c　**3.** b
2. a　**4.** a

UNIT 5: Workbook Pages 163–165

A. The Heimlich Maneuver 1

1. T
2. F
3. T
4. F
5. F
6. T
7. T

B. The Heimlich Maneuver 2

4
2
5
3
6
1

D. A Smoke Detector Diagram

1. b
2. c
3. b
4. c
5. b

E. Apartment Ad Abbreviations

1. bedroom
2. washer and dryer
3. air conditioning
4. eat-in kitchen
5. dining room
6. living room
7. bathroom
8. elevator
9. building
10. parking
11. transportation
12. heat
13. included
14. hot water
15. immediately
16. near
17. basement
18. large
19. available
20. utilities

F. Reading Apartment Ads

1. C
2. A
3. B
4. A
5. A
6. B
7. C
8. B
9. B
10. C

UNIT 6: Workbook Pages 166–169

A. Numeracy: *Word Problems about Money*

1. $2,175
2. $1,895
3. $645
4. $639.40
5. $869.40
6. Yes
7. $6.50
8. $16.95
9. $33.05
10. No
11. $0.98

B. Types of Bank Accounts: *Understanding Vocabulary from Context*

1. e
2. i
3. h
4. b
5. c
6. g
7. a
8. j
9. f
10. d

E. Numeracy: *A Cell Phone Bill*

1. $86.28
2. 6/27/18
3. $79.93
4. $49.99, $19.95
5. $2.20

UNIT 7: Workbook Pages 170–173

A. Symptoms and Medical Advice

1. muscle
2. knee
3. bump
4. swollen
5. low-fat
6. exercise

B. Numeracy: *Nutrition Amounts on a Food Label*

1. one
2. 110
3. 55
4. 13 grams
5. 0 grams

C. Informational Reading: *Using Medicine Carefully*

1. d
2. b
3. c
4. a

D. Reading a Medicine Label

1. T
2. F
3. T
4. T
5. T
6. T
7. F
8. T
9. F

E. Workplace Safety

1. corrosive materials
2. poison
3. high voltage
4. biohazard
5. combustible materials
6. flammable materials
7. safety gloves
8. safety glasses
9. no drinks allowed

10. helmet
11. first-aid kit
12. fire extinguisher
13. respirator
14. no food allowed

F. Map Reading: *An Evacuation Map*

1. N	3. Y	5. N
2. Y	4. Y	6. Y

UNIT 8: Workbook Pages 174–177

A. Job Interview Vocabulary

1. communicator
2. get along
3. attitude
4. skills
5. familiar
6. employed
7. specific
8. promotion
9. goals
10. position

C. Job Ad Abbreviations

1. excellent
2. assistant
3. company
4. references
5. driver's license
6. experience
7. required
8. certified
9. office
10. benefits
11. equivalent
12. available
13. diploma
14. opportunity
15. previous

D. Help Wanted Ads

1. d	3. d
2. c	4. b

UNIT 9: Workbook Pages 178–179

A. Informational Reading: *Employee Benefits*

1. F	6. T	11. T
2. T	7. F	12. F
3. T	8. T	13. F
4. T	9. F	
5. F	10. T	

B. Numeracy: *Reading a Pay Stub*

1. 37
2. $210.00
3. $360.00
4. $7,110.00
5. $4,435.00
6. $85.00
7. $1,085.00
8. $40.00
9. $40.00
10. $520.00
11. $40.00
12. 9.75
13. 8

UNIT 10: Workbook Page 180

A. Civics Vocabulary

1. j	5. a	9. c
2. h	6. g	10. l
3. b	7. d	11. f
4. i	8. e	12. k

B. Community Legal Services

1. C	4. D	7. A
2. D	5. B	8. D
3. A	6. C	

Correlation Key

Student Text Pages	Activity Workbook Pages
Chapter 1	
2	2
3	3
4	4–5
5	6–7
7	8–10
8–9	11–12
10	13
11	14
12	15–17
14a–b	155 Exercise A
14c–d	155–156 Exercises B–D
Chapter 2	
16	18
17	19–20
20	21
22	22–23
23	24–25
24–25	26–28
26–27	29–31
30a–b	157 Exercise A
30c–d	157–158 Exercises B–C
Chapter 3	
32–33	32–34
34–35	35–37
36–37	38–40
40–41	41–42
43	43
46a	159 Exercise A
46b	159 Exercise B
46c–d	159–160 Exercises C–E
Check-Up Test	**44–45**
Gazette	**45a–d**
Chapter 4	
52	46
53	47–48
54–55	49–52
58–59	53–54
62–63	55–56
64a	161
64b–d	162

Student Text Pages	Activity Workbook Pages
Chapter 5	
66	57–59
67	60–62
68	63
69	64–65
72–73	66–68
74–75	69–73
77	74–75
78a	163 Exercises A–B
78b	163 Exercise C
78c–d	164–165
Check-Up Test	**76–77**
Gazette	**77a–d**
Chapter 6	
84–85	78–79
86	80–82
87	83–84
89	85
90–91	86–89
94a–b	166–167
94c–d	168–169
Chapter 7	
96–97	90–92
98–99	93–96
102–103	97–99
106–107	100–103
108a	170 Exercise A
108b–c	170 Exercise B
108d	171
108e–f	172–173
Chapter 8	
110–111	104–107
112–113	108–109
116–118	110–113
120–121	114–121
124a	174
124b	175
124c–d	176–177
Check-Up Test	**122–123**
Gazette	**123a–d**

Student Text Pages	Activity Workbook Pages
Chapter 9	
130	124–125
131	126–130
132–133	131–132
134–135	133–134
136–137	135–138
144a–b	178–179 Exercises A–B
144c–d	179 Exercise C

Student Text Pages	Activity Workbook Pages
Chapter 10	
146–147	139–141
148–149	142–143
152–153	144–145
154–155	146–151
158a–b	180 Exercise A
158c	180 Exercise B
Check-Up Test	**152–153**
Gazette	**153a–c**

SIDE by SIDE Plus Activity Workbook Audio Program

The *Side by Side Plus* Activity Workbook Audio Program contains all Workbook listening activities and GrammarRaps for entertaining language practice through rhythm and music. Students can use the Audio Program to extend their language learning through self-study outside the classroom. The Audio Program is available on the Pearson English Portal.

Audio Program Contents

	Page	Activity
Unit 1		
	Page 3	Exercise C Listening
	Page 5	Exercise E GrammarRap
	Page 6	Exercise G Listening
	Page 8	Exercise K Listening
	Page 16	Exercise R GrammarRap
	Page 16	Exercise S Listening
Unit 2		
	Page 23	Exercise G GrammarRap
	Page 28	Exercise K GrammarRap
	Page 29	Exercise M Listening
	Page 30	Exercise O Listening
	Page 31	Exercise P Have You Heard?
Unit 3		
	Page 34	Exercise C GrammarRap
	Page 35	Exercise E Listening
	Page 39	Exercise L Listening
	Page 41	Exercise O GrammarRap
	Page 43	Exercise R Listening
Check-Up Test: Units 1–3		
	Page 45	Exercise D Listening
Unit 4		
	Page 49	Exercise E Listening
	Page 49	Exercise F GrammarRap
	Page 52	Exercise H GrammarRap
	Page 53	Exercise J Listening
	Page 53	Exercise K GrammarRap
Unit 5		
	Page 58	Exercise D Listening
	Page 59	Exercise E GrammarRap
	Page 63	Exercise J Listening
	Page 66	Exercise N Listening
	Page 73	Exercise U GrammarRap
	Page 73	Exercise V GrammarRap
	Page 74	Exercise W Listening
Check-Up Test: Units 4–5		
	Page 77	Exercise D Listening

	Page	Activity
Unit 6		
	Page 80	Exercise E Listening
	Page 82	Exercise G GrammarRap
	Page 83	Exercise I Listening
	Page 86	Exercise N Listening
	Page 87	Exercise P GrammarRap
	Page 89	Exercise R Sound It Out!
Unit 7		
	Page 93	Exercise E Listening
	Page 96	Exercise J GrammarRap
	Page 99	Exercise N GrammarRap
	Page 102	Exercise R Listening
	Page 102	Exercise S Listening
	Page 102	Exercise T Listening
	Page 103	Exercise U Have You Heard?
Unit 8		
	Page 107	Exercise C GrammarRap
	Page 108	Exercise E Listening
	Page 110	Exercise H Listening
	Page 113	Exercise J GrammarRap
	Page 118	Exercise O GrammarRap
	Page 120	Exercise Q Listening
Check-Up Test: Units 7–8		
	Page 123	Exercise D Listening
Unit 9		
	Page 129	Exercise G Listening
	Page 130	Exercise I GrammarRap
	Page 132	Exercise L Listening
	Page 137	Exercise P Listening
Unit 10		
	Page 141	Exercise D GrammarRap
	Page 143	Exercise F GrammarRap
	Page 145	Exercise J Listening
	Page 147	Exercise M GrammarRap
	Page 150	Exercise P Listening
	Page 151	Exercise R Listening
	Page 151	Exercise S Have You Heard?
Check-Up Test: Units 9–10		
	Page 153	Exercise E Listening